NATURAL CHILDHOOD

NATURAL CHILDHOOD

The first practical and holistic guide for parents of the developing child

JOHN THOMSON
General Editor

TIM KAHN MILDRED MASHEDER
LYNNE OLDFIELD MICHAELA GLÖCKLER
ROLAND MEIGHAN

RAHIMA BALDWIN Consultant

A GAIA ORIGINAL

A FIRESIDE BOOK
Published by SIMON & SCHUSTER INC
New York London Toronto Sydney Tokyo Singapore

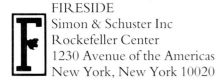

FIRESIDE
Simon & Schuster Inc
Rockefeller Center
1230 Avenue of the Americas
New York, New York 10020

First published in the United Kingdom in 1994 by Gaia Books Ltd, 66 Charlotte Street, London W1P 1LR

Printed and bound by Dai Nippon Printing Company Limited in Hong Kong

10 9 8 7 6 5 4 3 2 1

ISBN 0-02-020739-5

Library of Congress Cataloging-in-Publication Data

Natural Childhood : the first practical and holistic guide for parents
    of the developing child / John Thomson, general editor ; Tim Kahn
    ... [et al.].
        p.   cm.
    "A Fireside book."
    Includes bibliographical references and index.
    ISBN 0-02-020739-5
    1. Parenting--Religious aspects--New Age movement. 2. New Age
movement. 3. Child development. I. Thomson, John. II. Kahn,
Tim
BP605.N48N38 1995
649'.1--dc20   94-23147
                                                                                 CIP

NOTES TO THE READER

Throughout the book the child is referred to as either "he" or "she" in each alternate chapter, starting with "he" in Chapter 1.

The development of a child with a learning difficulty or disablement may not necessarily follow the patterns of development described in this book.

John B. Thomson
Lecturer at Emerson College, Sussex, England *General consultant for the book and author of Part 1, The Developing Child, pages 10–61*

John Thomson's original aim to be a lawyer was unsettled by World War II and his encounter with painting. His experience of teaching children left him dissatisfied until he realized that teaching is an art and he found himself inextricably entangled with Steiner education.

Tim Kahn
Journalist and parent educator *Author of Part 2, Communicating, pages 62–125*

Tim Kahn has worked in parent education for eight years. He runs parenting skills groups, writes in national magazines and newspapers and is a consultant for television on parenting issues. For five years he took a major share in the care of his two young children.

Mildred Masheder
Teacher and writer in child development *Author of Part 3, Play and Creativity, pages 126–213*

Mildred Masheder was a primary school teacher and later a lecturer in child development. She is the author of Let's Co-operate, Windows to Nature, *and* Let's Enjoy Nature, *and the video* Let's Play Together. *She is currently writing a book on preventing bullying.*

Lynne Oldfield
Director of the Lindens Waldorf Family Centre, Stroud, England *Author of Part 4, The Unfolding World pages 214–265*

Lynne Oldfield came to Waldorf education after teaching in England, Greece, and America. She is also tutor and co-director of the London Waldorf Kindergarten Training Course; co-editor of the UK Waldorf Kindergarten Newsletter; and lectures in child and human development and parenting.

Dr Michaela Glöckler
Head of the Medical Section at the Goetheanum, School of Spiritual Science, Dornach, Switzerland *Author of Part 5, Health and Healing, pages 266–289*

Dr Glöckler qualified as a secondary school teacher before studying medicine. She took further training in paediatrics, and worked in a children's hospital outpatient clinic and as school doctor at a Rudolf Steiner School. Since 1988 she has been head of the Medical Section at the Goetheanum, Dornach, Switzerland.

Professor Roland Meighan
Special Professor of Education at the University of Nottingham, England *Author of Part 6, Education and Schooling, pages 290–335*

Professor Meighan is an expert in education, particularly in home-based education. He has lectured and researched in teacher education and worked with the Open University from its inception. He is editor of the influential Educational Review *and is author or co-author of over a hundred books and publications.*

CONTENTS

Communicating 62 – 125
Tim Kahn

Play and Creativity 126 – 213
Mildred Masheder

The Unfolding World 214 – 265
Lynne Oldfield

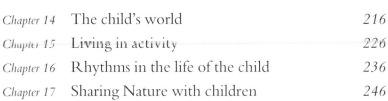

Health and Healing 266 – 289
Michaela Glöckler

Education and Schooling 290 – 335
Roland Meighan

Protecting childhood

This book is in defence of the child. It is written to defend childhood and to remind us of the child's world, to which the adult has too often become blind. Today's talk of the need for men to find the feminine in themselves expresses a dangerous vertical split in our society. There is also a horizontal split: a deep need for adults to uncover the true child within themselves, hidden and shut away by the infatuations and preoccupations of the grown-up world. Together, they form a divide which seals off the vast world of the child from the world of our everyday consciousness, where facts rule and statistics decide. For only the eye of the imagination can see the child. But we have preferred to exploit the child rather than see him.

How is it possible to say that the child is not seen? In which time has there been more written, discussed, felt, experienced about the child than in ours? Past ages hardly noticed children. But ours expends vast amounts of time and money on books, studies, health and education programmes, on child welfare. We have prenatal clinics and postnatal services, centres for child care, playgroups, kindergartens, shops full of toys and games (many of which are devised to be "educational"), entertainment programmes, playgrounds, scientifically researched food products – all of which make the 19th-century child seem positively deprived.

This "deprivation" is generally not our deprivation. I have no wish to diminish the real gains that have been made in child welfare over the last hundred years. But the problem has shifted. The shift is part of the dramatic scene change of the 20th century, where the character roles, too, have altered almost beyond recognition.

Imagine the late-Victorian family: the bearded, watch-chained, authoritarian papa and the bustled, corsetted, long-robed mama, with a family of five, six, or more offspring unquestioningly preoccupied with their contrasting gender roles, innocent of drugs or sex education. Compare them with their fourth or fifth generation descendants in the late 20th century: parents in unisex dress, explicitly democratic, one third of them impermanently united with, statistically, less than two children, car-borne and media-haunted. On Sundays, the first family might be walking to church, the second might be driving to the shopping mall. The outer differences are impressive. No other century has offered so much change so fast.

This grand tidal wave of novelty has swept the child along. The facilities, comforts, and medical techniques, as well as the threats, fears, and catastrophes, served up by our technology, have changed the child's life as inevitably and inexorably as the adult's.

But our attitude to childhood has changed at a far deeper level because what we think a human being is has shifted. In fact, the break-up of a constructive imagination of the human being has largely shaped the spiritual history of the 20th century. Lacking this imagination, childhood is diminished, birth becomes an illness and the utility of the child, like all other social units, is calculated and engineered.

Yet, today, a new awareness is abroad. Many people recognize that we do not come to understand the world, the child, society, or ourselves by only analytical procedures or surgical dissections. Understanding is an action carried out by a Self. It is not information laid over the factual world but the raising of facts into life through a conscious imaginative insight into the world and its contents, Nature, and humanity. This world is then no longer a conglomeration of material data, but a hierarchy of meaning, where secrets are accessed by the inwardly active mind.

This new awareness contrasts with the intellectual and cultural excitements at the end of the 19th century. Then, the Western world was intensifying its grip on material processes for the greater gratification of the ego. Colonization, dehumanized labour, and human inventiveness were all dedicated to this end. At the same time, ideologies of right and left floated above this hardening world. Instead of meeting and healing the social problems of industrialization, they hurled nations into a century of cataclysmic wars.

Rediscovery of the human

Today, all these ideals and ideologies seem dead. Who would have believed there was so little life in the doctrines that vanished with the Berlin Wall? What remains are purely impersonal forces, driving political and economic leaders without ideals; in the East as in the West.

But within and behind these changes there is a spiritual awakening grounded on both traditional ideals and lived experience. It is difficult to make generalizations, for in our pluralistic society change takes many forms. But I see at the core of change a new spirituality which is the successor of the scientific attitudes of the Western tradition. The impartiality and objectivity of science was its great merit and achievement. But it seemed to require that the human being could only be a spectator in his universe and this exclusion meant, ultimately, his abolition.

Many signs of this spiritual awakening indicate a rediscovery of the human being. The objective scientific spirit is crossing a frontier beyond which the human being becomes an apprentice in the service of his universe. His consciousness is raising him to a unique level of understanding in which he becomes the serving conscience of the world. Through him it rises or falls. This is not the humanistic pride of the Renaissance. We have been through too much since then to hold our heads so high. It can only be built on the humility of the one who serves.

Change comes into the world through ideas. The ideas which are felt and experienced through this new awakening spirituality can completely transform both our way of living and our understanding of the child. These ideas constitute a new vision, but a vision for the here and now, which can be practised.

This book is intended to be a contribution to this vision.

PART 1

THE DEVELOPING CHILD

John B. Thomson

*T*he work of the early psychologists attempted to give a structure to the psyche (soul) and to describe the operation of its complex forces. Some of the later psychologists felt the need to include in the picture a spiritual element capable of becoming active in the ego or Self as the source of human transformation. Rudolf Steiner is one of the enlightened thinkers who represents most comprehensively this enriched understanding of the human being. Chapter 1 gives a brief outline of some of the different views of childhood which have been current throughout the 20th century.

Steiner's picture of the human being forms the basis of Chapter 2, which deals with the different stages of development that the child experiences as she gradually awakens to her own sense of Self.

Such development is characterized by rhythm and the interplay of opposites. Chapter 3 shows how an understanding of these can be a help to every parent or teacher mindful of their child's wellbeing.

CHAPTER 1

Visions of child development

A new spirituality is changing our views of childhood. The old materialism, so strong in our everyday world, is weakening in our intellectual and emotional life. In practice, the reign of quantity is still with us and the child's world is governed by the spectator's perspective. Yet, even as we rediscover what it is to be human, we are learning what it is to be a child.

The spirit and the Self

What is this talk of a new spirituality really about? "Spiritual" is such a vague word. Its meaning seems to change with the speaker. Since World War II, it has gained currency and seems to embody new insights about the nature of human beings. The increased interest in Eastern religious teaching in the Western world since the 1960s has contributed to this.

But it is not merely a borrowed habit. It involves a changed experience of the Self. This is another tricky word that lacks clarity. At times, it is used to mean the "ego"; sometimes it is used in contrast to the ego. Some psychologists avoid it entirely as it harbours too many difficulties. Others, such as Abraham Maslow, use such words as transcendence and metamotivation in another attempt to encompass the meaning of the spiritual active in the individual.

However we define such terms, we know there has been a marked alteration in the understanding and conceptualization of the human being during the 20th century. The changed vocabulary that describes the range of human experience is a sign of this. In this chapter we shall look at the work of various psychologists over this period, as an illustration of this great shift in consciousness.

▲ **Early experience**
Freud believed that the child's personality is completed by around the fifth year, and so the quality of his early experience is vitally important.

Freud and the unconscious

We cannot picture a human being without including some notion of the unconscious, a term voiced by Sigmund Freud almost a century ago. Freud himself made no attempt to study children, but his radical theory of the personality utterly transformed our picture of the child.

Freud deduced that the adult is unfolding what has already been unconsciously established in childhood: "The little creature is often completed by the fourth and fifth years of life and after that merely brings gradually to light what is already within him".

Freud believed that the seeds of neurosis are planted during the first years of life. So psycho-analysis meant the exploration of the past through analyzing early memories: "It appeared that psychoanalysis could explain nothing belonging to the present without referring back to something past".

It was the task of Freud and his disciples to emphasize the role played by the unconscious in the everyday world and its consequences for education and social life. To them, the Self was suspect and not recognized as the real director of our actions. They assumed the processes and forces in the psyche were like those in the physical world and so analyzed and described it in much the same way as a physicist would.

The forces within us

All behaviour, thought Freud, is motivated by instincts, painful stimuli, homeostatic needs and sex, or by drives based on these. The child's instinctive search for pleasure expressed itself in sucking, in elimination, and in genitality. The child's experience of these expressions would determine his health as an adult. What Freud termed the "id"' points to this unconscious instinctual life and is full of unknown and uncontrollable forces, which direct our lives. What is called the ego had, for Freud, only a passive role to play.

For educators influenced by Freud's theory, the most important agenda was to liberate those repressed instinctual forces that led to neurosis. However, the image of the human being derived from such pathology was essentially a negative one. While their research undoubtedly brought to light significant aspects of behaviour that were trapped in unconscious bonds, it could neither envisage nor engage the autonomous part of the human being.

Love and maturity

Erich Fromm, a member of the Freudian school who never met Freud, developed a positive view of the parent–child bond. He wrote a series of popular books on psychology in which he explored the experience of love and freedom in the years after World War II. He wondered whether the popularity of psychology did not betray the fundamental lack of love in human relations in our time.

In *The Art of Loving,* Fromm highlights the differences between mother's love and father's love. The first, he writes, is unconditional: it has to be given and cannot be gained. This is the foundation of a child's security. A father's love is based on his authority and is conditional on merit: the child strives for it, and wants to aim for goals. Mature people, in becoming free of their mother and father figures, build motherly consciences on their own capacity for love and fatherly consciences on their own reason and judgement.

It was Fromm's view that the development from a mother-centred to a father-centred attachment, and their eventual synthesis, offers the basis of mental health and the achievement of maturity. This differs from Freud's picture of the adult, which incorporates mother and father figures into what he called the "super-ego": here, there is accumulation but not real transformation. Motherly love, writes Fromm, makes the child feel good to be born and instills a love for life. Milk is the symbol of this first aspect of love – that is, care and affirmation.

> "
> *If you love yourself, you love everybody else as you do yourself. As long as you love another person less than you love yourself you will not really succeed in loving yourself, but if you love all alike, including yourself, you will love them as one person and that person is both God and Man. Thus he is a great and righteous person who, loving himself, loves all others equally."*
>
> Meister Eckhart

To love someone is not simply a strong feeling; it is a decision, a judgement, and a promise. If love were only a feeling that comes and goes, there could be no basis for a promise. Love is, in fact, an act of Will, of commitment. To be able to love, a person must feel self-worth. Self-love, which contrasts with selfishness, must be present. "Love thy neighbour as thyself" requires a love of self, a respect for one's own integrity.

Fromm points out that love is indivisible as far as the connection between "objects" and one's own self is concerned. Genuine love is an expression of productiveness and implies care, respect, responsibility, and knowledge. The affirmation of one's own life, one's happiness, and the growth of one's freedom are deeply rooted in one's capacity to love. If an individual is able to love productively, he loves himself, too.

Selfish people cannot love others since they cannot love themselves. Neurotic "unselfishness" is often accompanied by depression, tiredness, inability to work, and failure in love relationships. The unselfishness is not separate from these symptoms but belongs to them and can be cured only if the underlying lack of productiveness is cured.

Children of an unselfish mother may be affected by her hidden hostility to life. The effects of selfishness and unselfishness are similar. The child is unable to criticize. But a mother with genuine self-love gives her children the experience of what joy and happiness are. This theme of deformed love is examined again, with great insight, by such contemporary writers as Alice Miller and Scott Peck.

ERIKSON'S LIFE CRISES IN THE CHILD

Life crisis	Favourable outcomes	Unfavourable outcomes
1. First year Trust – mistrust	**1. Hope** Trust in the environment and the future	**1.** Fear of the future; suspicion
2. Second year Autonomy – shame and doubt	**2. Will** Ability to exercise choice as well as self-restraint. A sense of self-control and self-esteem leading to good Will and pride	**2.** Sense of loss of self-control or sense of external over-control; the result is a propensity for shame and doubt about whether one willed what one did or did what one willed
3. Third through fifth years Initiative – guilt	**3. Purpose** Ability to initiate activities, to give them direction and to enjoy accomplishment	**3.** Fear of punishment; self-restriction or over-compensatory "showing off"
4. Sixth year through puberty Industry – inferiority	**4. Competence** Ability to relate to the world of skills and tools, to exercise dexterity and intelligence in order to make things, and make them well	**4.** A sense of inadequacy and inferiority
5. Adolescence Industry – confusion about one's roles	**5. Fidelity** Ability to see oneself as an integrated person and to sustain loyalties	**5.** Confusion over who one is

▲ **Erik Erikson**
According to Swedish psychologist Erik Erikson, the personality has to overcome various crises on the road to maturity. If negotiated successfully, each crisis leads to a favourable outcome. Should the ego stumble, however, the outcome is less favourable and problems develop.

The role of the ego

Erik Erikson, a successor of Freud, integrated psychoanalysis with the social sciences. For him, the ego, rather than instinctual drives, dominated human behaviour. Instead of being simply a passive entity, the ego can play a key role in the recovery of health by passing to the patient the ability and responsibility of participating in its own healing. He sketched a developmental cycle of the ego indicating the stages a personality has to traverse on its journey to maturity (see chart).

For Erikson, a person develops by overcoming obstacles which lie along his path. Each stage offers different obstacles which, if favourably dealt with, enable the person to move on to the next stage with new strength. Failure to cope successfully means that the individual will be haunted by the unresolved problem and this will hold up development.

Education: the emotions and the intellect

In his summary of A. S. Neill's educational principles, Fromm recognized some of his own efforts to help emancipate the child from the narrow bondage imposed by contemporary education. Emotions and feelings are as much a part of the educational field as the intellect. Furthermore, it is necessary to maintain faith in the goodness of the child, with his full potential to love life and be interested in it.

Nurturing independence

Education should be attuned to the psychic needs and capacities of children. This means accepting their aggression and self centredness, and not expecting maturity and altruism too early. Only in this way will children build up sincere values and attitudes, and avoid hypocrisy. The adult who exercises authority or enforces discipline will distance himself from children. Discipline and punishment create fear and, in turn, fear creates hostility.

Feelings of guilt in the child are rarely the voice of conscience and most often are caused by disobedience to an authority, whether parent, teacher, or church, and such feelings are an impediment to growth and maturity. They are usually associated with fear: fear of punishment, or fear that love will be withdrawn, or fear that society will ostracize him.

The goal of the educational process is the achievement of independence and personal responsibility. The child must therefore learn to break the primary ties with the parents, or later substitutes, and accept the loneliness of growing up. It is only in being able to accept oneself and the world, emotionally and intellectually, that one finds one's proper security.

> "
> *Freud showed that every neurosis is founded on sex repression. I said, 'I'll have a school in which there will be no sex repression'. Freud said that the unconscious was infinitely more important and powerful than the conscious. I said, 'In my school we won't censure, punish, moralize. We will allow every child to live according to his deep impulses'."*
>
> A. S. Neill,
> *founder of Summerhill School*

TEACHING INTELLIGENCE
Intelligence, or mental ability, is easily perceptible. We rarely hesitate to judge whether a child is bright or slow, especially if the child is not ours.

As a way of measuring a child's academic success, French psychologists Alfred Binet and Theophilus Simon invented IQ tests in 1904. The notion that a child has a fixed intelligence which can be given a number (100 for average, 120 for 20% above average) has had an enormous impact on teaching methods. Forms of these tests are still widely used today: for example, the Wechster Pre-School-Primary Scale of Intelligence (WPPSI) for children aged between four and six-and-a-half.

IQ tests are designed to measure different aspects of mental ability, reasoning, comprehension, common sense, quickness, and abstraction. However, the parent's or teacher's view of the child may be influenced by the results of IQ tests. As a result, they become teachers of mental abilities and not of people, and the experience of the whole child is fragmented.

▲ The interpretive phase

*Around the third year the child begins to
produce representational outlines of houses
and people which are expressions of his
experience of himself.*

Piaget's stages of development

Following a very different approach to cognition, Jean Piaget concentrated on understanding how a child's thinking evolves. He conducted his research with the rational approach of an experimental scientist. He realized that the way in which a child carries out a specially devised set of experiments reveals certain information about the structure of his intelligence.

Piaget concluded that the thinking, or cognitive, faculty develops in an inexorable sequence of stages. This sequence is part of the maturing process and cannot be speeded up. Each stage is the prerequisite for the next. Certain aspects of learning can only happen after a child's thinking faculty has developed the appropriate structure and is ready for the next stage.

Grasping the world

Up to the age of eighteen months, a child's learning is based on his sensory experience and activities. From then until the age of seven, he develops a capacity to grasp the world through mental imagery, language, drawings, and make-believe (see also pp. 154–5). Only after the age of seven, when he has internalized the world, can he undertake the reverse process: grasping the world through the manipulation of objects and through the application of practical logic. Only then can the child embark on reading, writing, and arithmetic in a systematic way.

Piaget assumes that the human being has inborn structures, whether biological or psychological, which unfold in an orderly way and permit ever-new levels of grasping the world. This notion of innate structures rejects the behaviourist view that the child is a clean sheet on which sense-experience writes, for these elements are not simply inherited, but belong to the very nature of what we call human.

The development of language

What makes us human is that we use language to express thoughts. How this comes about in the child is miraculous to behold. While we clearly do not inherit language, we are born with the ability to learn it.

There are two sides to the question: the acquisition of speech and the development of thought. When we search for words to express a thought, the thought must clearly exist already. We generally think in language, especially if we want to communicate our thoughts. But verbal thought does not encompass all forms of thought or speech – much of music, painting, and sculpture, for example, are beyond words.

Thought and speech converge

The outstanding Russian psychologist, Lev Vygotsky, set out to trace the development of thought and speech in the child. He maintained that, originally, these belong to different streams and stem from different roots. This means that young children form concepts before they speak intelligibly; and they master the sounds, tone, and words of language before they use them in the service of their thought. These two streams converge at about the age of two. Then speech begins to be rational and thought verbal. From the age of about two onward, language and thought interact and thought development is determined by language.

Forming concepts

Adults understand the world through concepts. So how do these emerge in the child? Vygotsky concluded that forming a concept is a creative process, which cannot be learned by repetition, memorizing, or artificial explanations. He quotes Tolstoy, who found out by bitter experience

▲ A rose by any other name…

The concept of a flower can be expressed in many different ways: in spoken and written words; drawings, paintings, and sculptures; music, song, and dance; perfumes and aromas.

when he tried to teach peasant children, that they resisted acquiring concepts that were forced on them mechanically. When the child hears a word which he does not understand, first in one context and then in another, he begins to have a notion of the new concept. Finally, he makes it his own. Giving new concepts deliberately is as futile and impossible as teaching a child to walk by the laws of equilibrium.

Vygotsky observed that most educational theories and methods assume the child can absorb concepts ready-made and with no "inward history". But forming a concept does not happen automatically, but arises out of an aim – the solution of a problem. As adults, we form concepts by alternating our thinking between the general and the particular within the pyramid of concepts we have available. The next time we have to do some hard thinking on a personal problem we can reflect afterwards on what we did and we will recognize what Vygotsky describes.

Concepts change

To arrive at what the adult is able to do, the child must complete a number of stages. Only at puberty (after twelve years of age) does a child begin to make new concepts for himself. Until then, he uses concepts he has learned from adults, but their content will not be the same and he will combine them differently. These pre-puberty concepts change as the child grows. This is why giving fixed concepts to a child is as inappropriate as buying him a jacket to use for the rest of his life. Concepts change and grow just as the body grows and needs larger jackets.

Overall, the language of a child has an image quality and only later does the abstract element appear. As the child grows toward adolescence, the image is in contest with the concept and the image gradually loses out.

▲ **Development expressed in art**
Drawings express the child's stages of development. Crenellated roofs and window shapes are often depicted by children who are losing their milk teeth.

Looking beyond the senses

In the first half of the 20th century, the different aspects of the child were explored, but without any healthy integration of the parts. The instinctual life, the life of Feeling, the forces that shape behaviour, and the life of cognition were each studied separately but were not united into an understanding of the human individuality – the Self – in development.

The world-view of Rudolf Steiner provided a powerful integrating tendency. Although he founded the first Waldorf School as early as 1919, his work echoes throughout the spiritual attitudes that have emerged in the West since the 1960s. In his image of the human being, Steiner grasped the different Soul elements of Thinking, Feeling, and Willing in their dynamic interplay. As they interpenetrate, the elements are differentiated in their relation to consciousness and in their interface with the world. The human individuality expresses itself bodily, psychologically, and spiritually, and it is essential that all levels are understood and known.

Observing and perceiving

Everything we call knowledge, insisted Steiner, must be based on observation and on the thinking we bring to bear on what we perceive. He also insisted that observation must not be limited to what the senses take hold of, for human beings can also perceive supersensible data.

When I perceive my friend, it is not just her skin and shape and clothes that I perceive, but through these, her personality and inner qualities, which are supersensible. Steiner maintained that this capacity to perceive the supersensible can be greatly heightened by deliberate training.

It is up to parents or teachers to relate Steiner's ideas to their own experience and understanding. His statements on child development are similar to those made by Piaget, but whereas Piaget focused more on what can be observed by the senses and then measured, Steiner looked beyond the senses.

The quotation (left) illustrates Steiner's research clearly. It raises many questions, yet it can be weighed like any other that is made about the human being: does it accord with reality, with experience? It is not always possible to make a sound judgement straight away. Thoughts and perceptions which have any depth usually need time to be considered and to unfold. The passage quoted is typical of many statements which Steiner made on the child's development. Some of these will be looked at in the later chapters of this book.

Correspondence of ideas

Although Steiner's research has a different basis from that of the child psychologists we have mentioned, there is often a correspondence between them. For example, the stages of child growth are also recognized and described by Erikson, Piaget, Gesell, and others.

"

If, for instance, we study the child up to the age of the change of teeth, we see that his development is primarily dependent on his physical organism. The physical organism must gradually adapt itself to the outer world, but this cannot take place all at once, not even if considered in the crudest physical sense... And the conclusion of this process of the physical organism growing into the outer world is indicated by the appearance of the second teeth at about the seventh year. At approximately this age the child's physical organism completes the process of growing into the world.

"During this time, however, in which the organization is chiefly concerned with the shaping and fashioning of the bony system, the child is only interested in certain things in the outer world, not in everything. He is only interested in what we might call gesture, everything that is related to movement...

"In the inner nature of the organism speech develops out of movement in all its aspects, and thought develops out of speech. This deeply significant law underlies all human development. Everything which makes its appearance in sound, in speech, is the result of gesture, mediated through the inner nature of the human organism."

Rudolf Steiner,
from a lecture in 1924

"

The child lying with half-closed eyes waiting with tense soul for its mother to speak to it – the mystery of its will is not directed towards enjoying (or dominating) a person, or towards doing something of its own accord; but towards experiencing communion in face of the lonely night, which spreads beyond the windows and threatens to invade."

Martin Buber

The freedom to develop

Transpersonal psychology, which has developed over the last 30 to 40 years, carries important influences from Eastern spirituality, yet its values and orientation mirror those in Steiner's teaching. It assumes in every individual the existence of a central essence, or Self, which motivates and guides the psyche. For Steiner, this Self already exists before conception; it is the informing principle in growth and development, until it has achieved in its body and soul the mature basis to act out of its own centre in adult life.

Abraham Maslow, among the first transpersonal psychologists, describes the function and goal of education as, ultimately, self-actualization. When the higher needs of the human being – for respect or freedom to develop – are seen as fundamental, the perspective on education and learning will have shifted in a beneficial way.

The transpersonal preoccupation with the Self may seem to be an extreme form of individualization. When philosopher Martin Buber said, "I am against individuals and for persons," he meant that an individual who lives well with the world and with others is a person, but one who is merely individual, however strongly, is not necessarily a person. For the humanistic school of Maslow and Carl Rogers the quest for self-actualization does not limit itself to an individualism in isolation from society.

Faith and trust

The optimistic view of human nature expressed by Maslow and Rogers has set the tone for new approaches in education and therapy. The active engagement of student or patient is crucial to the process. The therapist does not act on the patient, with a superior insight, to dislodge the obstacle in his personality, but endeavours to

▲ **Safe places**
We all need three safe places on which to stand – the earth, our relationships, and our own power of thought.

activate the Self as the essential source of future healing. Similarly, the educator's task must be to awaken and nourish the child's learning potential and not just to inform and instruct.

Faith and trust are necessary companions in the growth and unfolding of the child. Development is open-ended because it is a soul and spirit process. Meaning and values among adults are needed to support the evolution of the child's own meaning.

The intent of a child

The fiery vision of human development which Joseph Chilton Pearce expounds in *Magical Child* and *Evolution's End* gives a new slant to the transpersonal viewpoint. Building on Piaget's work, Pearce interlocks behavioural, emotional, and intellectual development with development in the brain–nervous system. A kind of inbuilt programming organizes a sequence of stages toward maturity. Each stage, which he calls a "matrix", is a specific set of interrelated conditions, and there are five in all.

The impulse that moves the child from one stage to the next Pearce calls "intent". This is the will to interact with the world around (the "content") and, through this interaction, to develop. We should not frustrate the child's intent which is provided by Nature, but should nurture it – as well as understand how a child develops.

"

We must rekindle our knowing of a personal power that can flow with the power of faith in all things and never be exhausted…. Only through faith in yourself and in your own life can you respond to a new life given you, according to the needs of that new life."

J. Chilton Pearce,
Magical Child

Natural childhood

In this chapter we have looked at images of the child created by 20th-century psychologists and educators. What connects these images with the popular social attitudes prevalent at the time? In his book *Miseducation, Preschoolers at Risk,* David Elkind speaks of three consecutive attitudes to childhood in the 20th century. Until the 1930s or '40s, the child was perceived as basically sinful. Education was seen as the process of overcoming this sinfulness and enabling children to become members of civilized society.

After World War II came the sensual child, whose mentor was the paediatrician Benjamin Spock and whose chief threat was maternal deprivation. Provided that his sensual needs – to be mothered, to have play-space, and so on – were met, it was not necessary to pay special attention to the sensual child's intellectual abilities.

The competent child

In the 1960s and '70s, the image of the competent child emerged and inspired programmes aimed at giving the child a head start in learning. Jerome Bruner proposed that "We begin with the hypothesis that any subject can be taught effectively in some intellectually honest way to any child at any stage of development". This is the maxim of the competent child.

The competent child's intellectual abilities are placed in the hands of learning technicians who try to use his innate capacity to learn a language to master other disciplines, especially reading and mathematics. Mastery of key concepts is the essential step to intellectual progress.

> "
> *If you want your children to be brilliant, tell them fairy tales. If you want them to be very brilliant, tell them even more fairy tales."*
>
> Albert Einstein

> "
> *The child is a gift of nature, but the image of the child is mankind's creation."*
>
> David Elkind,
> *Miseducation, Preschoolers at Risk*

Pressures on parents

"Will you handicap your child for his 21st-century future unless you buy him a computer and an assortment of software for his third birthday?" asks Joan Beck in *How to Raise a Brighter Child.* Her implied answer is: if not now, you will in the near future when an educational gap opens up between the kids with home computers and the kids without.

The persuasive image of the competent child brings enormous pressure on parents. Commercial interests make it worse. As a result, a child is taught at the wrong time and in the wrong way for purposes that belong to the parent not the child. Childhood is sacrificed for the sake of parental egoism and commercial profit.

It is against this illusory image that natural childhood must be placed. Like natural birth, which affirms a reality that medical practice often ignores, natural childhood is an affirmation in the face of destructive tendencies in education. We are not seeking a lost paradise of childhood, but to rediscover a meaningful human tradition increasingly threatened by technological change.

Childhood is especially vulnerable. Viewing the brain as the basic instrument of our humanness ignores the life of Feeling and of Will that equally characterize human-ness. Failing to observe this imitative learning is linked with our failure to act meaningfully as adults.

Children who do not experience a natural childhood will lack the strong foundation it gives to adult life. The way we bring up our children has far more importance for the world than the technical advances made for their comfort.

▲ Mother Nature's child

An adult who can look back on a child-hood of honesty, freshness, and naïveté has truly experienced a natural childhood.

CHAPTER 2

Planes of development

A "holistic" approach means that the point of departure is the whole rather than the part. The parts find their significance in their relationship to this whole. So, what is the whole in human development? This must defy definition which works by fixing limits. The whole must include the physical, psychological, and emotional as well as the spiritual dimensions of the human being.

The wholesome imagination

Every culture that came before our own carried an imagination of what it is to be human. This imagination penetrated social, individual, and religious life. Our culture today, lacking that imagination, has a special task, a remarkable one: to create individually out of our own capacities this whole picture of what it is to be human, so that it becomes the uniting, vivifying element in our understanding of whatever meets us in life.

What we are calling the whole, this wholesome imagination, is not some subjective fantasy. With it, and through it, we are mothering, fathering, educating, and the child is there with her needs, challenging us to understand her, to give her our care, to love her. And the way we are with the child enables us to make clearer, more vivid, and real this imagination of what it is to be human. Building the whole, the imagination, and knowing the details, the parts, is a two-way process. It is not an intellectual idea, rather a feeling, thinking way of understanding.

But the process makes its demands. The child for whom we have taken responsibility is not there for our ends, but for her own. Her hidden goal is to become more and more her individual self, not a reflection or a product of her parents. And we must recognize and support her own need for growth, her own aspirations.

Pre- and post-natal life

Embryology maps out in great detail the stages of physical development that take place from the moment of conception to birth. This amazing evolution, in no matter which race or culture, follows a universal pattern, repeated endlessly in each individual.

Throughout the pre-natal stage, the embryo is protected in its fluid environment from the effects of gravity and the sudden shocks and changes in temperature, light, and sound. After birth, this is no longer the case and we must introduce the new-born child gradually to her new environment.

The pattern of development continues after birth, although this may show great individual variations. But all normal children develop spectroscopic vision, have first teething, stand and walk, reject the first teeth, and push out the second dentition at more or less pre-ordained stages in growth. These changes are physically obvious, but other changes also take place which, although not as evident, are just as real. It is on the understanding and support of these more hidden stages that the art of being a parent depends.

Understanding inner stages

In fact, the more we understand and perceive these inner stages of growth the more we can support the development, encourage the external active learning, and strengthen the growing self-confidence of the child. We are not aiming to make the child conform for the sake of conforming, or obey for the sake of obeying.

Warmth, comfort, and nourishment are the primary needs of the child when she arrives on earth. The newborn puts herself, with total trust, into the hands of her parents for her physical requirements and also for the relationship which she must have for all the learning she undertakes in the first years.

Almost immediately after birth the mother and the child communicate with each other; the infant (without language) responds to the speaking mother, who intuitively understands the meanings of her child's varying murmurs and cries. It is in this shared communication that the

◀ **Starting a long journey**
From the beginning, the baby is feeling, touching, and tasting her mother. The strength drawn from her mother's milk begins a long journey of awakening.

emotional and cognitive life of the child develops in the first years. The mother's care and protection create a foundation for trust in life. The gesture and speech of the mother draw from the child the language that will enable her to understand and communicate with the world around her (see also pp. 68–73).

The physical, psychological, and spiritual growth of the child passes through a number of stages. Development is not a uniform process, for at all three levels, one part will progress faster than other parts, which will, however, catch up at a later stage. For example, at birth, physically, the baby's head is more developed than the limbs. At the psychological level, however, her will to move and act is far in advance of her ability to cognize and reflect.

Stages of development

We can characterize the main stages briefly as standing, speaking, and the development of an inner conceptual world. These stages overlap, but they represent the enormous achievement of the first seven years of a child's life, the essential preconditions of all that will emerge later in the human capacity to communicate, to create, and to evolve a personal life of worth and satisfaction.

It is as if, in these first seven years, the individuality of the child has to prepare a house in which it can live for the rest of her life. The role of the adult is to understand all the stages of

▶ **The steps of development**
The first step is when the child is standing and ready to walk. The second step is when language is being established and she says "I", making an important step in her consciousness of herself. The third step is when she can express what she has in her mind and begins to imprint her own character in the language she uses.

this house-building and to help the child with it. This is easier said than done.

The Self

Why does the human take so long to grow up physically? This phenomenon sets us apart from all animals: the duckling swims a few hours after leaving the egg; the wildebeest calf runs with the herd the day after it is born. The animal is mature when it is equipped to fulfill its behavioural role in that unique space made available for it by Nature. All its special attributes – claw, hoof, wing, fur, feather, or hide, assign it its special place. Not so the human! Lacking the nar-

row specializations of the animal, she is both a creature of Nature and a creature who confronts Nature, but with undefined capacities.

Where the animal is a specialist, the human is a generalist. The animal is enclosed in Nature, the human is partly liberated from it. What liberates her are her upright posture, her speech, and her thinking power. But aren't the primate and the penguin upright? Don't the bee and the bird have language? Don't the chimp and the gorilla reason? Things which resemble each other are not necessarily the same. Human language is not confined to expression of pain or pleasure or signalling where food is. Language and thinking are the basis of all culture. The reasoning of animals is incapable of reaching those levels at which the human thinks about her situation and reflects on how she thinks. The human moves beyond Nature as farmer, builder, technician, artist, gardener, and polluter.

The human signature

Uprightness reveals the presence of the Self. Speech enables the joint attentiveness between one Self and another to take place. The "I" can be co-present with the "Thou". Animals share the same moment. They can be co-operative or competitive in it, but they are never jointly attentive in it, as humans can be. Thinking enables the human to encompass the world of things, of Nature, of humanity.

Uprightness, speech, and thinking, which are the signature of the human, also determine her developmental path. This is the incarnating path of the human Self.

STEP 3
Thinking

3–7 years

1–3 years

STEP 2
Speaking

0–12 months

STEP 1
Standing

▶ **The human hand**

The hoof is shaped for running. What is the hand shaped for? Making fire and axes and automobiles; pointing, painting, and piano-playing; climbing, swimming, and writing. It is limitlessly, and unspecifically functional, and our upright-ness allows the hands to perform.

Step One

From the moment of birth, the baby has an innate Will to reach toward the world, represented at first by the mother, and to engage it in dialogue. This Will (see pp. 226–33) is the impulse to be alive, to learn, to become. It is the fundamental expression of the individuality, of the soul and spirit of *this* being. This unique being follows steps of development which are both universal and idiosyncratic. They are universal because every human being follows them in a set order. They are idiosyncratic because each individual chooses her moment to enter on a certain stage and has her own way of doing so.

We shall try to describe these steps in broad brush strokes. At first, the newborn's eyes do not focus at will, the hands cannot hold, and the mouth only seeks. By six weeks, the vision can focus. Then the hands meet and clasp and the baby smiles. The total movement-system of kicking legs, flailing arms, and arching back becomes differentiated. Within the total organism of muscle activity the head begins to separate its movement. In the second month the baby can turn her head and begin to raise it. This process of separation works downward from the head (see also p. 217). After freeing the head, the baby learns to roll over. Soon she will be able to sit with support. Then her limbs become further differentiated in their movements as she crawls, rises on to all fours and sits unsupported. This is usually attained by the eighth month. The sitting position offers a new view of life. She can reach for, and grasp, objects and bring one moveable object into contact with another. She can beat the table with a spoon and move about the room with surprising speed.

In the ninth or tenth month the baby tries to stand with support. She can throw things, and in a short time can bring herself upright and stand by holding on to something. By the end of the first year she can stand freely and begin her first steps. Much else is also going on that will only fully emerge at a later stage. Gestures, eye movements, and cooing sounds of the child are the signs of dialogue with her parent. This communication is a kind of pre-speech, but it already carries nuances of feeling, of intention, of understanding, and even of humour.

Step Two

At first, the child walks forward with arms aloft. As her stride becomes firmer her arms are freed from the leg rhythm and so her hands can refine and develop their very different skills. Language development follows walking. The preparation has been in the gurgles, cooings, and gestures with the parent; language exists and is understood long before it is spoken. If the child's walk is strong and sturdy her speech will be more articulate, and if hand and arm movements are harmonious, her speech will be flowing. There is a powerful link between the development of walking and talking.

Because the child learns by imitation (see also pp. 48, 136, 174, 225), it makes a great difference if, in the first year, she hears adult language that is clearly pronounced, not just baby-talk.

In the second year, utterances such as, "mama", "dada", and "bye-bye", become clearly names for mother, father, or saying goodbye. But at first, "dada" may represent a whole sentence, such as "dolly has fallen on the floor" (see also p. 37). Gradually, words separate out – mainly names at first. In the second half of the second year adjectives such as "pretty" or "good" and verbs such as "fall" or "like" emerge.

Slowly, language becomes specific and appropriate to the thing or event, just as, earlier, the child's movements in space became more and more directed to handling objects.

Language develops through imitation. The child's mimicry is not like the adult's. There is no sharp focusing of attention, rather a kind of dreamy absorption. It may be some time before the child brings out what she has absorbed.

But the child's role in acquiring language is not a passive one. Both in the absorption of the parent's words and in the active uttering when a new event arouses similar-feeling impulses, the child seems to have a wide, unfocused consciousness, which will gradually give way to a more awake, focused self-consciousness. The child's power to imitate diminishes in this process of gaining the sense of Self.

In the first two years perception and activity are closely united. For example, during a walk, the child may see a dog and wander after it. A boy may pass on a bike, and she will turn to watch, then she may see a flower and run to pick it. In the third year the Will is sufficiently strong inwardly so that her actions are more independent of sense impressions. But in this second stage, when speech is developing, the word and sense impressions are joined and out of this union the world begins to make sense.

▲ The beginnings of form

The child experiments, building a vocabulary of "scribbles". Human shapes may be depicted in body "spirals" (far left), and spiky limb lines (above).

Step Three

In the third year, Step Three begins. The child starts to articulate her experience of the world. By the end of the third year she will have acquired most of the vocabulary needed for everyday life. Her activity is not so closely bound up with sense impressions. She will begin to refer to herself as "I" instead of Joanna or Susie. The moment she intuits that she is an "I", she makes a significant step in self-awareness (see p. 220).

We experience our individuality because we live consciously in time. We remember yesterday and anticipate tomorrow. This conscious living in time becomes part of the three-year-old's experience. She begins to have a personal biography. Future self-respect is built on this.

Piaget describes the first two years as sensory-motor, and years from three to five as symbolic-representational. This corresponds with our description, which is also borne out by children's drawings. The stories and fairy tales that appeal to children in this third step nourish the symbolizing capability of the child. With the adult, the symbol is not the same as what it symbolizes. With the child these two are one.

The three-year-old child is able to enter deliberately into the logic of a situation. She makes thought-connections with refreshing imagination and originality. The toe of a shoe she may call the shoe's "nose". She is beginning to bring the world into conceptual order. This is human thinking at a level which even the higher mammals never attain.

The three-year-old frequently says "No". She likes to refuse or to reject and even show her negative will in tantrums. This can be very frustrating for the parents. But from her point of view, she is experiencing what is going on from a new centre of consciousness. The old dreamy, diffuse consciousness is being transformed by a new focusing. The growing self-awareness carries an inner world of feeling which cannot be expressed. The parent may now find it even more difficult to know what is going on. The child's need is now to develop her language so that she can express her inner experience. It is important for parents to understand this difficult transition and the frustrations it may bring, and to give the child support in her need to separate herself, in order to find her identity.

Physical changes

Physical development means growth in height, increase in weight, change of shape, and the completion of the structures of the different organs of the body. It also implies increased control over the body, the ability to move the limbs, to use the hands, to co-ordinate hand and eye, to stand, to run, and to jump. This development is driven by an inborn force. There is no need for the child to be trained or motivated.

Teething signals change

The creation of the permanent teeth in the seventh year is an important developmental sign. They have been produced by growth forces and when these forces are no longer needed in the creation of the hardest material in the body they are free for other activity: furthering the development of intellect and memory. The change signals that the child is ready for her next stage of learning. This learning is directed and asks for conscious and deliberate teaching from adults.

The changing face

The changing proportions of the head are expressive of the incarnating process. In the baby's face, the horizontal line through the eyes is below the middle of the head, as the lower part of the face is relatively small and the nose still undeveloped. At three months, the forehead is beautifully domed and the child may look like a Buddha. The toddler's chin begins to come forward, although the upper lip still protrudes over the lower. While the face shows more expression, the features remain soft and formless. By the fifth year, the nose is more pronounced and the forehead is less dominant. The eyes, which appear smaller, and closer together, are now above the horizontal middle line.

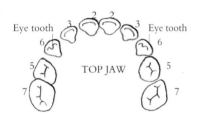
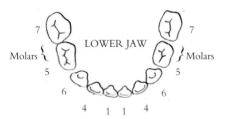

▲ **How the teeth grow**
Before the eighth month, the first teeth appear. In the sixth or seventh year the extra molars and new incisors emerge. The other teeth are gradually changed during the eighth year.

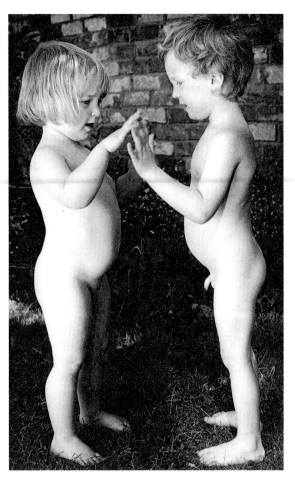

Shifting proportions

The whole body also shows transformations in its proportions. At birth, the head is relatively large and grows more slowly than the trunk and legs. In the third year, the neck seems slightly longer and the head and shoulders are more separated. Between the third and fifth years, after the broadening of the chest comes the lengthening of the limbs. By the seventh year, the characteristic round tummy has disappeared and the waist separates the chest from the abdomen. When the child reaches school age she is slim and elegant. In movement she is rhythmic and agile, and her expression is more alert. Head, chest, and limbs are more clearly differentiated. This corresponds to a new level of integration of the Soul activities of head, heart, and limbs.

▲ **Changing body shape**
As the toddler changes from "walking baby" to upright child, the limbs lengthen, though the head is still large and the tummy protruding.

7 YEARS

4 YEARS

18 MONTHS

NEWBORN

▲ **Changing face shape**
At birth the lower part of the face is small and the nose undeveloped. At 18 months the chin is more obvious. At four the nose is more pronounced and the forehead less so, while at seven the eyes seem smaller and above the middle line.

The senses

The first sense-experiences of the baby are the warmth and touch of the mother, and the taste and smell of her milk. Literally, and metaphorically, the child is drinking in the world.

The child is also perceiving what is going on in her own body. Sensing the movement of her limbs is as much a sense-experience as hearing a noise. This sense is called the muscle-sense, or proprioception. The sense of balance is experienced by the baby when she raises her head and later sits, comes into the upright, and walks. Those sensations associated with different organs of the body, such as thirst or hunger, pain or wellbeing, are called life-senses. Touch tells us the limits of our body as well as the surface we are pressing against.

The child is wide open and defenceless against the sensations she encounters. She is unable to ignore dazzling lights or loud noises. Today's environment provides many powerful sense-experiences which are very harmful for the young child. The parent can shield her from strong light or penetrating smells, but it is difficult to give protection against the pervasive "noise" of modern, everyday life.

Scents and smells make a deep impression on the child. There is no barrier to their penetrating influence. The tastes of different foods have a strong effect and we must cultivate in the child a taste for healthy foods. Warmth is also an important sense for the young child. She cannot hold her warmth like an adult and so her body needs to be well protected (see also p. 284).

Looking and seeing

Our understanding of the world is dominated by our visual and auditory senses. When the new-born baby opens her eyes, her gaze does not rest on an object. After a time she can focus on her parent's face 10 inches (25cm) away. She learns to direct her gaze first, as a kind of reflex, without having any object in focus. Finally, at about two months, she can follow with her eyes an object about 10 inches (25cm) away. She also turns her head in the direction of a sound.

The baby achieves this ability to converge and direct her sight by about three-and-a-half months and she then begins to explore the world around her attentively. Hand–eye co-ordination quickly develops and the child is ready to satisfy her curiosity by reaching out for things to look at, to feel, or to suck.

As humans we see many things but actually look at few. Looking is active seeing. It is a long, quiet process. We should help the small child to develop her looking. She can become absorbed in the appearance of an object such as a stone, or an insect. The scurrying images of television excite her to see, but do not educate her to look (see also pp. 53, 140–1, 223).

Hearing and listening

The sound the baby most likes to hear is the sound of her mother's or father's voice, whether speaking or singing. The disembodied voice of radio lacks what she wants – the living presence of the adult. For the development of spoken and written language the habit of listening is essential. Listening is active hearing. It is not a question of training the child to listen, but rather of not hindering listening, or looking. A distracting or confusing home atmosphere works against the child being able to experience that inner quiet necessary for proper listening. This is a major problem in our society, where we have become so used to constant noise that silence has become unbearable. We must recover some of this lost territory of silence.

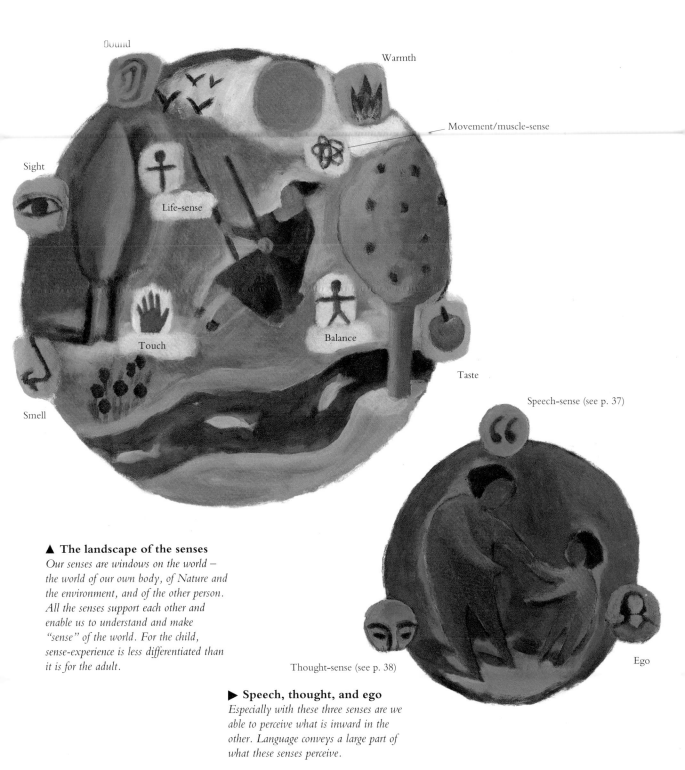

Sound

Warmth

Movement/muscle-sense

Sight

Life-sense

Touch

Balance

Taste

Smell

Speech-sense (see p. 37)

Thought-sense (see p. 38)

Ego

▲ **The landscape of the senses**
Our senses are windows on the world –
the world of our own body, of Nature and
the environment, and of the other person.
All the senses support each other and
enable us to understand and make
"sense" of the world. For the child,
sense-experience is less differentiated than
it is for the adult.

▶ **Speech, thought, and ego**
Especially with these three senses are we
able to perceive what is inward in the
other. Language conveys a large part of
what these senses perceive.

The emotions

The bond of attachment between the baby and her mother is essential for her healthy development. This bond already exists before birth. Even if the mother gives the baby up for adoption it is still there. It is still there if the parent ill-treats the child. For the baby, the bond is made up of trust and acceptance, but it is not the same for the mother. She has to adjust her life to make a place for her newborn and this may mean sacrifice. But she may also experience a new sense of fulfillment. How she copes will affect the baby's feelings.

It takes a few weeks before the baby first smiles. By then the mother has already learned the meaning of her different cries. Happiness and joy, sadness or discomfort, are the primary feelings of the young baby. When the baby smiles or laughs, she breathes out and when she cries she sucks in her breath. With joy or happiness her smile expands. We say she beams with joy. With sorrow, her face and body contract inward.

The whole emotional life is carried and expressed in the breathing. The blood circulation and heartbeat also register feelings. The rhythms that belong to the heart and lungs are continually modulated by the feelings that take hold of us. Stress or fear makes us pale; anger or shame makes us blush. The bonding between mother and child is an emotional one affecting the rhythms in the chest. Cramped feelings and feelings of tightness in the chest, which many adults experience, may well have their origins in

the relationship that they had with their mothers in their early years. This may be because of parental manipulation. The mother may threaten to withdraw her love in order to bring about certain behaviour in the child. In order not to lose this love, the child learns not to express certain feelings (see also pp. 50, 96).

Until the child is able to speak and express her feelings she must rely on the perception and sensitivity of the adult to read them. The four-year-old who can now express her anger or

◀ **The first smile**
We can feel so honoured when a tiny baby smiles at us. It is very different from the smile of an adult, which can show pleasure, happiness, irony, superiority, or embarrassment. We lose ourselves in the smile of a baby, glimpsing already the being who is making her way into the life on earth.

frustration but does not have the words, needs the adult to understand and acknowledge her right to express these emotions and to be given the chance to do so.

Before three years of age, the child has little capability of controlling her emotional state. After the change in self-awareness of the third year she begins to learn to deal with her fluctuations of feelings. These don't appear so directly in bodily expression. They swing between opposite states, between, for example, the need for affection on the one hand, and the wish for a certain independence on the other. Of course we all swing between these polarities during our whole lives. Parents who long only for, say, an affectionate and cheerful child, do an injustice to the natural pendulum of emotions.

The growth of language

We do not inherit our language. A new-born baby has the potential to acquire any one of the 6000 languages that humanity speaks. She needs only to be placed among speakers of one of them.

The newborn has the ability to vocalize and also to respond to language. She acquires it without learning grammar or structure, yet these belong to all languages. Her capacity to grasp structure is inborn.

The child's speaking begins with coos, gurgles, and babbling. At first, certain vowel-like sounds emerge, then more consonantal sounds are heard. The more guttural sounds, like g, k, or r, tend to express comfort or satisfaction, whereas nasal sounds and consonants like w, l or h are audible whining cries of discomfort or distress. Still later, as her lips and tongue grasp the stream of air more firmly, we hear p, b, d, m, and n. After six weeks, the child continually repeats strings of sounds. Rhythm, change of pitch, stress, and sound-groups are endlessly rehearsed and enjoyed. In the fourth month, the child responds, with contented sounds, to the parent's delighted comments. Actions soon become linked with words and eventually the sound "No" makes the baby desist and "bye-bye" is met with a tiny hand wave. At first, words like "mama" or "dada" have large meanings encompassing different situations. "Mama" might mean "Pick me up, mama" (see also p. 30). It is only gradually that the word and the object come together. So at eighteen months, "mama" becomes the name for the mother.

Through language we utter our thoughts and feelings. A child develops language in the presence of an adult, who is thinking and feeling. So she hears more than just words; she is hearing the inwardness of the speaker.

GRASPING MEANING
A little girl is learning the word "pittie" (pretty). Between 1 year 9 months and 2 years 4 months the child applies the word to the following: a piece of ribbon, a green pencil, a woman on a bus, a dress, a light when switched on, the reflector on a bicycle, beads. How can we explain this application of one word to such diverse and yet appropriate objects? It cannot be just abstracting a common element. So what is the common element that unites them? Perhaps the diverse situations must have the same feeling and will character to evoke the word "pretty". The child is experiencing deeply in its feeling and will a quality which calls up the word.

THE MAGIC OF WORDS
For the child words have magic as well as power. Hence she likes to hear again and again their rhythm and sound. For there is a secret link between the sound and the name. Adults may lose connection with this side of language and hear only the meaning. The poet keeps this child-like sense for language where every vowel and consonant has its special quality. That is why nursery rhymes are so enjoyable for children. The meaning can be strange, but their sounds are magical (see also pp. 162–3).

Thinking

When the baby begins to observe the world, she begins the process of thinking. Not of course the abstract, logical thinking of adults. She begins to make sense of the colours and shapes that surround her and learns to name now one thing, then another. This is the most primary kind of thinking. We don't actually see a chair. We see a configuration of upright and horizontal parts whose function we grasp and whose name we learn. For the adult this is second nature. For the child it is original activity. The child grasps the essence of the chair, which is its function. So an upturned bucket can be "my chair". The child also shows a kind of practical reasoning. For example, if a toy cannot pass through the bars of the playpen one way, then it can be made to pass by turning it. This kind of reasoning one can find among the primates and higher animals. It is always based on a situation.

▲ Coming in from the cosmos
The concept of the child taking up her place on earth, or incarnating, can be brought alive in vivid imagery for the small child who asks the question, "Where did I come from?" The child before birth has a dwelling place with the moon, planets, and stars and is welcomed on to earth into the outstretched arms of her parents.

Pictorial thinking

The child's thinking has a more pictorial character than the abstract thinking of the adult. This sentence is from an Irish fairy tale: "A king went out hunting one day, but saw nothing till near sunset, when what should he come across but a black pig". We can read this by making a picture in our mind as we read of the king, his riding out, and the black pig. We can also skim off the information with the minimum of picturing. It is the first way that appeals to the young child because the picture is more alive than the mere informational content. This "picture"-consciousness is appealed to by fairy tales. At the age of ten or eleven it gives way to a more abstract thinking. If this is pushed too early, it affects the young child's feeling relation to the world and is a barrier to healthy thinking in adulthood.

Intuitive thinking

It must surely amaze parents when they hear a five-year-old use such words as "because" or "although". It is quite hard for most adults to explain their meaning, yet the child intuits it. "That's true 'cos my Mum says so", is a reasonable statement for a five-year-old. The child has already embodied in language the idea of "because", but it is some years before she grasps it as an experience and perceives it in the laws of physics: "The wooden block floats because the water it displaces has the same weight as the block". To grasp this logical connection inwardly, the child has to grow down into her body and experience her own physical structure, as she begins to do before puberty.

Sexuality

Meeting the child's need to understand sexuality is not simple. There are no rules, but if parents cannot give the child the answers she needs because of embarrassment, then they are failing her. As a guide, her questions show what she is ready to know. It is important that the parent is neither evasive nor presumes what may not be present in the child's mind. The four-year-old's question will not be the same as the nine-year-old's, although the words used may be identical.

The origin of the soul

It is important to realize that the little child is not just asking about physical birth, but also about the root of her Self, her Soul. Much formal sex-education may imply for the child that the human being is only a physical apparatus, created randomly for a meaningless existence. If the child is able to overcome this picture it is because of her own intuitions rather than the guidance of her culture. As she grows older, her questions will be more searching. If the parent has established trust, the child will continue to be open and will derive great strength from a parent who can speak wisely.

CHANGES IN THE 6TH OR 7TH YEAR
In the fifth and sixth years the child begins to use language in a new way. Her talk is directed outward; private talk is now inward and silent. It is the beginning of an inner reflective experience. Speech is more integrated with what she is doing. The child begins to ask questions of metaphysical profundity. By the sixth or seventh year the parent finds she has a companion with whom to share conversation. The child is beginning to be able to see the world through another's eyes and can also play the role of another. Now we see a fundamental reorganization of the child's mental life. There is a blossoming of the imagination and picture-thinking, which is visible in the child's drawings and play, and in the kind of stories she chooses. In the seventh year we notice that the language is more and more the child's own and less and less an imitation of what the parents have given her. Her face will change and it may begin to look less like the parents', more and more herself. Then we realize that childhood in its infant stage is coming to an end, and a new phase is beginning.

▶ **The temperaments in symbols**
The temperaments can be symbolized as a Jack-in-the-box, a tea set, a drum, and a mask. The Jack-in-the-box is the choleric, who likes to lead, to win, and is full of energy and vigour. The tea set is the phlegmatic, who enjoys home comfort and may be over-indulged. The drum is the sanguine, who is fiery and light-hearted. And the mask is the melancholic, who lives, to some extent, in a world of her own making.

The temperaments

Various attempts have been made to classify human beings according to constitutional, psychological, or personality types. In these we can recognize a certain number of ways in which the uniqueness of the spiritual part is related in life to the inherited part.

Typology

Steiner's typology is especially helpful in understanding the later years of childhood and can give useful guidance to parents. The four temperaments he describes are the choleric, the sanguine, the phlegmatic, and the melancholic. These names go back to the Greeks, but the perception they entail is entirely contemporary. Children respond in different ways to the same situation. For example an obstacle in the way of one child may make her sit down and cry, while another kicks it and steps over it. Such different reactions may be due to temperament. Temperamental differences ask for different treatment from the parent or teacher. Temperament shows itself more clearly from about the fifth or sixth year and an understanding of it is helpful through puberty. Temperament can change significantly from childhood to adulthood

Identifying the temperament

A child's temperament is usually a combination of two or three and it is especially important to identify the most dominant one. This can sometimes be done by observing which temperament is missing. It is not the aim to suppress or alter the temperament. We help the child by making her aware of what she feels inclined to ignore, through her temperament.

THE CHOLERIC

Choleric is an extroverted temperament and the child likes to assert himself. He is usually ready to tackle a job which would make others pause. He is not shy, but looks at you with a steady gaze. He walks with a firm step. His will to be out in front marks him as a leader. He likes to have the main role in a play or to organize others. He can inspire the group to complete a difficult task. It is not unusual to see him red with anger and with eyes flashing. This temperament likes to win, but seldom bears a grudge. Opposing the Will of such a child generally gets the parent nowhere. He needs to be appreciated and given things to do which challenge him and use up his excessive energy. He learns best from people who can do things well and whom he can admire. He doesn't easily learn from his mistakes. If guided well the choleric brings initiative and originality to his play. The temperament is fiery and this shows in his paintings, where strong colours, especially red, and strong forms dominate.

▲ Choleric
The choleric child is very intense and very quickly roused to attentiveness.

▼ Sanguine
The sanguine child is not very intense but can be easily roused to attentiveness.

THE SANGUINE

The sanguine temperament is an extroverted temperament. The child lacks the fiery inner purpose of the choleric and is activated more by what is going on around her. She has difficulty in concentrating on one thing for long and a new event easily distracts her. This restless changeability can be a bane for parents and teachers. A sanguine is often light-footed and rhythmical, but also light-headed and lighthearted. The interest she shows in everything makes her popular and a good social bridge-builder. Parties are great fun for her and she is seldom alone. Her face is expressive and mobile and her eyes easily sparkle. She is more likely to have curly hair than straight. It is hard for her to bear antipathy from a friend or an adult, for she is most herself when she feels loved. In extreme forms, the sanguine can appear superficial and may be unable to concentrate on a game or to amuse herself for long. It is good to encourage the sanguine to stick to a task.

THE PHLEGMATIC

Phlegmatic is an introverted temperament. This child doesn't easily connect with what is going on around her, for her interest is not easily aroused. Eating may be a prime attraction and she may be rounded and clumsy. She is generally easy to bring up, so she may not get the attention she needs. She enjoys comfort and doting parents may over-indulge her. She needs to be stimulated to action or to take interest. She is generally placid and doesn't anger except when extremely frustrated. She is methodical, keeping her things in order unless she is so spoiled that, for the sake of comfort, she abandons her orderly ways. She can be counted on to do what she sets out to do, although speed is no object. She has a certain stubbornness, making her resistant to new ideas. She adores routine. Her love for food makes her gain weight and parents should impose a sensible diet. She needs to be encouraged to join in with other children and to try new activities. When she has found an interest in others, the phlegmatic is loyal and steadfast.

▲ Phlegmatic
The phlegmatic child lacks intensity and is not easily roused to attentiveness.

▼ Melancholic
The melancholic child is a rather intense personality who doesn't easily become attentive.

THE MELANCHOLIC

This child experiences his physical body as somewhat of a burden. Instead of moving with a light skip (sanguine) or a firm step (choleric), he drags his feet. A minor physical injury causes excessive pain and while he likes others to know this, he doesn't want to be consoled. Cold water is to be avoided for he needs warmth. He usually avoids social life and prefers to play by himself. Remarks easily wound and are long remembered. When surrounded by different goings on, he chooses what interests him and is not diverted by other things. He gives himself up easily to his own-world fantasies, which tend to be rich. This preoccupation with his own world appears very egocentric and further increases his isolation. But it is an isolation which he appreciates. This inner concentration gives the melancholic a special depth and understanding which parents can appreciate. He asks profound questions about God or death. Such lonely souls need a great deal of love and understanding, but too much sympathy is unhelpful, for he is to some extent in love with his own suffering. Making him aware of the suffering of others can often help to take him out of his self-centredness. While he never wants to be the heart and soul of the party, he appreciates a warm social environment.

Physical characteristics

The different temperaments tend to have a certain physical appearance, but it can be surprising to find a particular temperament in a body that doesn't quite suit it. This is because other factors, such as inherited constitution, are also in play. Nevertheless, there is a physical type we can associate with each temperament.

The choleric is often short and sturdy with a strong neck, while the sanguine has a light and graceful build, with finely shaped hands. The round shape of the phlegmatic has already been mentioned and this contrasts with the thin, even lanky, form of the melancholic. The eyes of the melancholic are frequently downcast, but have a fine attractive gaze. They also tend to be dark. It is important for the adult to pay great attention to details and not to jump to quick conclusions. One can discover that a child one thought of as sanguine can show a phlegmatic or a choleric side. The important thing is to understand from what level the child acts and how to respond appropriately.

▼ **Temperament combinations**
Temperaments which are opposite are not present together, but the temperaments on either side of the main type are usually present to some degree.

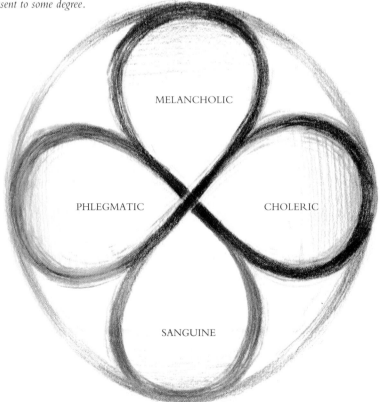

MELANCHOLIC

PHLEGMATIC

CHOLERIC

SANGUINE

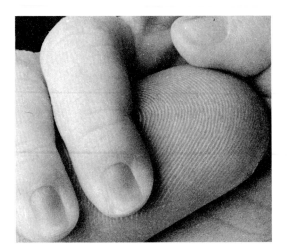

CHAPTER 3

The rhythm of development

Rhythms belong to life. They manifest in every living thing. The wing beat of a bird, the crawling caterpillar, the sap's rise and fall, the human heartbeat, express the rhythmic essence of life (see also Chapter 16).

Rhythms of the body

The experience of rhythm begins before birth. The mother passes her blood rhythm to the fetus so that the fetal blood is already pulsing before the heart is formed.

Other rhythms pervade the whole body. The fluid in the spinal column rises and falls. The muscles of the stomach and intestines are swept by rhythmic movements. Such rhythms interweave. Sleep is Nature's way of restoring order to the rhythmic system of the body after the stresses of the day (see also p. 283).

Growing up is itself a rhythmic process. The baby has to find new rhythms in sleeping and waking, in digesting and evacuating. His early chaotic limb movements find rhythm in the crawling and toddler stages. When he stands, arms and legs are rhythmically united, but in the second year he frees his arms from this bond so that he can use expressive rhythms in playing, in moving, in making, and in doing. In the development of the senses, language, and memory he also experiences rhythm.

The organic rhythms affect and are affected by the psychic life of the child. Anxiety and stress are registered in heartbeat and breathing, and if these are regularly experienced the child's development may be injured. Parents need to have an understanding of the child's rhythmic development. It is no mere metaphor to speak of the heart as the place where love has its dwelling.

Day, night, seasons

Not only do rhythms permeate living organisms, they are also experienced in the relationship of the earth to the sun, moon, and stars. The cyclic rhythms of the heavens influence the earth itself and all plants and animals. Technological developments, such as artificial lighting, have to some extent freed humans from some of these cycles. We have greater independence from the exigencies of day and night and the seasons of the year than our ancestors and the other species on the planet. The seasons of growth and fruits for harvest in the plant world, and for migration and hibernation in the animal world, are regulated by this cosmic interaction.

Rhythm for living

The newborn baby ignores day and night, alternating as he does between periods of sleeping and eating. After a few weeks, he begins to adjust to sleeping more during the night. In his second year, meal-pattern rhythms also change: he will be sitting in his highchair, eating with the family. He has learned to conform to the day–night rhythm and the social pattern of family life. Helping to bring this about is part of the art of being a parent. Without imposing a rigid discipline, and by avoiding the attitude which lets the child decide everything, the parents can bring the child to a healthy daily rhythm by firm, but gentle, encouragement.

Only slowly does the child become aware of the larger rhythms – the seasons and the years. When Sarah says proudly, "I am four," her three-year-old brother admires uncomprehendingly. Birthday celebrations are joyful occasions which mark steps on the stairway to being grown-up. Celebrations (see also pp. 254–65) can have a strengthening force in the education of the young child.

Day

Spring

Summer

Winter

Autumn

Night

▲ Celebrations

Festivals confirm that there is an order in the universe and a miraculous balance of forces which make human life and creativity possible. These call for wonder and reverence. Such feelings give a healthy foundation for the child's growing understanding of the world. Some festivals have, unfortunately, lost their meaning for many people, but with conscious effort we can find a renewed connection with the cycle of the year.

Living in space

Growing up is learning to be more and more at home in space. Through his senses, and with his increasing ability to move, stand, and walk, the child explores space. From the first opening of his eyes and moving of his hand, he belongs to space. At the same time, he is experiencing his own increasing sense of being separate from the objects in space.

Growing into time

How does the child grow into the experience of time? For the baby time is either a sleep or a dream: islands of soft awareness in a sea of sleep, without memories or anticipations. Yet from the beginning, almost, there is a kind of memory. In the intricate process that goes on between mother and baby there is a dialogue, although only the mother speaks. This rhythmic exchange increases in complexity. When the situation is repeated, say, each time the child is nursing at his mother's breast, he recalls the experience of before. Memory is there, but it is not the developed picture-memory of the older child. When a fourteen-month-old child comes back to his grandparents' house two months after his last visit, we know he remembers an object he played with because he immediately goes to it. This kind of memory is attached to a place and is called "locative". The phrase "out of sight, out of mind" describes it.

Rhythm has a significant role in memory. The repetition of sounds and words which children love link them in memory. Sounds similar to "gee-gee", "bow-wow", and "tick-tock" are part of early language in all cultures.

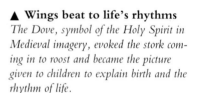

▲ **Wings beat to life's rhythms**
The Dove, symbol of the Holy Spirit in Medieval imagery, evoked the stork coming in to roost and became the picture given to children to explain birth and the rhythm of life.

In the third year, the child develops another memory which is essential for our experience of being a whole person. This is picture, or conceptual, memory and it gives us a firm relationship in time to the past and future. The child is now able to form an image of what he did two days previously. This capacity to remember also enables him to anticipate what he will do, say, at the weekend, since he remembers what happens at weekends. The child is now awake in the stream of time. About the same time, or a little earlier (two-and-a-quarter-years), the child begins to say "I" instead of "Sarah". As nobody

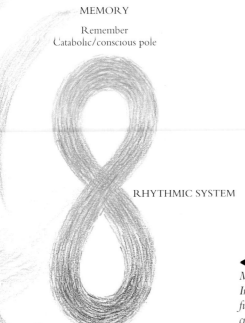

MEMORY

Remember
Catabolic/conscious pole

RHYTHMIC SYSTEM

Anabolic/vital pole
Forget

FANTASY/IMAGINATION

◀ **Past and future**
Memory delves into the past, into the old. Imagination has to do with the new, the future. Memory conserves, imagination creates. With the awakening of memory and "I" consciousness, a big step is made. The child now asks questions about the great rhythm of life, asking for the whole story in pictures. Where does the "I" come from before birth, and where does it go after death?

else uses "I" to mean Sarah she must have grasped its meaning out of her own consciousness of Self (see also p. 54).

Remembering and forgetting

Rhythm characterizes human life and development. In the same way opposites or polarities are also characteristics of our being. Waking and sleeping, action and reflection, practice and theory, change and conservation, society and the individual, and so on, are examples of polarities. We cannot live for long in one extreme, and so we move toward the opposite.

Remembering and forgetting form just such a polarity. We usually think of forgetting as a negative: something we could do without. Learning to write is often a painful process for the child (see also p. 58). He has to be so conscious and remember which way the d and the b go. But once he has mastered the letters he forgets the rules and can concentrate on the meaning of the word. All skill-learning is of this nature.

In the education of children the role of forgetting is usually ignored and we try to keep everything in the "remembering" area. The significant experiences from which the child learns pass through the field of forgetting and when, later, they are remembered, there is enrichment.

Memory and imagination are opposites and both are essential, but we have to cultivate them. Our earliest memory is often one which is painful, such as the arrival of a sibling which threatened our place. However, highly painful experiences, when, for example, the child is abused by the adult, can become deeply suppressed and may not be remembered, although they will continue to affect later life. Interest and enthusiasm, however, are stimulants for the memory.

The imagination referred to here is not the fantasy which leads people to wallow in the unreal. It is the faculty which allows us to create the future. Planning an outing involves imagination. Scientists, artists, and the rest of us all require imagination. It is a way of seeing the future in a fresh way which can be realized from the present. All healthy personal and social change depends on it. It is in play, free play, that the child practises imagination (see pp. 142–3).

How the child learns

The child learns in the opposite way to the adult, who considers the task, reflects on the best way of going about it and then applies himself. We generally start a job in the head, and, after some thought, use our hands. The child starts with doing, and out of the activity reflection stirs. Learning is at first movement which eventually becomes cognition.

Stones, watering-cans, sand, water, wooden bricks, cups, and spoons are the teachers of the little child. In the playgroup and kindergarten the activities instruct and the parent, leader, or teacher is there to make space and to provide opportunities for the child. If the teacher is busy in her own activities, making things or baking, the child will want to do this too, and will come to his own learning out of his own Will. The mania for early "teaching" of children to enable them to "get a head start" on their peers, which is evident everywhere today, arises out of an inability to see how little children actually learn and a complete lack of understanding.

Learning by imitating

The adult mode of learning is generally intellectual and analytical. The child's is imitative. The child imitates spontaneously (see also pp. 136, 174). His imitation also includes less obvious aspects of his environment – the atmosphere of the room, physical warmth and colour, and also soul warmth and colour. The adult's attitude, feelings, and integrity belong to the environment where the child imitates and will be absorbed and will influence his development.

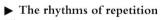
▶ The rhythms of repetition
The two-year-old is scooping water into a plastic container and pouring it over her legs. When the last drop has gone she scoops up more water and starts again. She is absorbed and relaxed, but learning.

Doing and knowing

The toddler plays with his blanket, his "softy" – it has many other names. He draws it over his eyes and then pulls it away, peeping and laughing. So he makes things disappear and appear again. The child's consciousness is not yet centred within him but belongs to all that is around him. It is peripheral consciousness rather than centric, but now he is beginning to experience the world and the Self as two separate entities.

Interchange and conversation

At eighteen months the child offers the adult a spoon. Moments later he toddles back to recover it and immediately gives it back again. All the adults in the room are brought into the game. If the adult, with his habit of doing things for a deliberate purpose, tries to channel the game, the game is spoiled. It is common for adults to feel they are being "given" the object to "keep". But giving and then taking back again is free interchange, open dialogue. In this activity is the predisposition for the give and take of social exchange, for true conversation.

In the action of filling and emptying a container (see facing page) we also see an archetypal gesture in the child. She is exploring the relationship between inner space and outer. These childish games contribute to the psychological development of the child, where within and without, me and not-me gather significance. From the age of three or four the child loves to make dens. Why this house-building mania? He is constructing a bodily house for his Soul. We see how, in his marvellous economy, he takes hold of the most earnest things in life uncompromisingly and playfully.

The landscape of feelings

Our feelings put us in touch with the world. They tell us what we desire or dislike, admire or despise, love or hate. Such contrasts are typical of our emotions, moods, and affective states. The one tends to take us toward the object if we desire, admire, or love it; and the other tends to put us at a distance from it. In the extreme, we embrace or we repulse the object. Sympathy and antipathy describe the two extremes, the opposite poles of our feelings.

We should not see the sympathy pole as positive and acceptable and the antipathy pole as negative and unacceptable. Both belong to our psychic life and are necessary for our wellbeing. The baby expresses mostly sympathy toward the world. Buttons, sand, or worms he may put in his mouth to taste or to lick, out of sympathy for the world. Growing up means acquiring the ability to separate, to reflect, and to say "No". The three-year-old who is perfecting the use of "No", and rejecting the parent's help at any cost, is working on the antipathy pole. Self-assertion is accompanied always by distancing and by antipathy. It is a necessary part of growing up.

Generally, the baby cries before he learns to laugh. In the first weeks, crying expresses discomfort. After four or five months the child may cry because he wants the parent's attention and he is unhappy if this is not given. The attention of the parent reassures the child that the world is safe and benevolent.

The parent's feelings of anxiety or anger, or an exaggerated sense of hygiene also affect the child. Adults may also have suppressed feelings which originated in their own childhoods and which are most difficult to deal with. These induce the parent to deny space for the child's expression of feelings, whether of anger or suffering. The mother threatens to withdraw her love and the child learns that the price to be paid for showing his feelings is too high, and so he conceals them (see pp. 36, 50, 96). Being parents challenges us and continually asks us to make steps in our own inner lives.

Thinking, Feeling, and Willing

The human being is usually studied merely as a higher animal or else as a complex mechanism.

▲ **The balance of the emotions**
If the Soul experiences rejection and loss of love (left), balance is upset, while acceptance and love (top) pave the way to growth of Thinking, Feeling, and Willing.

Processes and interactions are measured, because measurement is considered essential to scientific method, but in all this it is not possible to grasp the meaning of "truly" human.

Humans as works of art

Suppose we consider the human being as a work of art. Now we have a different understanding, where the qualitative becomes more significant than the quantitative. To do this will seem, at first, to be unscientific. However it gives, in fact, an insight or imaginative understanding of the human which is more deep and comprehensive than the mechanistic model allows.

I have written of rhythms and polarities (see pp. 44-7 and 50) to describe the child and his development. If we are dealing with a work of art, this makes sense.

The three-fold soul

To describe the human soul as being three-fold, as having three fundamental capacities – to think, to feel, and to will, is to characterize it pictorially and artistically (see diagram, right).

Howard Gardner, in his *Developmental Psychology,* describes three systems that develop during childhood – the perceiving system, the making, or action, system, and the feeling system. Outwardly, these resemble the nerve–sense system, the limb system, and the heart–lung system that Steiner described. Steiner, however, links these physiological systems with the psychic concepts of Thinking, Willing, and Feeling. This enables us to relate, in a pictorial way, these three systems directly to child development from birth to adulthood.

The human Soul

The Soul is made up of Thinking, Feeling, and Willing. Thinking is making inward, through

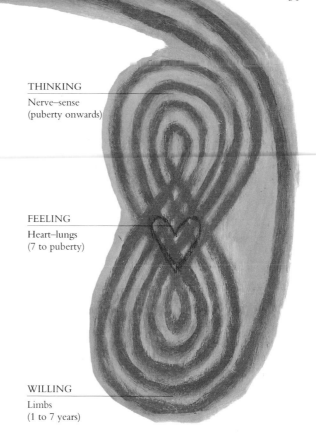

THINKING
Nerve–sense
(puberty onwards)

FEELING
Heart–lungs
(7 to puberty)

WILLING
Limbs
(1 to 7 years)

▲ Harmonizing the capacities
Proper attention to the successive development of the capacities for reflection, loss of love, acceptance, and love can strengthen each one in turn and harmonize them in adult life.

cognition, the world we encounter outside us; Willing is expressing our inner life, impulses, intentions, on the world outside; and Feeling is the play of emotions and moods between the world and the Self. In the first seven years, the Will is the dominant Soul capacity and, by being good parents, we provide the right environment for it to express itself in activity. From seven to puberty, Feeling is the dominant capacity and education should unfold Feeling through artistic activities. At puberty, the child begins to look for intellectual challenge.

▲ Love of repetition
The child loves to hear the same story told in the same words, day after day.

Repetition and habit

The child learns to handle things, to stand, to walk, and to speak through repeating the action again and again. Failure never discourages him. Eventually, such skills become habits. Repetition is the essence of the active learning of the child. He likes to hear the same story, today, tomorrow, and the next day. If a word is altered, he will notice. Regularity in home-life is deeply satisfying. The world can be trusted. It is a safe place to grow in.

The child's way of learning

Later, the thinking, cognitive process enters into learning, and the more childish way diminishes. Parents should ignore the pressure to follow "early learning" programmes, which force the intellect. Such programmes do not, in the long run, produce more capable intellects, and the loss at the level of the Will and Feeling is not easily measured. If children are awakened intellectually too early this can be counter-productive to healthy development (see also p. 48).

Educating the Will does not mean forcing the child to conform either to a set of rules or to adult preferences. The challenge is to guide, not suppress, this wilfulness. Guidance, example, and confirmation of love are ultimately more effective than threats or sermons.

The moral health of the child is linked to this guidance of the Will. We do not make a child moral by just telling him what is good and what is bad. The only way is for the adult to foster good habits in the child by showing him, by example, the meaning of goodness. This can be no pose or pretence. Children see more than we realize (see also p. 234).

This stimulating world

The young child is profoundly affected by all the sensations he receives from the world around him. Normal development depends on a rich sensory experience. Institutionalized children may lack normal development because of their sense-impoverishment. They do not have the same wealth of experiences, the games, the songs, the speech which a parent continually provides. These sense-experiences are usually inherent in the family setting, where the child feels his world is a whole. New experiences are, therefore, easily integrated in a meaningful way into this whole. Today, however, the child is also faced with impressions that change rapidly, lack context, and are incoherent. These may come from living a pressurized life in a city, or from television. Instead of enriching, these sensations can lead to nervousness and an overstimulated sensitivity. The "smart" child is often the victim of this way of life. He is drawn too quickly into adult preoccupations and short-cuts the full experience of childhood.

The impact of television

When watching television, the child is not in an interactive situation. He is learning language and behavioural modes passively, in relation to a world which is unreal. The adult, through self-consciousness and experience, is able to clothe this world of television with a certain reality and to give it coherence and meaning, but for the little child it is basically chaotic and destructive. Television also teaches. It teaches short attention spans because of the "rapid fire" editing techniques in fashion today, and also because of the habit of "browsing" with the remote control panel. It also teaches that the unreal world is more colourful than the real.

> **"**
> *Attention to rhythm and the environment can work wonders in home life, helping to avoid most discipline problems and direct confrontations with your child. Because the young child is so centred in the body, and in imitation, rhythm is one of the most important ways to discipline."*
>
> Rahima Baldwin,
> *You are your Child's First Teacher*

To help the child grow up and develop healthily in the midst of modern technology, parents have to make choices. It is a fallacy to believe that exposure to television and the latest video games, and other sophisticated electronic toys will give your child the best start in life. It may in fact be the worst (see also pp. 140–1, 207, 223).

Give childhood its due

It is certainly a major task for parents who wish to give support to the idea of "natural" childhood to become discriminating and to distinguish clearly between the real needs of the child and those imposed by commercial interests or adult fascination for technology. I am not criticizing the products of technology, but insisting that the world of the child is not the same as that of the adult and childhood must be given its due. If it is, it will lead to adulthood which can make technology its servant and not its master.

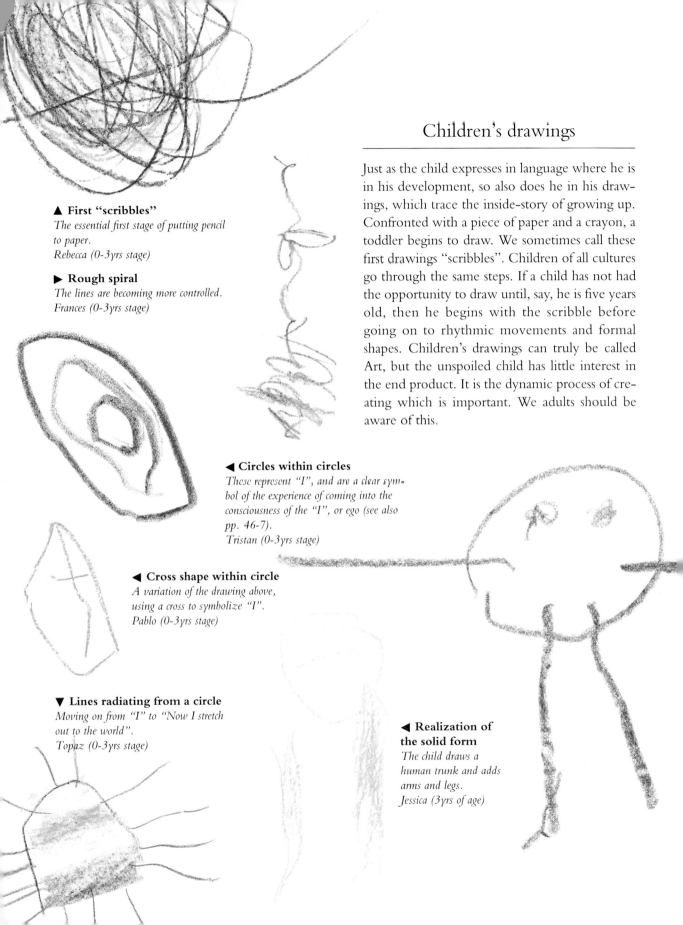

Children's drawings

Just as the child expresses in language where he is in his development, so also does he in his drawings, which trace the inside-story of growing up. Confronted with a piece of paper and a crayon, a toddler begins to draw. We sometimes call these first drawings "scribbles". Children of all cultures go through the same steps. If a child has not had the opportunity to draw until, say, he is five years old, then he begins with the scribble before going on to rhythmic movements and formal shapes. Children's drawings can truly be called Art, but the unspoiled child has little interest in the end product. It is the dynamic process of creating which is important. We adults should be aware of this.

▲ **First "scribbles"**
The essential first stage of putting pencil to paper.
Rebecca (0-3yrs stage)

▶ **Rough spiral**
The lines are becoming more controlled.
Frances (0-3yrs stage)

◀ **Circles within circles**
These represent "I", and are a clear symbol of the experience of coming into the consciousness of the "I", or ego (see also pp. 46-7).
Tristan (0-3yrs stage)

◀ **Cross shape within circle**
A variation of the drawing above, using a cross to symbolize "I".
Pablo (0-3yrs stage)

▼ **Lines radiating from a circle**
Moving on from "I" to "Now I stretch out to the world".
Topaz (0-3yrs stage)

◀ **Realization of the solid form**
The child draws a human trunk and adds arms and legs.
Jessica (3yrs of age)

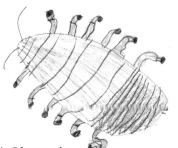

▲ Observation
The child begins to look at things as they really are and wants to "get it right".
Daniel (7yrs of age)

▼ A bridge with arches
The child's organic life sets its imprint on his drawing. When his second teeth emerge, crenellated forms appear.
Joseph (6yrs of age)

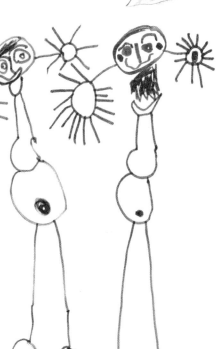

▲ Riding a snail
Houses, animals, trees, the sun, plants, the ground, and perhaps the sky find their relationship to each other.
Raphael (5-7yrs stage)

▶ Sun, flower, and dinosaur
The child begins more and more to illustrate.
David (5yrs of age)

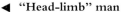

◀ "Head-limb" man
The human being is at first a head with lines emerging for arms and legs. These lines may express nerves and senses as much as limbs.
Alexander (4yrs of age)

◀ Hands and feet
A great feeling of "life" is present.
Hannah (4yrs of age)

▼ A body below a head
The drawing works downward, as if the child grows downward. Feet appear.
Zoë (3 ½ yrs of age)

▼ A house
An angular, beehive shape.
Thomas (3yrs of age)

Play

When we say "it's child's play", we mean it is easy, anyone can do it. How has it come, then, in our society, that there is an increasing number of children who can't play, who don't know how to play? For the child who is brought up naturally, it is, of course, easy. No one teaches him rules or shows him how. He just plays. Play is his natural life. Soon after birth he begins to respond to the caresses and endearments of his parents with looks and sounds. When he walks, there are the social games he plays of giving and taking, hiding and finding (see p. 49).

Imaginative play

What we see as inanimate objects are animate for the child. He does not make this distinction. A rough piece of wood can be a doll, a dog, a boat, or a spoon. The child's imagination completes the object, fills it out to become what he wants it to be. If children are given manufactured toys that are exact replicas of objects from the adult world, there is no room for the "play" of the imagination (see also pp. 142–3). Fortunately, lively children can convert a replica toy into something the adult never intended.

Co-operative play

In the fourth year, the child begins to enjoy playing with his peers. Two or three children can now co-operate to build a castle, dig a trench, or move a large log from one end of the garden to the other. Games at this age are usually creative and relatively unstructured. It is the activity which is important. There is usually no further purpose. Froebel, who invented the idea of the kindergarten, meant it to be a garden where children could play. He called play, "spontaneous self-instruction". The pressure today to change

▲ **Fairy tales**
Told in the language of fantasy and fable, fairy stories describe real life in vivid images and symbols.

kindergartens into pre-school learning establishments, with pedagogical methods, ignores the true educative value of free play, when the child is still building his body, developing language, and acquiring natural skills and aptitudes.

The inability to play means that the imitative faculty, natural to normal children and the basis of learning new skills, has been attacked. Memory and imagination have no field for their natural development. Play is the child's work, the way he explores and learns about the world; his entry into life's reality.

The story

There was a time when fairy tales were accused of being false-to-life and unhelpful to children who were growing up in the "real" world. This attitude no longer prevails, although most of us would find it difficult to explain their value, except that children seem to like them. Stories of all kinds are coming back into their own; adults as well as children thirst for them. The fairy tale is only one of many kinds of stories. The best open out some of life's secrets for the child, not in any intellectual way, but pictorially in images and symbols (see also pp. 158–9).

Themes and meanings

In spite of the changes in our society, many traditional stories still have power to move and to educate because they are about good and evil, right and wrong, and the human condition. Stories that are told are better than stories that are read, but read stories are much better than no stories at all. To read or tell the stories well, the parent should form inner pictures of what the story is describing. Stories should not be presented in a highly dramatic way. They can then refresh us, as well as the child.

At first, we may look at a picture-book with the child and tell why the acorn fell on Henny Penny. Stories for three-year-olds tell of simple things like why the hedgehog sleeps in winter. Then there are stories like *Billy-Goat Gruff* who pushes the horrible ogre, who frightens the little billy-goats, off the bridge. What we do not have the strength for when we are small we can achieve when we are big. How reassuring for a three-year-old!

Fairy stories (never about fairies!) usually begin with a perfect world. Then some difficult trials follow. Finally, the good is rewarded and the wicked are condemned. The ending is always happy for the one who has passed the trials. Out of experience comes a new understanding, symbolized, perhaps, by marriage. From innocence, through separation and hard times, comes a true love and union. "False!" "Unreal!" cry the sceptics. If we look at the surface of human life, where the good are often punished and the wicked escape, then the fairy tale is false. If we are willing to look deeper, another wisdom emerges which the child recognizes. The story is a form of play which lights up the true world of fantasy for the child. Instead of being escapist, it shows up our notion of sentimental love as shallow indeed.

Writing and reading

For many children, learning to read and write can be something of a torment. Since the time of Ancient Greece, debate has raged on the best way of teaching these skills, and there is no consensus of opinion today.

Active and passive learning

Broadly speaking, there are two approaches – the passive and the active. In the passive the child is simply taught the alphabet and is then made to practise it in words and phrases using simple letter combinations. It may be some time before he can read anything that is alive with meaning for him. The active approach engages the child's Will and understanding from the beginning by letting him meet the power and magic of the word immediately. No banal phrases like "The cat sat on the mat". Better might be, "The King of the East had a beautiful garden and in the garden grew a tree that bore golden apples". Surely more exciting. The difficult letter-combinations are dealt with gradually. If the child already knows the story of the Golden Bird the motivation will be there to find more of it in the written word. If the child learns to write the sentence and acquires reading from his own writing, the skills of hand and eye are joined together.

Learning and hearing

Hearing the word is also an important part of learning to read. Linking together the visual and the auditory with the movements of the hand

▼ **First writing**
Because of the difficulties of the task, writing is the first real "work" that the child has to face. However enjoyable the teacher is able to make it, it can never be just a game.

supports the active approach. In the learning of writing, Steiner recommended that the letters should be taught out of pictures. For example, the picture of a snake suggests the letter S (see also pp. 176–7) so the child moves from a picture to the abstract letter. This active approach arouses the involvement of the child and the alphabet becomes more alive and understandable.

When to start?

There is little agreement on when the child should be taught to read. Some reading schemes start in the third year, while some educators favour starting at the age of seven. Those who believe that reading should be related to the whole development of the child show a clear preference for the later start.

▶ **The physical relationship to number**
Each child should be allowed to develop his own natural relationship to number, freely and without stress.

Numbers

The child's experience of number begins in his first years (see also pp. 178–9). He soon learns that he has one nose, two eyes, two shoes, three buttons. He hears the sequence of the numbers. Each number has to wait until a certain other one has been said before it makes way for the next one. This experience of sequence has already begun in games like dropping stones, one by one into a watering-can. The muscle movements involved in such a game, or in crawling, with its rhythmic sequence of movements, underlie the real experience of arithmetic.

Arithmetic is mental movement. Like physical movement it is rhythmic and directed. Multiplication tables are rhythms and can be a joy for children if they learn them through physical movement. Number is then not just a head experience. The pre-school child has a rich contact with numbers without any formal teaching and in this way he has a basis for later learning.

Grasping arithmetic is a process in which the rules should be taught systematically, but the teacher should be aware that children can sometimes see number relationships which don't fit the procedure. Confidence is an important companion to number-work; if it is missing the child will acquire a permanent distaste for it.

Home-making

Making a home in which a child can grow up happily needs the positive will and determination of the parents. It doesn't just happen by itself and it is not easy if both parents work full-time, whether for economic reasons or for personal fulfillment. Today, families are thrown very much back on their own resources. Friends or relatives may not live close by. The home may be small and, if there is no garden and neighbours are anonymous, the parent at home can feel isolated.

The experience of childhood has changed since the 1950s. Today's child is much nearer the adult world in anxieties, in desires, and in the frenetic pace of life. The child-dream is fractured. Exposure to the fears and threats of daily life is more blatant. The walls of Froebel's garden (see p. 56) have been, for the most part, pulled down. Consequently, the child comes earlier to an experience of loneliness and the adult presumes a maturity which the child doesn't have.

Where there are two parents, it is important that they both share the same goals in bringing up their child. They will probably have different ways and this is fine if these complement each other. This means having a common picture of how a child grows up, and of what it is like to be a child. As adults, we usually forget this, but we should try to recover the experience without sentimentality and without blame.

A home is a convivial space. Each family member has to be comfortable there. A home has an individual style created by the parents; an individual rhythm, colour, and warmth. It can be a place in which things happen, in which people make things, make music, make conversation, or it can be immaculate, super-hygienic, and somewhat sterile. In home-making, the parents create a culture. Nothing is anonymous; everything is personalized. This home-culture gives the child substance in which to grow, in the same way that a plant has earth.

Responsibility

The child arrives in the world full of trust. He is helpless and comes in the hope that people will be there to care for him. If this trust is not met or is abused the result is devastation. For parents, meeting this trust can mean a hard commitment. Babies, toddlers, and young children are demanding and tyrannical. They can bring out similar qualities in the adult. It is also tempting for the parents to claim ownership. The child then becomes the object of their ambition or convenience.

Answering the child's trust means meeting him in his needs. It means recognizing that, stage by stage, he is going to step into his own responsibility and so release us, his parents. This is a long process which is only completed when the child is approaching adulthood.

Responsibility can be a burden for the adult. It is acceptable when we act not out of compulsion, but in freedom. Usually we feel we do what we have to do and there is not much freedom. We get glimpses of this freedom when we see how each task belongs to the wholeness of life. A young child should not be burdened with responsibility. To appreciate that he has a right to his preferences is to acknowledge his personality, but this does not exonerate us from taking decisions which he is not yet capable of taking for himself. For example, it is our responsibility as parents to decide what school our child should attend, if, indeed, we have a choice (see pp. 314–335). He should not be burdened with such a decision but we should take his views into account and let him know that we are doing so.

◀ **"Living arrows"**
We must be aware of our responsibilities to the child in our care. He needs us to show him how to come into his own responsibility. For, "You are the bows from which your children as living arrows are sent forth". (Kahlil Gibran)

A helping hand

To help the child into his responsibility, parents have to know theirs. We make sure the child has a secure and convivial home life, eats the right food, wears warm clothing, and has enough sleep. When he is at the "no saying" stage we must understand that this is the development of his growing self-awareness and not bad behaviour. We must give him space for free-flowing play, for making things, for drawing. We must recognize his right to his own feelings and give him opportunities to express them. We must be active in our loving.

PART 2

COMMUNICATING

Tim Kahn

*T*his section challenges many commonly held assumptions about the emotional development of the infant, about the way children learn about themselves and the world, and how we as parents can best support our children in this process – while remembering our own needs. As parents we are particularly vulnerable to advice – mostly conflicting – that is thrust at us from all directions as to how we ought to bring up our children, and the advertising and media images that tell us all the things we need to buy, give, and do for our children.

However, the essence of love and the ability to nurture our children is already within us. If we can learn to listen to ourselves then we will find many of the answers to the question, "What does my child need?". And it is the same with children, too. They don't need us, their parents, to fill them up with answers. They need us to help them to find the answers that already lie within.

This section offers information and practical suggestions to help you and your family on this journey.

CHAPTER 4

An early start

Technological developments such as intrauterine scanning and other obstetric advances mean that we can now watch an unborn baby developing physically. But we also know much more about the baby's own experience. What we once thought was a world of "nothingness" is, in fact, rich in sounds, feelings, and sensations.

Sensing before birth

From around the fourth month of pregnancy the baby can hear the muffled sounds of her mother's body; the heartbeat is a regular, soothing sound. She can hear stomach rumblings, eating and drinking noises, and from the outside world the shrill voices of sisters and brothers.

Dr Thomas Verny, in his book *The Secret Life of the Unborn Child*, discusses the evidence for pre-birth awareness. The baby has a growing sensitivity to what is happening in her mother's body and in the outside world. Investigations indicate that the quality of a mother's relationship to her partner is almost as important as her attitude toward being a mother in determining how her baby will develop. So the supportive role of the father is critical at a much earlier stage than we might think.

Some researchers believe that the unborn baby responds to her environment from conception. We do know that she responds actively to noises and vibrations, that her body moves in rhythm to her mother's speech, and that a newborn can recognize her father's voice in the first hours of life, if she has heard him speaking to her before birth. What are the implications of all this? Certainly that the baby needs and deserves sensitive and nurturing care in the womb, just as she does outside it.

A good start

We can use the evidence supporting intrauterine bonding to encourage us to support expectant mothers rather than as an excuse for blaming them for any of their children's later difficulties. Expectant fathers need to be supportive of their partners through pregnancy and play their part in ensuring that the pregnancy goes well. An emotionally secure environment will give the baby the best start in life. Daily ups and downs don't matter, but long-term anxiety in the mother may transmit a sense of unease to the baby. Equally importantly, the father's attitude to the mother and the unborn baby will also have a marked influence on them both. The first steps of bonding between the parents and the unborn baby take place in the womb.

"

I knew my [unborn] baby could hear because she seemed to dance in rhythm with my music… I practised a particular phrase in a Chopin waltz over and over the last few months of pregnancy… When she was three months old… I started practising again. As I played through the waltz, she was playing on her back looking at her mobile. When I got to that particular phrase, she turned to me, looking surprised, as if 'There it is again!' I know she recognized it."

(told to Dr T. Berry Brazelton by a pianist, taken from Touchpoints)

"

In each baby is a vital spark, and this urge towards life and growth and development is a part of the baby, something the child is born with and which is carried forward in a way that we do not have to understand. For instance, if you have just put a bulb in the window-box you know perfectly well that you do not have to make the bulb grow into a daffodil. You supply the right kind of earth and the rest comes naturally, because the bulb has life in it."

D.W. Winnicott,
The Child, the Family and the Outside World

◀ For fathers

Position yourself as shown left, or in whatever way feels comfortable for you both. Gently stroking your partner's abdomen and talking to your baby in a warm and reassuring tone are the first steps in bonding with your baby.

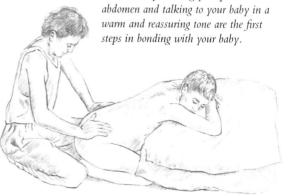

"

[In therapy] I treated [a man] who had been a severe stutterer since the age of six… In one session he remembered having a painful series of tonsil infections between the ages of three and five; in another, he recalled being born with an umbilical cord looped around his neck. Because his birth records were not available, I was not able to verify this recollection. But in the weeks following the emergence of his birth memory another, more meaningful form of corroboration presented itself. The man's stutter gradually began to disappear."

Dr Thomas Verny,
The Secret Life of the Unborn Child

▼ Support in labour
In the early stages of labour a variety of positions will help to ease the pain and discomfort of the contractions, particularly if the birth partner supports the mother's weight and massages her lower back. Kneeling and squatting can often relieve the strain, but the woman should allow her own intuition to guide her.

The birth experience

Birth is the first great transition. Unborn babies are aware of much that is happening to them and around them, both in the uterus and in the world outside. At birth these two worlds merge. Parents and health-care professionals focus their attention on making sure that the birth goes smoothly and that the mother gives birth safely to a healthy baby. However, we generally tend to give little thought and attention to the baby's own experience of the birth.

Throughout pregnancy contractions have been taking place in the uterus; in the last month these contractions grow stronger. As the baby gets used to them they become pleasurable; part of a sensual game. But at birth they are ten times stronger. To us this may seem frightening for the baby, but we do not know how the baby experiences them. We can be reassured to know that labour is a process that prepares her for her entry into the world and thinking of the contractions as hugs for the baby can help the mother welcome their increasing intensity. Through labour the baby is massaged and squeezed, making the lungs and chest expand and contract, which facilitates her breathing when she is born.

Out into the world

For nine months the womb has nurtured and given security to the unborn baby, but now she is being pushed out of the womb and into the narrow birth canal. In travelling down this narrow passage, the unborn baby twists and turns and, completing her journey, is suddenly pushed out into the world.

Experiments conducted under hypnosis show that we retain birth memories in our unconscious. Such memories are, of course, difficult to corroborate, but they do seem to suggest that the

"
*We must accord the greatest respect to this
fragile moment of birth. The baby is
between two worlds, hesitating on a
threshold. It must not be hurried or jos-
tled; it must be allowed to enter at its
own pace. This is an extraordinary
moment; it is no longer a fetus, but not
yet a newborn baby. It is no longer inside
its mother but she is still breathing for it.
An elusive, ephemeral moment."*

Frederick Leboyer,
Birth Without Violence

▲ **The warm welcome**
*What is important is a welcoming atmos-
phere for the newborn. All parents give
their baby the best possible start to life.*

birth experience has a long-term effect on a
child's personality and how she will relate to and
experience the outside world. Studies show a
correlation between the level of complication
occurring at the birth and the level of difficulty
that an individual experiences in life.

Preparing for birth

We can take into account the struggle that the
baby is undergoing in the way we prepare for the
birth. The mother needs to feel safe and secure
wherever she has chosen to give birth (whether
at home or in hospital) and trusting of the people
with her. If both parents prepare for the birth
that they want and acquire the knowledge they
need, their confidence will increase.

Taking all this into account will make a
straightforward, uncomplicated birth more likely,
and the mother will be able to communicate her
expectant yet confident feelings to her baby.

Sensing and responding

When a baby is born all she knows is one-ness. She cannot differentiate between Self and other-ness. It is as if all experiences wash over her, as if all senses and sensations are both a part of the Self and a part of the world. There is no separation. Within a few hours of birth she can recognize her parents' voices. She enjoys being held and, after some practice, can latch on and suckle contentedly. Within a few days she can recognize her mother's smell and identify her face. She is, at times, alert to the world and other people.

Both mother and baby adapt and respond to one another during feeding and holding, although at first the newborn has little interest in face-to-face encounters. Although she only responds in a limited way and is often in a dreamlike state, the way she develops suggests she is already aware of feelings and the surrounding world. By six weeks she can concentrate on the sensations of sight, sound, and touch. If any of these are too strong she will shy away; if they are too weak she will fail to notice them.

"

If all children aged six or under were cradled or rocked or held and sung to, or they could just sit on your lap and you read to them, once a day every day until they are six, it would revolutionise the world."

(from a talk given by Dr Viola Brody *at Parent Network Parents Conference, March 1990)*

▲ **Parent–baby contact**
Contact is vital for babies. It is not for anyone to tell us that we should carry her constantly or take her into bed every night. Rather, we can pay attention to what she is "telling" us about her needs and respond in ways we think are right.

The importance of touch

How much closeness and physical contact does a baby need? This would be a simple question to answer if we could recognize our intuitive feelings and our baby's real needs. But we are so confused by society's conflicting messages about what babies need and whether we ought to ration closeness and physical contact so that we don't "spoil" them that it is hard for parents to know what is right.

In the womb the mother nourishes her baby's every need at every moment: the baby has constant contact with the mother and the massaging effect of contractions stimulates her for life in the outside world.

In this outside world the newborn is on her own for the first time. She must cope with the after-effects of the birth and she has to adjust to being out of constant contact with her mother.

What does a new-born baby need?

"Every nerve ending under his newly exposed skin craves the expected embrace; all his being, the character of all he is, leads to his being held in arms." Thus writes Jean Liedloff in *The Continuum Concept,* which is based on her experience of living with the Yequana Indians, who carry their babies constantly. These babies have no reason to scream because there is always an adult at hand to respond to their needs. This is very different from the experience of babies in industrialized countries. We are not suggesting that parents should carry their babies constantly. Our way of life is very different. We tend to live in small families, with, at best, only tenuous support networks. Often both parents go out to work. Yet we can acknowledge how important closeness and physical contact are and make time for them in the hectic rhythms of the day.

Early contact

When a mother sees her new-born baby for the first time she may reach out to hold her. If she puts the baby directly to the breast this early suckling releases hormones that help the uterus contract, provides nutritious colostrum before the milk comes in, and gives the baby physical contact with her mother. Skin-to-skin contact is important and has been described as the glue of bonding. As little as an hour spent in close contact after the birth can have a lasting effect on the relationship between mother and baby. Studies show that a baby who has been allowed to bond at birth is physically healthier, more secure, and more active than a baby who has not and these mothers (and fathers who attend the birth) feel a stronger connection to their babies. However, if circumstances dictate that you cannot keep your baby with you right from birth it is never too late to bond.

QUESTIONS: MEMORIES OF TOUCH

● What memories do you have of being held as a baby?

● Were you kissed and cuddled as a child, or was there little touching in your family?

● Were you perhaps abused in some way by those whom you trusted most? If you were, there are organizations you can approach for support in resolving these issues (see pp. 336–40)

"

It is through the hands that we speak to the child, that we communicate. Touch is the first language ... It is skin speaking to skin; and from this skin all other sense organs derive. And these in turn are like windows in the wall of skin that contains us and holds us separate from the world. The newborn baby's skin has an intelligence, a sensitivity that we cannot conceive of."

Frederick Leboyer,
Birth Without Violence

▼ **Body talk**
Gently massaging your baby fulfils her need for bodily contact and brings trust and co-operation into your relationship.

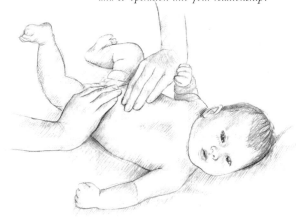

The value of communication

From the very beginning a small baby responds to and also initiates interactions with people who give her sensitive attention. Both parent and baby share control of the "conversation" and negotiate an exchange in which both smile or laugh and are amused in unison. If one party takes over the conversation (usually the adult), the other may become dismayed or intimidated.

What is taking place between parent and baby is rather like the performance of a pair of highly practised dancers. Nobody teaches a parent how to play face games with her baby, yet all parents actively initiate and join in such activities with great sensitivity.

Parents exhibit impressive intuitive behaviour with their babies. They raise the pitch of their voices, they slow down the rhythm of their speech and add a singsong quality; and they speak in five- to fifteen-second intervals. This combination of timing and sound is ideal in holding a newborn's brief attention span and seems to resonate with an in-built rhythm within the baby. It is as if some kind of human programming ensures that babies and parents respond to each other in ways which complement their needs.

Tuning in to each other

Right from the moment of birth (if not before) both parents and baby are sensitive to each other, and adapt their responses to one another.

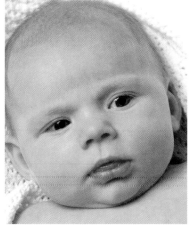

▲ **Pre-speech**
The tiny movements of head, hand, tongue, and eye in the early weeks and months are the beginnings of gesture and articulation which will eventually lead to speech. We think of this as real communication, and we are right to do so.

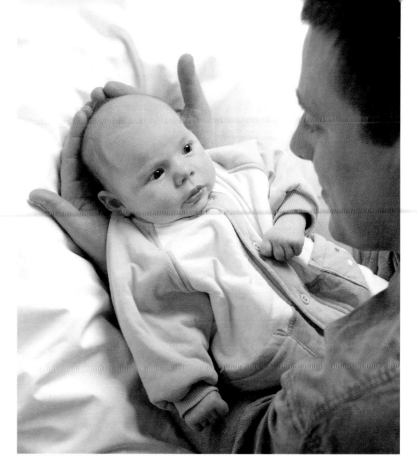

▶ Attunement
Father and baby spend time tuning in to each other, laying deep foundations for their future lives together.
Communicating is far more than just learning to speak.

"
Once a pair of smiles has passed between a mother and a baby of this age [four-and-a-half months], a process has already been set in motion. What happens is this. Joey's (the baby's) smile and his mother's are slightly out of phase with each other. That is as it should be, since a smile takes time to grow on the face, to reach its peak, and to fade. When his mother's smile is close to its peak, it triggers Joey's smile. And when Joey's smile hits its peak, it reanimates her fading smile. By remaining out of phase, they keep restarting the other and prolong the duet ..."

Daniel Stern,
Diary of a Baby

Researchers call this process "attunement" and believe that it is the first step in the process of the baby learning to speak.

The more a baby interacts with her parents and others, the more she wants to be able to communicate with them. As her needs become more complex, she will want to be able to express them more clearly, and she will start to use words. So the motivation to speak comes from within: the baby acquires language as she needs it. How does this process develop?

Child–parent interaction

By about two months the communication between parent and baby has developed into face games, in which each plays a part in a dance of expressions and gestures.

Over the next few months, face games develop into body games as the parent lifts, bounces, pushes, and pulls the baby about while making excited and dramatic sounds. The baby shows her enjoyment by eager attention and laughter and makes her displeasure obvious when her parent has been overly physical. This lets parents "attune" their actions and expressions to the baby again.

The parent's and baby's range of expressions increases: they both laugh and exclaim in glee and mock surprise and they put on exaggerated expressions of anger and sadness as part of their joyful play. When the baby is around five months old, the parent starts singing action songs and nursery rhymes, again intuitively. Even though the baby cannot sing the words she can learn the actions and respond to the rhythm. She is not just imitating her parent, she is also following the rhyme and co-ordinating her hand and body movements in response.

Language and learning

At around six months, babbling begins as the baby gets better at controlling her vowel sounds and the pitch and quality of her expressions. Then, at around nine months, a significant development takes place. For the last few months the infant has been able to either play with an object or to interact in person-to-person games, but she has not yet learned to do both at the same time. Now she can play a game in which, for instance, she follows her parent's instructions and puts wooden dolls into a toy truck and takes them out again. She could not have done this before. This shows she can now understand, and follow, her parent's instructions and that she is reaching a point where she herself will want to be able to communicate what is in her mind to others. She now begins to need to speak.

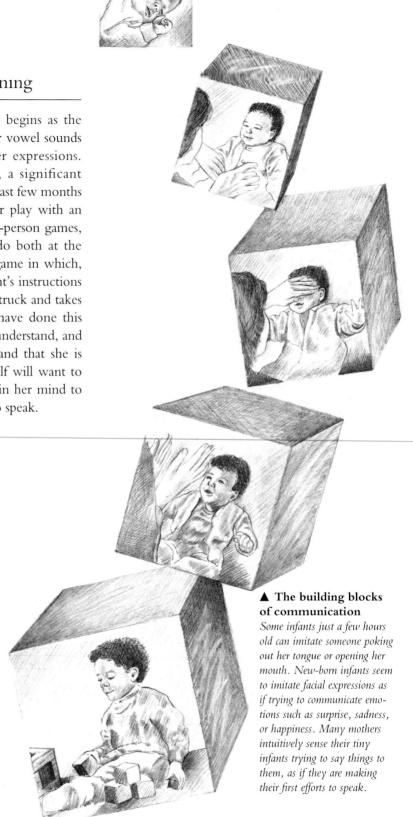

▲ **The building blocks of communication**

Some infants just a few hours old can imitate someone poking out her tongue or opening her mouth. New-born infants seem to imitate facial expressions as if trying to communicate emotions such as surprise, sadness, or happiness. Many mothers intuitively sense their tiny infants trying to say things to them, as if they are making their first efforts to speak.

ACTIVITY: **COMMUNICATING WITH YOUR BABY**

While you are playing together, let a part of your mind watch what you are both doing and see if you notice some of the stages discussed in this section.

● What kinds of games are you initiating with your baby and how is she responding?

● What kinds of games is she initiating and how are you responding?

● How does your baby show you she does or does not want to play, and how do you respond?

The beginnings of speech

The young child combines gestures of reaching, pointing, and pushing away with sounds and intonations which communicate her needs, thoughts, and feelings. She is deliberately trying to attract another person's interest and get them to act in the way she wants. In essence she is communicating without words. Next she starts to learn names for people, objects, and actions.

As she becomes more mobile, her world expands. She can reach and handle many new objects and she needs to be able to talk about these new activities. From this point on her communication increases rapidly from "baby language", which is understood only by her own family, to "child language", which can be understood by all. There is a wide variation in the speed and clarity with which children develop language. Once a child can understand language, she will usually learn to speak in her own good time.

Intuitive response

As the child begins to speak, the parent continues to respond intuitively to her in a way that helps her in her speech development. If she says "dolly", then we may say "there's your dolly", and as her comments lengthen, so do our repetitions. A child needs to hear her parents using language that is at the frontier of her own abilities, so that she can then start using new words, sounds, and structures in imitation. At the same time it is important to leave gaps for the child to make her own contribution.

Children inevitably make mistakes as they learn new words, and they have difficulty with certain sounds. These will mostly correct themselves. But if you feel that your child may have a problem with language or understanding, seek professional advice either to get assistance for the child or to lay your anxieties to rest.

How can we help?

We must acknowledge our huge range of intuitive skills and knowledge that is finely tuned to our child's needs. As we play with our child we need to talk with her about what we are

◀ **Parts of speech**
From gesture, to name-saying, to baby language, to child language – the human makes the gradual journey into communication with the world around her.

both doing. This encourages her to want to communicate with others. Parent–child games are essential to our child's development, perhaps because they are an expression of our love for her. Our child automatically learns, explores, and communicates her experiences to others. We do not need to teach her how; we just need to enable her to make this developmental journey.

We must remember to see our child as a thinking and feeling individual right from the start. She may learn some things faster and some things more slowly than other children, and we may be anxious that she should perform according to the "norm". However she "measures up", she needs us to be pleased with her and have confidence in her. She is fine just as she is.

CHAPTER 5

A time to learn

Learning springs naturally in new-born babies and young children. Though we do not need to teach a baby how to see, we can place him in interesting and colourful environments. We do not need to teach him how to feel, but we can offer him new things to touch and explore. The new-born baby's interest and curiosity in people and the world are already there, inside him. They are in-built. And so it is with the other senses. He just needs us to offer him the right opportunities, and he will develop at his own inner pace.

Teaching and learning

What are these opportunities, and how will we know if we are offering the baby what he needs, when he needs it? Many of the interactions between a baby and his parents takes place at an intuitive level (see p. 70). He behaves sponta-

neously in the only way he knows how and we respond to him intuitively.

As the baby grows and changes we adapt our behaviour to suit him. Face games turn into body games and body games develop into nursery rhymes, without anybody teaching us to do it (see p. 71). And nobody needs to teach the baby what to do next. The pattern of a healthy relationship is there right from the start. What is important is that it is maintained and can develop and flourish.

An important aspect of the relationship between parent and child is teaching and learning. We don't think of ourselves and our children as teachers and students, but teaching and learning go on between us all the time.

Unfortunately we have lost touch with much of this innate human sense. Experts who "know best" tell us what our child ought to be doing

"
What babies seem to be showing their mothers is, 'I know how to be in a conversation, and, if you'll be polite and listen to me, I will talk to you and learn from you'. In this way, the baby acts like it knows what it is doing."

Professor Colwyn Trevarthen

"
Children are born passionately eager to make as much sense as they can of things around them."

John Holt,
Learning All the Time

"
No matter what our family situation or lifestyle, we as parents are our children's first teachers. The importance of what they learn in the home and through their relationship with us cannot be underestimated. By understanding how children develop and some things we can do to help their balanced and healthy growth – physically, mentally, emotionally and spiritually – we will not only help our children, but also increase our own enjoyment and growth as parents.

Rahima Baldwin,
You are Your Child's First Teacher

"
Six-year-old Ben took the one-litre measuring jug and a half-litre bottle. I said, 'If we fill the bottle with water and pour it into the jug, how full will it be?' He realized it would be half full. He poured the water in and found he was right. Then he said, 'Let's do it again', and quickly realized that another half-litre would fill the jug. He poured the water in and found he was right again. Ben's final words were, 'Now I understand litres'. Ben set up his own 'lesson' and decided what he wanted to learn from it."

Tim, a father

when, and what remedial action to take if he is a "late developer". We may feel great pressure for our child to "achieve", and we may be tempted to push him at too fast a pace. This may appear to reap rewards in the short term, but it will only cause tensions in the end (see p. 136). We should trust ourselves and our intuitive senses as to what our baby needs, and trust our baby to know when he is ready to do what he needs to do.

Anticipating needs

We cannot know what goes on inside a child's head. We can only guess at it from his words and actions. Let's look at the needs of a young child as he travels on his journey exploring and learning. Some of his needs do not involve us, some of them require us as observers, and others require our participation. Our role is to sense what our child needs from us and when.

What does a child need?

The child is "at work" all day and every day. He is learning all the time. For him there is no distinction between learning and playing, between work and play. There is no need to set up special learning opportunities for a child. We just need to acknowledge that he is learning about life at every moment.

Good feelings about himself

We learn best when we feel good about ourselves. If we are upset, we are distracted from the task in hand and we need to take time to resolve our upset so that we feel better in order to be able to concentrate fully. Then we can get on with our work. So it is for a child. When he is upset he cannot learn. Helping him deal with whatever is on his mind will let him get on with enjoying himself and so with learning.

A sense of success

Every moment is an opportunity for the child to learn. Learning is a process. Learning to walk, for instance, is composed of all the attempts to stand upright, move one foot in front of the other, fall over, scream with frustration, take a few steps and finally, walk unaided.

The child needs our active encouragement and our confidence in his ability to succeed. We can say, "You can do it". We can put his efforts into perspective for him when he feels frustrated or despondent by saying, "You couldn't read that word last week, but now you can!".

He will feel encouraged by successful attempts at tasks that are at the limits of his ability, but he may feel discouraged by failing at tasks that are too difficult. Our job is to judge these limits, guide him toward success, and help him see the achievement in what he may see as failure.

PROJECT: **ESSENTIAL NEEDS**

- Food, warmth, exercise, sleep
- Love and a sense of belonging
- To explore, question, experience, and learn

To help him grow you can:

- Listen to his ideas
- Point out his achievements
- Think through difficult situations with him
- Let him learn by his mistakes
- Stop being too busy for him
- Stop telling him what to do
- Stop telling him what he's doing wrong

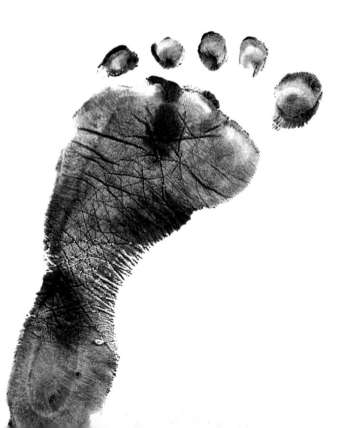

Experiences to learn from

The child cannot learn through our experience. He must learn through his own. He must have his own successes and make his own mistakes. As much as we might like to, we cannot protect him from the knocks of life, and it is important that we do not try to. They are an essential part of growing up. When our child approaches a new task, such as tying his shoe-laces, he is likely to find it difficult and he may take many weeks to master it. He may struggle, he may scream in frustration, he may beg us to do it for him.

A belief in himself

If he is ready and able to learn a new and difficult skill, then we do him a disservice by doing it for him or helping him when we have not been asked (or even when we have). Instead we can express our confidence in him. When he masters the skill, not only will he have learned to tie his shoe-laces, but more importantly, he will be strengthened in the feeling that he is able to do things. He has learned that perseverance brings success. This attitude will affect his approach to every task throughout life. The child's sights are limited if he starts out with the feeling that he cannot do it and that he needs help.

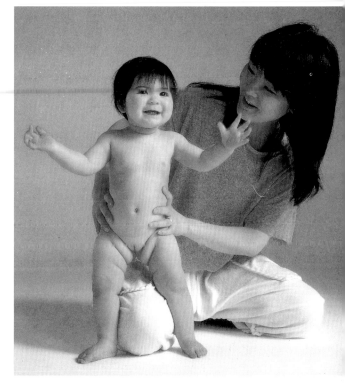

▲ "I am truly human"
When the child finally comes into the upright and stands by herself she is doing something that is unique to humanity.

Control over his own learning

Your child learns things as he needs them and is ready for them. He learns to speak when he needs to communicate ideas to other people and he learns to walk when crawling or shuffling fails to give him enough mobility. He needs us to introduce him to these activities – in the case of walking, he needs to have us there as examples to copy (see also pp. 174, 225).

Parents who are relaxed with his progress

Paradoxically, if we are desperate for our child to learn a particular skill, then he will be less likely to learn it until we have let go of our desperation. Children seem to have invisible antennae that pick up our unexpressed feelings, which then influence their behaviour.

Parents who know when not to interfere

If we are observant we will see what piece of learning our child is currently undertaking. We will then be able to give him the appropriate assistance, or sit back and not interfere if he does not need us. Not interfering while still giving our child attention is a great skill. We adults find it hard to keep our mouths shut. Instead we offer suggestions as to how he could do things better and then we feel hurt when he sends "leave me alone" or "let me do it" signals.

A broad range of experiences

We can try to structure our child's world very carefully so that he only experiences what we think is good for him. But he needs to explore and experience life to the full. For example, when a young child is starting to feed himself, he will make a mess. Only some food will go in his mouth; he will play with it, mess up his clothes and throw it on the floor. He needs the freedom to experience food in his own way without our intrusion. We need to set boundaries, such as no food can be thrown around the room, and he needs the security of boundaries (see p. 120), but they must be flexible so that they do not interfere with his need to experience life. He needs to get himself soaked, have some choice over what he wears, "taste" stones and earth, and this is all

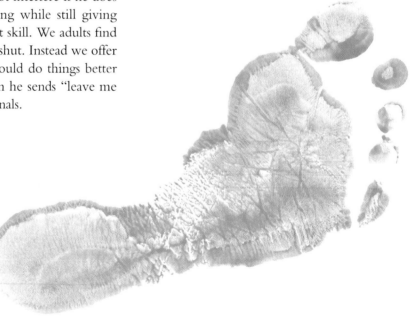

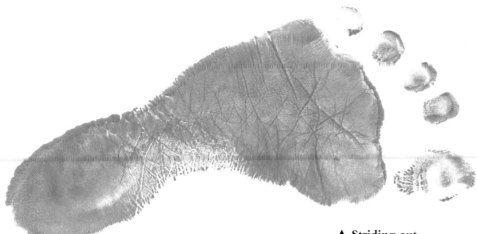

▲ Striding out
The two-year-old has perfected his first hesitant attempts at walking and now explores his world with steady strides.

"

I wanted my son, David, to dress himself. He was quite capable of pulling his clothes on, but he refused to. Each morning was a battle. The more I cajoled, the more he resisted, until I gave up and started dressing him myself. With the pressure removed, in time he was dressing himself without any fuss!"

Susan, a mother

EXERCISE: HELP YOUR CHILD LEARN A NEW SKILL

● Is your child really ready to learn the skill? Or is it just that others of his age can already do it and you fear that he is "behind"?

● Can he already do part of it?

● Does he still need you to do part of it?

● Does he seem ready to learn part of it?

right. He needs to take risks. Our role is to ensure that he does not put himself in danger and only suffers the necessary knocks and bruises of experience. So we need to set limits on his activities; we do not let him pull a plastic bag over his head in the name of exploration, and we may need to set very firm boundaries on the child who does not yet have a realistic sense of his own abilities and limitations.

Appropriate information

Our role as parents is to give our child access to the world. His curiosity and desire to learn unfold and develop as he grows older. As adults, we possess knowledge and experience that is useful to him and we can share it with him as and when he needs it.

We need to tell him as much as he wants to know, no more and no less. For example, when a five-year-old asks, "Where do babies come from?", he may only need the answer, "From their mothers' tummies".

Satisfying answers

How can we know how much information to give our child? If we pay enough attention to him, we will be aware of his lack of interest when our answers are too long, of his dissatisfaction if our answers are incomplete, and of his pleasure if we get it just right. Taking time to get to know him properly will help us to answer his questions appropriately.

It's fine to show our ignorance too. To be honest and say, "We don't know", and perhaps offer, "Let's go and find out", helps the child see that we are not super beings who know everything. Sharing our weaknesses in this way lets him be imperfect too.

A child asks questions about all kinds of subjects, including "difficult" ones such as sex, death, and God. It is important to answer these questions openly and with detail appropriate to his age and understanding. In answer to questions we find embarrassing it is useful to admit to our embarrassment (the child will sense it anyway) and do our best to give him satisfactory answers. If we try to hide our embarrassment, all we are likely to do is communicate loudly and clearly our reluctance to discuss the subject and any information we do give will be "lost". The child is likely to feel embarrassed too, and reluctant to ask further questions. By acknowledging our feelings of embarrassment we show our child that it is all right to be embarrassed. And if we attempt to answer all his questions he will learn that it is good to ask questions about anything and everything, and that he will get honest answers.

Freedom to make mistakes

Mistakes are to be celebrated, not avoided. As a child learns new skills he will make many mistakes. We cannot perform new skills perfectly the first time. Without mistakes we do not learn. It is the fear of making mistakes that prevents a child from going into new situations and learning new skills. Once infected with this fear, learning stops. Pointing out and correcting a child's mistakes plays a central role in giving him the fear. If we notice the achievement in a mistake he can learn from it too (see example, right).

◀ **Opening up, not closing down**
Our answers need to open up a subject, not close it down. We could answer the question, "Where is God?", with, "That's a good question. Let's talk about it". The child can then start exploring spirituality for himself, rather than just accepting our view.

Examples to imitate

The child is constantly observing and imitating adults. We see this in the games he plays. Whether "mothers and babies", "doctors and nurses", or "teachers and pupils", he comes to understand by experiencing their roles in imaginative play. These games satisfy an inner need and they come and go in new guises as the child grows and plays them in different ways. They form an integral part of learning.

Examples to learn from

Our child learns from our example. Our actions speak far louder than our words. If we approach every problem as a challenge, or a joy, then our

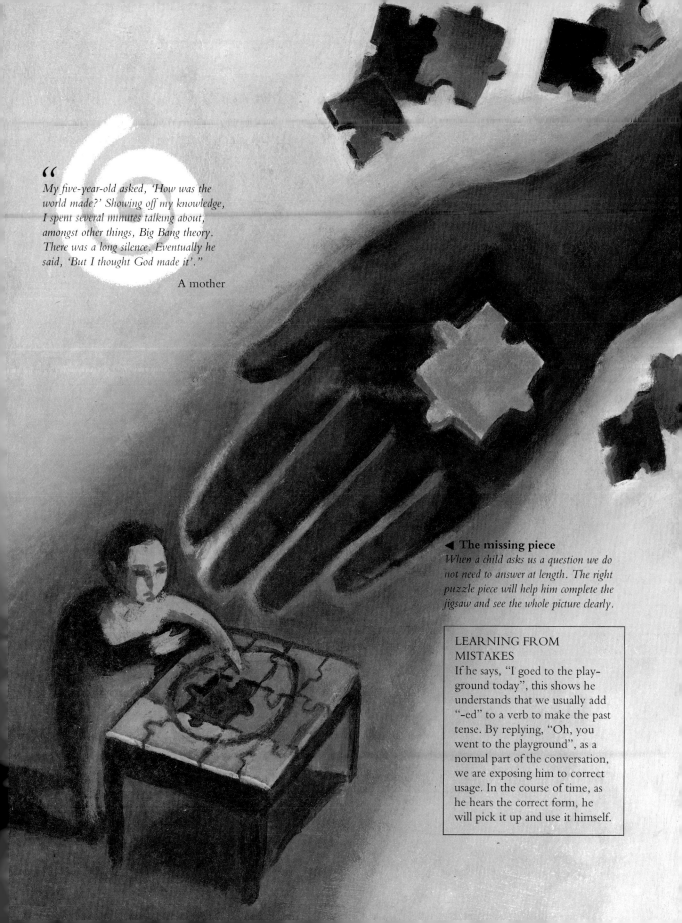

"

My five-year-old asked, 'How was the world made?' Showing off my knowledge, I spent several minutes talking about, amongst other things, Big Bang theory. There was a long silence. Eventually he said, 'But I thought God made it'."

A mother

◄ **The missing piece**
When a child asks us a question we do not need to answer at length. The right puzzle piece will help him complete the jigsaw and see the whole picture clearly.

LEARNING FROM MISTAKES
If he says, "I goed to the play-ground today", this shows he understands that we usually add "-ed" to a verb to make the past tense. By replying, "Oh, you went to the playground", as a normal part of the conversation, we are exposing him to correct usage. In the course of time, as he hears the correct form, he will pick it up and use it himself.

▲ **He needs to feel useful**

The child enjoys entering the adult world. He wants to help in the kitchen and the garden, to make and repair things. He derives great satisfaction from seeing his work being used in real life, rather than just making things for amusement.

child may take on the same attitude. However, if every problem seems to be an insurmountable barrier to us, then, whether or not we try to hide that feeling from our child, he is likely to pick up the same attitude. The more we can grow to overcome the obstacles in our lives, the more powerfully will we enable our child to develop the inner strength to face life's challenges.

> "
> *Children do not move from formal ignorance about a given thing to knowledge of it in one sudden step, like going to a light that has been off and turning it on. For children do not acquire knowledge, but make it."*
>
> John Holt,
> *Learning All the Time*

His parents' loving presence

There will be times when our child will be playing contentedly on his own, but when we try to slip away unnoticed he will demand that we stay. We may not think that we are of any use to him because he does not constantly turn to us for reassurance and encouragement, but he still wants and needs our attention and our presence.

His parents' pride in him

When we, as adults, are unable to solve a problem on our own, we may, by confiding in a friend, suddenly see the answer. It can take the aware presence of another to draw it out, almost as if we become aware of ourselves when we are "seen" by another. Our child needs this kind of attention. If he proudly shows us a model he has made, he may not really want our opinion; he just wants us to see him with his creation. It is as if he is bathed in sunlight by our attention.

YOUR ACTIVE PARTICIPATION

Your child needs you to intervene actively at times; your presence alone is not enough. Instead of initiating or taking over his game, pay attention and follow his cues. If he is sitting quietly, sit quietly too. If he wants to be boisterous, join in. Follow his lead and stick to his rules. The more you do this, without taking over, the stronger your child will feel in himself. He will feel that he is valued and that adults listen to him. He will know that he is at the centre of his world rather than being just a child in your adult world. This may sound simple, but as adults we are conditioned to believe that we "know best" because of our greater experience and we often find it hard to allow our child to take the lead.

CHAPTER 6

Responding to your child

Being parents is the most important job we do – and perhaps the most difficult. Yet we are ill-prepared by society for the challenges ahead and we have little support. A growing number of expectant parents attend pre-natal classes; we are prepared for the birth and some of the early practical tasks. But all too quickly the tiny baby grows into an infant, then a toddler, and then a young child, and we struggle, with little guidance, to adjust to these transitions. Outside support is mostly available only at crisis point, and then we, the parents, are usually the ones who are blamed for what has gone wrong, and made to feel inadequate.

Learning how to be parents

It is generally assumed that we instinctively know how to be parents when we have children. In fact we learned how to be parents from our own

parents, or from whoever brought us up, and we tend to repeat what we learned from them with our own children. The criticized child will often become the critical parent while the child who receives affection is likely to become an affectionate parent.

Some parents who were unhappy as children try to be "opposite parents" and give their children a different experience of childhood from the one they had. But even these parents may unwittingly pass on underlying patterns of behaviour (see p. 92). In fact, neither being a "same" nor an "opposite" parent is appropriate. Our children are different people from us and they need us to respond to them in fresh ways, as separate individuals.

So what can we do? Fortunately there are skills we can learn to help us in the job of being parents. This chapter introduces many of these

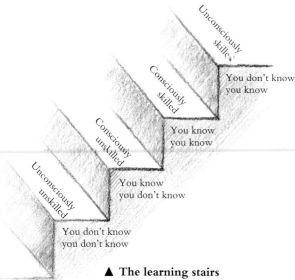

▲ The learning stairs
These are the steps involved in undertaking a new strategy. As you learn about new ways of relating to your child you are already on the second step. People experience this as the most frustrating place to be. As you practise the skills you move up the stairs.

Unconsciously skilled
You don't know you know

Consciously skilled
You know you know

Consciously unskilled
You know you don't know

Unconsciously unskilled
You don't know you don't know

"
My parents had the best of intentions. They pointed out my mistakes so that I could learn from them. But I ended up feeling I was no good. So I promised myself I would be different with my own children. My daughter, Sophie, is now ten. I have constantly made a point of praising her, but now her school tells me that she only does her work if her teacher praises her."

Jane, a mother

"
Advertisement: parent wanted
Person to work 24-hour shifts, 7 days a week, no holidays, low status, much criticism, little appreciation. Must be flexible, with manual, intellectual, managerial, and personnel skills, endless patience, energy, and good ideas. Life contract. No grievance procedure. No qualifications required, no training given. No salary or pension."

skills, which can help make being parents easier and can enable our child to develop into a sensitive, responsible, and independent adult.

Listening partnerships

No strategies work by themselves. Only we can make them work by adapting them to suit our own style. Some of the skills are easy, others are more difficult and can often point to unresolved issues from our own childhoods.

Patty Wipfler of the Parents Leadership Institute in California (see pp. 336–40) talks about the importance of "listening partnerships" in which parents get together in pairs and talk about their relationships with their children (for some guidelines on listening, see p. 98). Sometimes, when we try to relate to our child in a new way, we may become aware of strong feelings that stem from memories of our own childhoods. Finding an understanding friend and creating a "listening partnership" can be very helpful.

PRACTISING NEW STRATEGIES

These are typical stages that you may pass through:

● You are aware of using a habitual response (e.g. "Don't!") but it's hard to change it

● You learn to interrupt this response, but you cannot find a new response to replace it

● You find new words. For example, you say, "Hold it tight", rather than, "Don't spill it", but you feel self-conscious

● You integrate the new skills into your daily life. You say, "Hold it tight", and it feels right

▲ **Relaxing with children**
*Bringing up children sometimes gives us
the chance to behave in "childlike" ways,
which is good for us.*

Appreciating our children –
and ourselves

Educationalists stress the importance of appreciating our children and encouraging them in their efforts. Yet, despite this, many of us seem compelled to point out our children's mistakes and tell them what they are doing wrong. At the same time we often neglect to tell them what they are doing well, so they feel discouraged.

Encouragement creates confidence
The compulsion to point out mistakes may arise from our fear that if we don't, our child will never learn from them. But, as in the case of Jane and Sophie (see p. 85), such actions may have the opposite effect from that intended (for alternative responses see p. 90). We may also feel that we should limit the amount of appreciation we give to our child so that she doesn't get " bigheaded". But most "big-heads" have low self-confidence born out of a lack of appreciation and encouragement, which they try to cover up by acting "big".

It can make a crucial difference for our child if we appreciate her and tell her what we like about what she does. Focusing on the positive tends to reinforce the positive.

We all need to know that we are liked and loved by the people close to us. Saying, "I like being with you", can mean so much to a child.

THE CHILD AS TEACHER

As adults we may forget that our child has a lot to teach us. We have greater knowledge and experience, but she offers us many new perspectives on life, if we are open to receiving them. She will awaken a depth of loving and she will love us unconditionally. There will be moments when she will be extremely angry with us, but she will not hold grudges. She will forgive us when we are in the wrong. We may shout at her impatiently, or we may not take her views into consideration, but she will accept our apologies without hesitation.

Children have a simplicity and directness. They live in the present and can bring spontaneity back into our lives. Our routine may include little, if any, play. A child is sure to involve us in play and fun.

If we have difficulty in expressing feelings such as anger, sadness, or fear, she will give us countless opportunities to learn how to deal with these feelings, both in her and in ourselves. She will constantly question us and challenge us. This will often feel uncomfortable, but nobody else is likely to do it for us.

It is said that our need to love is greater than our need to be loved. Our child gives us the opportunity to love non-stop.

Support to face life's challenges

Our child needs encouragement when she is learning new skills. We can, for instance, say, "You're really doing a good job with your knife and fork tonight". When our child knows that she has our complete support, she feels empowered to face the challenges of daily life.

Just as we appreciate our child, so we can also appreciate ourselves. It may sound easy, but so many of us notice our own "failings" and constantly run ourselves down inside our heads. As we learn to concentrate on what we do well, we feel better and achieve more through our increased sense of self-worth.

QUESTIONS: WHAT DO YOU LIKE ABOUT YOURSELF AND YOUR CHILD?

Make a list of things that you like about your child. Congratulate her on at least one thing, choosing something that you have never told her before.

● I like the way she shows concern for other people

● I like the way she helps me sometimes, without me asking her to

● Her paintings show a good sense of observation

● Some of her craft projects show a lot of fine detail

● She is making a real effort not to whine

● She is trying hard to keep her room tidy

Make a list of things that you like about yourself as a parent. Remind yourself of these things especially when you feel low.

● I think I show extraordinary patience when my daughter whines

● I think, all things considered, I keep the home pretty tidy

● I have a good sense of humour

● I managed to stay calm when she threw a tantrum last week

● That costume I made for the school play was a big success

● That fruit cake I made was really delicious

◀ Superperson?
As parents, we may feel that we have to be Superpeople. Asking our child for help will not only make things easier for us, it will teach her to be considerate of others.

QUESTIONS: RECHARGING YOUR BATTERIES

Make a list of the things you enjoyed before you became a parent. For example: soaking in a hot bath, staying in bed late, going out, listening to music, reading a book, cooking and eating a favourite meal, talking on the phone.

● Which of these things do you still do, now you are a parent?

● Do you do enough for yourself? Could you do more?

● Take some time to do things you enjoy. Everyone will benefit from the pleasure it gives you

Parents' needs

In Chapter 5 (see pp. 74–83), we considered children's needs, but, as parents, our own needs are just as important. A new baby makes it hard to find time for ourselves, but as she grows we begin to have more free time. It is important that we use this time to do the things that refresh us and give us energy.

Mothers' guilt

This can be harder for mothers than for fathers because mothers often feel guilty about doing things for themselves; society gives them the message that they should "sacrifice" themselves for their children. But we all need to look after ourselves, both for our children's sake and for our own. If we are constantly fulfilling our children's needs and neglecting our own, we will reach the point where we have no more to give (see p. 236). We will feel exhausted, resentful, and angry because nobody is looking after us. It is better to ask for what we need. If we always put our child first we are showing her that our needs don't matter. But by looking after ourselves we are giving her a healthy role model.

Helping our child meet her needs

As parents we often feel that we have to do everything for our child. This is a necessity when she is a baby, but at a surprisingly young age she can start to take on some responsibility for herself. From early on we can, for instance, involve her in tidying up toys rather than doing it for her. She can start to decide what clothes to wear and then dress herself, and she can choose, within reason, what to have for breakfast. The earlier we involve her in sharing such responsibility, the more quickly she will be able to take on greater responsibilities (see p. 230).

▼ Help her to help herself

A small child can learn to put on her own coat, the Montessori way. First she puts the coat on the floor, inside upward, with the collar toward her. Then she puts her arms in the armholes and lifts the coat over her head. She then brings her arms forward as the coat goes down her back.

QUESTIONS: HELPING CHILDREN HELP THEMSELVES

● What are you doing for your child that she could do for herself? For example, does she drop her coat on the floor when she comes home? Do you automatically hang it up?

● How do you feel about hanging up that coat? How would you feel about not doing it?

● Could she do it herself? Could you stop doing it?

● Could she take over or share in some other tasks?

This does not mean neglecting her or forcing her to be independent before she is ready. It does mean assessing what she can do and giving her the opportunity to start doing it. We can also agree to her requests to do things herself by asking her how she would like us to help her.

A child feels good about doing things for herself. If she has lost a toy, we can refuse to look for it because it is her toy. When she finds it, she will feel pleased with herself. If we look for it, she may assume that we will always search for her lost things and will take us for granted. Once we have created that habit it can be hard to break it.

QUESTIONS: LABELS

● List the labels used about you as a child. Noisy? Clumsy? Helpful? Quiet?

● What were you actually doing when the label was used?

● What are the long-term effects of these labels?

● What labels do you now use for your child? Were these used about you?

● What is your child actually doing when you use these labels?

● Think up a description of her behaviour to replace the label, and use it

▲ **Unwanted labels**
It is all too easy to give a child an unhelpful label which may stick to her and influence her self-image as an adult.

The power of our words

Our words have power over our child. When we call her "lazy" or "mischievous" or "demanding" she starts to believe that she is lazy or mischievous or demanding. Then she behaves in a manner that is all the more lazy or mischievous or demanding, because that's what she believes she is. Labels become self-fulfilling prophecies and problematic because the labelling words are ours, not hers. So we, the adults, are defining the child and as a result she starts to wonder, "Who am I? Am I me or my label?"

Avoiding labels

Describing our child's behaviour is more useful than labelling her as a person. Rather than saying, "You're so messy", we can say, "The toys are still on the floor." This has two advantages: it avoids the danger of the label "messy" being attached to the child and it says precisely what the mess is, giving her the chance to do something about it. Otherwise the "messy" child may honestly not know what we are talking about.

Many of us can remember the labels that were used about us when we were young, which may still be following us around. When we become aware of this, we see how labels can affect our child in the long term.

The danger of positive labels is often harder to recognize. Surely, it seems, we are only helping our child if we call her "bright" or "good". But these words are our definitions of our child, who may start to feel that she has to behave in ways that fit the labels, in order to earn our love.

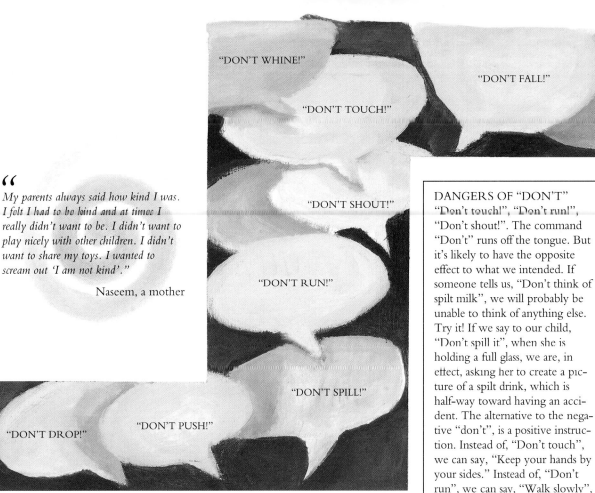

"DON'T WHINE!"

"DON'T FALL!"

"DON'T TOUCH!"

"DON'T SHOUT!"

"DON'T RUN!"

"DON'T SPILL!"

"DON'T DROP!"

"DON'T PUSH!"

DANGERS OF "DON'T"
"Don't touch!", "Don't run!",
"Don't shout!". The command
"Don't" runs off the tongue. But
it's likely to have the opposite
effect to what we intended. If
someone tells us, "Don't think of
spilt milk", we will probably be
unable to think of anything else.
Try it! If we say to our child,
"Don't spill it", when she is
holding a full glass, we are, in
effect, asking her to create a picture of a spilt drink, which is
half-way toward having an accident. The alternative to the negative "don't", is a positive instruction. Instead of, "Don't touch",
we can say, "Keep your hands by
your sides." Instead of, "Don't
run", we can say, "Walk slowly",
instead of, "Don't shout", we can
say, "Talk quietly".

▲ **"Don't"**
*We may feel overly aware of children's
shortcomings – their undeveloped skill,
grace, and balance – and it is all too easy
to say "don't" before anything else.*

Creating new images

Giving a child a label is a dangerous thing, even
if it is unvoiced. We may treat our younger child
as "the baby" and she is likely to respond by naturally falling into the role of the child who
demands the most. Our images of her greatly
affect her image of herself – whether we put
them into words or not.

Offering new images

When a child who is "demanding" asks us to do
yet another thing for her, we can say, "I know
you can do it by yourself". When the child who

is "self-reliant" sits down on her own, we can
say "May we sit with you?"

It may not be easy to relate to our child in
such a new way, but we need to offer her new
images of herself, even when she fights against
them. The "demanding" child will not gladly
give up her need for your help. She is likely to
have a tantrum and cry and be angry with you
for refusing to help her. She needs you to allow
her to let out the painful feelings, while you
insist lovingly, "I know you're angry with me for
not helping you, but I know you can do it yourself. That's the best way I know of helping you".

▲ A true image

We must appreciate ourselves for what we are, and teach our child to appreciate herself for what she is. Beware of projecting on to the child, but accept that she is herself; a separate human being.

QUESTIONS: **THINKING ABOUT ROLES**

● What roles did you play when you were a child? Were you "demanding", "the helper", "the quiet one", or what?

● What roles do you play as a parent? Are you "the martyr", "the problem-solver", "the angry one", or what?

● Which of these roles do you want to change? How can you start to break out of them?

● What roles does your child play? They may be some of the roles that you played as a child

● Does your child need your help to break out of any of these roles? What new self-image does she need from you?

Breaking out of our own roles

Very often we are so close to our child that we hardly know where she begins and we end. One mother, herself the eldest of five children, who had always been left to "fight her own battles" as a child, would step in to sort out even the most minor problems which her eldest son encountered. She found it hard to separate herself from her child and presumed that, without her constant intervention, her child would suffer in the same way as she had in her childhood.

In order to help our child break out of the roles she is stuck in we need to learn to step back and view her, and our relationship with her, from a distance.

Successes and setbacks

Learning to help our child in this way takes time and there will be setbacks along the way as we get angry with her and despair of her ever changing. However, we can keep offering the new image and the child will embrace it in time.

Another part of helping our child to break out of her role is to break out of the roles we play ourselves.

Upsetting the system

Roles in families tend to mesh with one another. For example, the parent who plays the martyr is likely to have demanding children, and the demanding child is likely to have a self-reliant sibling who seldom seeks attention. If we start to break out of our roles, then we upset the whole system and those around us need to change their roles too. Breaking out of our roles is a very effective way of enabling our child to break out of hers. This can bring about great change.

" *One of my children was demanding and the other was independent. The younger child, Jordan (the demanding one), would nag the older one, Janie, until she got so fed up she would give in. So I decided to help them. I encouraged Janie to stick up for herself and I told Jordan that he could not always have his own way. Then I decided to change my own behaviour. First I decided to stop dressing Jordan every morning. After two days of tantrums he started to dress himself. But Janie started asking to be dressed. My change enabled Jordan to learn self-reliance and Janie to ask for what she wanted.*"

Hilary, a mother

▼ **Family puzzle**
Every member of the family is a piece in the puzzle; each one has to fit in somewhere. But if it is allowed to happen, one member (even a tiny baby) may acquire more than the allotted space, leaving the others to battle over what is left.

STRATEGY: **GIVING YOUR CHILD A NEW IMAGE**

● Appreciate your child for the very qualities that you are encouraging in her

● Let her overhear you talking positively about the side of her that you are encouraging

● Help her to see herself differently. If she finds it hard to share, give her a bag of sweets to divide between her friends

● Be a storehouse for your child's successes. If she is dejected by her "failures", remind her of past achievements

Body language

Most of our communication takes place at a non-verbal level; it is not enough to focus on words. When we have a good rapport with another person, our non-verbal communication tends to instinctively match theirs: if they sit, we will sit; if they talk quietly, we are likely to talk quietly; we may even adopt similar postures. We communicate empathy with our bodies as well as with our words.

As adults, we tend to focus on the words people say. We are generally not aware of the non-verbal communication, though it affects us.

On an intuitive level our children tend to be much more conscious of body language. There are several ways in which we can raise our awareness of non-verbal communication in order to create better rapport with our children.

Giving clear messages

If a child is running around with a pencil in her mouth we may say, "If you run around like that, you may fall and hurt yourself". If we do not express the extent of our fear, she may not take any notice of us. We are giving a mixed message. This is called being "incongruent".

If our words and actions are incongruent, they are likely to confuse the child and our words will have limited effect and even be ignored. Remembering that the child is particularly aware of our non-verbal communication we need to ensure that our whole bodies communicate what our words say. If the child ignores us we will become more and more frustrated until we really say (or shout) what we mean. The child has forced us to be congruent by ignoring our incongruent messages. Only when we communicate with our whole selves are our messages really heard.

▲ On her level

To communicate with our child we need to devote time and energy to building rapport. Talking with the child on her level and keeping eye contact is important.

BODY LANGUAGE
The American anthropologist, Dr Ray Birdwhistel, who coined the phrase "body language", analyzed interactions between people in pairs and small groups to discover what proportion of communication was non-verbal. He came up with the following statistics:

- Words – 7%
- Tone of voice – 23%
- Facial expression – 35%
- Gestures – 35%

STRATEGY: **RAPPORT THROUGH BODY LANGUAGE**

- When talking or listening to your child, lift her up to your height or crouch down to hers

- When your child is talking to you, give her your full attention

- Try to match your child's speech in speed and volume

- Pay attention to your child's body language

- Your child may stomp around making angry noises. Joining in playfully may break the tension

- Saying, "Stop it!"quietly will probably not get your child's attention. Stand still and raise your voice (without shouting)

- Saying, "I love you", may not be enough. Express your love with a hug, a kiss, or a gesture

▲ **A child's view of adults**
"They boss you around."

Acknowledging our child's feelings

A child shows her feelings at every moment. These may include excitement at a new discovery, or frustration at shoe-laces that won't tie up. If we feel comfortable with these expressions of her emotions she will intuitively sense our ease. But if we do not feel comfortable with them, we may unwittingly try to find ways of preventing her from expressing them.

We may find it difficult to cope with our child's sadness. When she cries over a broken toy, we may quickly tell her that it can be mended rather than first comforting her with a few understanding words. If we were never allowed to express sadness as children we can find it difficult to deal with hers.

We may respond to her outbursts with harsh words or just with painful expressions on our faces. Our child will intuitively learn that certain feelings are unacceptable and she may stop expressing them to avoid our reaction. Acknowledging her feelings helps her to learn that all feelings are acceptable.

There are times, however, when we need to contain the way she expresses her feelings. We can show her that we still love her with her angry feelings, while channelling the expression of her anger. For example, if she is angry with a brother, we can hold her while saying, "I can see that you are angry with him, but I will not let you hurt him. You can show me how angry you are". She may scream and hit out in the safety of our arms, or vent her feelings on a cushion.

QUESTIONS: THINK BACK TO
YOUR OWN CHILDHOOD

● Think of a time when your
parents didn't pay attention to
your upset feelings

● How would you have
preferred your parents to have
responded?

● Which of your child's feelings
do you find it most difficult to
deal with?

● Acknowledge your child's
feelings. It can make a difference
to how she deals with them

▲ **The importance of tears**
*The more we can let our child cry out her
hurts, the more effectively she can recover
from them. The pain stays locked inside
when the tears cannot flow.*

Acknowledging our own feelings

Acknowledging – and expressing – our own
feelings goes hand-in-hand with acknowledging
our child's. As parents we may put our own feelings aside (see also p. 88), and lock them away so
securely that we don't even know they are there.
As we lose touch with our own feelings, so we
also lose touch with other people's.

Acknowledging our feelings can help us feel
better in ourselves and also shows our child by
example that it's quite all right to have and show
all kinds of feelings.

Sharing our childhoods

A child enjoys hearing stories about our childhoods. Often a story about one of our childhood
struggles can reassure a child facing a similar situation. A child who is fearful of the dark can be
comforted to hear that we were too when we
were young and that we overcame that fear.

"

*When Mackenzie, the older of my two
children said, 'I wish I were a baby', I
had to stop myself from saying, 'But
there are lots of advantages in being the
big brother'. I realised it seemed to him
that his younger sister had the better deal.
Instead I said, 'Part of you wishes you
were a baby', and he looked so pleased to
be understood. Now we spend a few minutes each day when he sits on my lap and
I rock him like a baby."*

A father

Listening to our child

It is surprising how difficult it is to really take in what people are saying to us. This is often most true of our closest relationships. Because we know our child so well it is easy to assume that we understand what she is telling us without really paying attention. Or we may find what she says uncomfortable and steer her away from it. Another "blocking" technique is to reassure our child when she is feeling bad about herself in order to "make her feel better". For example, if she says that she thinks she is ugly, we may spontaneously say, "But you're beautiful". Such words of reassurance will discourage her from talking about her bad feelings, when she actually needs the opportunity to talk about them.

A special kind of listening known as reflective, or active, listening can be of great help. The adult listener reflects back to the child what she understands the child to be communicating. For example, we might say, "You look sad", rather than, "Cheer up!" if our child has a forlorn look.

Very often a simple "reflection" of what our child is communicating to us through her words and actions is enough of an invitation for her to be able to share her upset with us, and we can continue to reflect back the content of what she says until she has finished. If we give her the chance to express her fears, problems can resolve themselves "magically": ordinary questions may be experienced as an interrogation and lead to silence whereas descriptive statements of what you see and hear can help to open a locked door.

Be pleased with yourself

This chapter contains many suggestions of how we can relate to our child in new ways. At times we will find ourselves able to apply them, but at others we will fall back into our old habits.

QUESTIONS: HOW DO YOU DEAL WITH BLOCKS?

● In what ways do you block your child from talking about what is upsetting her? Do you reassure, criticize, give advice, change the subject, become defensive, interpret her problem for her, or interrogate her?

● What is happening inside you at such times? You may be feeling tense and tight, or panicky, or you may feel you have to "know all the answers"

● Where do you think your listening blocks came from?

● Practise using reflective listening with your child, starting with minor upsets first. As you become more skilled you can start using the technique for more important concerns

Rather than acknowledging our child's feelings we will find ourselves disregarding them; rather than describing her behaviour, we will hear ourselves labelling her. "Don't" will come tumbling out of our mouths; and there will be times when we realize that we have prevented her from talking about her upsets.

That is all right. Part of loving our child means accepting that we have done our best up to now and that we will strive to do our best in the future. We can notice our successes and be pleased with ourselves. We are involved in the complex task of replacing well-practised habits with new and unfamiliar ones.

▼ Reflective listening

A father uses reflective listening with his daughter, who has mild cerebral palsy, affecting her balance (which she calls "wobbly legs"). The daughter has been attending gym club, but she is not sure whether to continue.

1. Elisabeth: "I don't want to go to gym club."

2. Father: "You don't like it there."

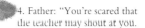

3. Elisabeth: "I don't like the teacher. He shouts at the children."

4. Father: "You're scared that the teacher may shout at you."

5. Elisabeth: "And I don't like the other children watching me doing gym so I always stand at the back of the class."

6. Father: "You stay at the back so nobody can see you."

7. Elisabeth: "Yes, I think they will make fun of my wobbly legs."

8. Father: "You're scared that they'll laugh at you."

9. Elisabeth (after a pause): "But I do like gym so I think I'll go."

THOUGHTS: THE ADVANTAGES OF REFLECTIVE LISTENING

A reflective listening response is a simple description that reflects back what we see and hear.

● The child is in charge of the exchange and has the chance to resolve her own difficulties

● Both child and adult can find out what is really concerning her, by finding out what lies underneath the problem

● Reflective listening can help us listen to the things that our child is telling us that we used not to hear

● If we misunderstand what the child says and reflect back incorrectly, she can easily correct what we have said and move on

CHAPTER 7

Fitting into society

The way we experience the world as adults can be determined by our own babyhood and childhood experiences. And the way our baby experiences the world, whether friendly or hostile, depends to a great extent on how we relate to him.

A joint venture

We need to be aware that a baby cannot be "badly behaved"; he does not know how to manipulate people. He is stimulated to act by whatever grabs his attention in the present. When we feel annoyed by his behaviour it is easy to assume that he is trying to "get at us". If we approach our relationship with him as a battle, then a battle it will become. But if we approach it as a joint venture, then it can become a journey of co-operation.

If our baby grows up in a family that is responsive to his needs, he will sense that the world is his oyster. He will expect others to treat him respectfully, just as he respects them. He will feel able to ask for what he wants and needs and to stick up for himself; he will have an inner sense that he will be heard.

Every baby is unique, as is every relationship between a baby and his parents. There are no rules as to how to respond to him. Each individual baby needs the particular attention that is suited to his needs. One baby might be easy to care for, feed easily and sleep contentedly; while another might find life more difficult and spend long periods crying for no apparent reason. We need to look and listen, try things out, make mistakes, and learn. If our baby senses that we are trying to respond to his needs, he will also sense that we are on his side.

▲ George is five weeks old

George has been happily looking at shadows on the wall, but has started to cry. If his mother does not come and he is repeatedly left to cry, he will "learn" that people are not interested in his needs. He may then reach a point where he won't even bother to cry because he knows nobody will come. This is called "learned helplessness" and he may grow up feeling that the world is a lonely place and that he does not deserve attention and help.

•

But if his mother regularly comes straight to him, picks him up and finds out what he wants, he will learn that she responds to his needs. He will learn to trust her. If other adults treat him likewise, he will learn that the world is a good place and that people care about his needs.

▲ George is six months old

George is sitting in his high chair, picking up pieces of food and dropping them on to the floor. His sisters call their father. If his father comes and scolds him, George may feel frightened. If this is a typical reaction, George is likely to "learn" over time that he has to watch his behaviour carefully so that his father does not lose his temper with him. George may become anxious about all adults.

•

George will feel very differently if his father, despite feeling exasperated about the mess, sets about cleaning it up. And if he says to George, "Food belongs on your plate and in your mouth, not on the floor", George will remain relaxed while learning over time what behaviour is expected of him.

▲ George is nine months old

George is starting to crawl. He is outside rubbing dirty water into his hair and licking his fingers. If his mother scolds him for being a bad boy, as she often does, he is likely to become anxious and to worry about his mother's reactions to whatever he does. His natural curiosity will be inhibited and he will modify his behaviour to anticipate her moods.

•

If his mother says, "I can see you're having fun, but the water is dirty and you might get sick", he may, initially, cry angrily despite her understanding. If she responds to him regularly in such a way, her boundaries will not inhibit his natural desire to explore.

Sibling rivalry

Friction is normal between siblings and we can be prepared for and accommodate it as a part of family life. It is a vital aspect of growing up, and it may be more noticeable at times of change.

A new baby in the family

The arrival of a new baby is a major time of adjustment for the whole family. We parents will be making practical preparations for the baby's arrival and siblings will be preparing themselves for the addition to the family. Many children will look forward with excitement to the newcomer because they like the idea of having a little brother or sister. Some look forward to being able to care for the new arrival, and many will assume that they will have a new, ready-made playmate. The reality does not usually match the fantasy, however, and our children will experience a mixture of feelings. At times, they will feel loving and caring, and at others angry and jealous. This confusion may manifest itself in more tantrums and upsets than usual.

Fighting

When children fight our first reflex as parents may be to step in and stop them. We try asking questions such as, "Who did what?" and "How did it start?", with a view to "refereeing" the fight. The problem with this approach is that once we get involved in sorting out the problem we become a part of it. Not only will the child who is deemed to be in the wrong be angry and upset with us but all our children will come to rely on us to sort out wrangles whenever they arise. If we analyze such situations, what is happening is that the children's angry feelings have become hooked together and they are trying unsuccessfully to release them while acting them

"

My two children were quietly building a model space ship. Suddenly I heard a scream and a bang. Stephen had hit Jennifer and she had bitten him in retaliation. The model had been kicked aside and broken, and the children were at each other's throats. I went into the room and separated them. I said, "You both look really angry." Stephen said, "She wouldn't let me have the wheels. I hate her." I allowed him to express his angry feelings and then asked Jennifer how she felt. When they had both had their say — and been listened to — they calmed down somewhat. Jennifer agreed to let Stephen have his wheels if he promised to help her mend her broken model. I helped repair the model and after a few minutes I was able to leave the room because they were playing happily again."

Sharon, a mother

out on each other. As parents we can help our children by acknowledging their painful feelings (see p. 96). Our aim can be to listen to each of them in turn, not with a view to sorting out the problem, but first to lower the tension and then to help them find a solution.

This can be difficult if our negative feelings were not acknowledged when we were children. If we were only-children, it may be far more difficult for us to understand our children's rivalries.

There are also times when our children need to fight and argue and sort out their own difficulties. We can learn ways of stepping back and only intervene when they really need a hand. It can be hard to decide whether to intervene or not (see right).

◀ A new sibling
The child will have mixed feelings about the arrival of a new baby brother or sister, but if we think carefully about his feelings we can predict possible trouble spots and smooth the way ahead (see also p. 244).

▼ Ups and downs
In their day-to-day lives siblings have ups and downs together as in all relationships. They play amicably, and they get into arguments, which they can often sort out by themselves. We need to step back and only intervene when necessary.

STRATEGY: **COPING WITH FIGHTING**

● Ask your children if it is a play fight or a real fight. It can only be a play fight if both children agree that it is. You then need not intervene

● Agree on boundaries for fighting children (for example, no shoes, no hair-pulling, no biting). With reminders, they will learn the rules over time

● Regular pillow or balloon fights can help drain tension if siblings fight a lot. If you join in, the ensuing laughter will help ease general family tensions

Family position

Our child's position in the family is important in determining his behaviour and outlook on life. The first child often has a very special relationship with his parents. When a second child arrives he may enjoy helping to care for the new arrival although he may also be outraged at being ousted. The first child breaks new ground for the siblings that follow. When he enters the outside world, by going to nursery or playgroup, his excitement may be tinged with jealousy toward a younger brother or sister who will be spending time alone with his parents while he is out. We need to talk to the older child and acknowledge his jealousy. By showing special interest in him and what he is doing, we can help him sense our continued love and concern.

Parental confidence

We, as parents, may feel more confident in caring for our second and subsequent children, who benefit as a result. Such children have never had their parents' undivided attention and so do not miss it in the way a first child does. A second child sometimes enjoys being "the baby", but at other times will want to "catch up" with his older sibling, or strike out for his independence.

When a third baby comes, the younger child is himself ousted and becomes a middle child. He may need support in this as he adjusts to his new position in the family. He may yearn to play with the older sibling whilst wanting to be a role model for the younger one.

Only-children enjoy the freedom and lack of competition from siblings for their parents' attention, but they may also feel lonely. They may find it difficult to mix with other children because they have not had to negotiate relationships with siblings.

STRATEGY: **DEALING WITH SIBLING RIVALRY**

● If a new baby is born into the family give an angry older sibling a doll to pound and punch as if it were the baby. This allows the sibling to express his angry feelings safely without damaging the baby

● Avoid making comparisons, favourable or unfavourable – this sets up rivalries between siblings. Show each child what you like about him instead

● Equal is never enough. In trying to be fair we may try to treat equally. Instead of giving equal love to each child, love each one uniquely for who he is and for his qualities. Instead of giving equal time, give each child the time he needs

"
I took my daughter Aisha to the cinema on her own. When we came out Aisha asked for some sweets from the kiosk. I said 'Shall we go to a restaurant to have a proper meal?' Aisha's eyes lit up and her mouth fell open. 'It really is my special day', she said."

Susan, a mother

"
When I went to secondary school, my two younger sisters teamed up together against me. I was left out of their games and their conversations and they sniggered at my developing body."

Wendy, the oldest of three

"
As an only-child, I have a much greater capacity for solitude than my sibling-blessed friends, and I think this is an attribute. The bond I have with my parents is very strong if sometimes a little suffocating. There is a great deal of guilt for single children."

Jill, an only-child

"
Being the youngest of four brothers was always a double-edged sword. One of the benefits was that I could watch and learn from their behaviour – their mistakes and successes – all the things that made my parents angry or pleased, or just plain indifferent. But, at the same time, my brothers could indiscriminately turn on me as a scapegoat, or treat me as being of little or no consequence. In general, my parents were far too concerned about the progress of my brothers to pay much attention to my development. In retrospect, I feel they simply crossed their fingers and hoped I would be all right."

Robert, the youngest of four

A wide range of roles

It is important to encourage children to develop broad personalities and help them to play a wide range of roles in the family. We need to ensure that the oldest child who cares for siblings can also be a child without responsibilities, that we encourage the youngest child to see himself as a strong and independent being, and also ensure that middle children are not forgotten. Only-children may need encouragement to explore their feelings about being only-children.

A child's relationships with his siblings set the scene for his relationships with his peers. The skills he learns at home will stay with him in the outside world and will help him negotiate sharing and competing with others.

Special time

Somewhere inside every child is the desire to have his parents' total attention. This is, of course, difficult enough when there is only one child in the family. When there are two or more children it can be almost impossible to find time to spend with each child separately and even if we put aside time for each child the others may try to disrupt the special time. Children have a sixth sense about such things.

All children need to have an adult's undivided attention some of the time. It helps them to feel special as individuals to know that they do not always have to compete with their siblings or others for our attention. And if we can regularly spend some time alone with each of our children, we may find that any tensions that exist between siblings will diminish.

When we spend time with our children in this way, it is useful to let them be in charge of whatever we are doing together. It is a time for them to choose what they want to do and set their own agenda.

▶ Winning

A child needs to have the experience of winning. For him there is no distinction between playing and living, and so, if he loses he may feel quite devastated. He needs to win, and his victory is a moment for him to treasure. He needs to beat us in his games, but we must put up enough resistance so that he is challenged. If he experiences "real" victories with us, he is less likely to need to win constantly against his friends.

"

I try to make the effort to sit and talk to each of my two sons on his own, without the other being present. They are very competitive with each other and the older one always tries to put the younger one down. I am always surprised at how much they both relax at these times."

Alison, a mother

Playing together

From the age of about three children start to be able to play together. Until this age their play tends to take the following forms. Very young children can play on their own for short periods, mostly when they are in the security of their own homes, or if a known and trusted adult is nearby. They can play a game with an adult or older child; the game may be initiated by either party, but is focused on what the young child wants. They can play in parallel with a child their own age, which means that they can play side by side, sharing the same or different toys, but each playing their own game. As long as their games do not interfere with each other's they will play happily. They enjoy the company of other children even though they do not play "together". Usually during their third year children start to

▲ Cheating

A child will often cheat in order to avoid losing, which he may find too painful. So if we are aware of this, we can be relaxed about it. We can make playful comments or join in, so that everybody can have a good laugh. This will help take the tension out of the situation and help to diminish the child's need to cheat.

◀ Sharing

A child may need encouragement to share, but he should never be forced to. As a starting point we need to respect the child's ownership of his property. From a position of security in his possessions, he will come to share with others. We can explain to him how his friends feel if he does not share his toys and we can jointly set guidelines on sharing some toys. We can also agree to put special toys away so that visitors will not come across them.

❝

James and John were both three and had known each other for over a year. James was playing with his model farm and John joined in. They were putting all the cows in the field when John started to put sheep in the field as well. James got upset because cows and sheep didn't belong in the same field. John couldn't understand this. I suggested that they make a second field and put the sheep in there. John liked the idea and James wanted to help put sheep in the field too.❞

Dan, a father

▲ Losing

As the child matures he will learn to lose "gracefully". We can help him by giving him a foundation of victories on which to stand. Losing is likely to bring up strong feelings of anger and disappointment. From time to time, we can ensure that we win so that he can experience losing and let these painful feelings out with us. Victories and occasional defeats prepare him for losing while playing with friends.

play "together". At first their attempts may be hesitant and their co-operation will only last for a short time. But with practice they will learn to play together for longer and longer periods of time. They will learn to negotiate difficulties without their games turning into fights and they will be able to devise and enjoy increasingly complex games (see also pp. 204–5).

One area of difficulty for many children is winning, losing, and cheating. Most children like to win but many of them find losing difficult and get terribly upset about it. They will try almost anything to avoid it. Another area of difficulty is sharing toys. On the one hand, children want to be generous toward their friends but on the other, they often cannot bear to see a friend play with one of their special toys. They need patience and understanding to help them come to terms with such concepts.

Transitions

Life is marked by transitions, large and small. Birth is the first great transition, when the baby moves from the inner to the outer world, and perhaps the next major one is starting school. This is a time in a child's life when he moves toward independence and begins to take greater responsibility for himself. But the time between birth and school is marked by many other important milestones (see right).

Dealing with separation

Separations often cause distress and anxiety for a child, but they also bring up powerful feelings for parents. Preparing our child for the time when he must be separated from us will help him understand what will be happening and minimize his anxiety. We need to expect tears and sadness, especially if our child is not used to leaving us and if we feel emotional about the change. We need to separate our anxieties from our child's (see p. 114). Our child needs us to have confidence in him and in his ability to cope with the separation.

If we are confident, then he can feel and express all his fears knowing, somewhere inside him, that he really will be all right. In this way he will be growing toward greater independence and we will be taking another step in letting go and standing back.

Uneven pace

A child does not develop at an even pace. One moment he may seem mature for his age and the next he may seem to regress. This often happens when he is facing difficulties. For example, if a mother goes back to work full-time, her child may become "clingy", may not sleep through the night, or may start wetting the bed. If a father has to go away for a long period his child may start behaving in a disruptive manner because he misses him. On his father's return the child may express anger at him for having left and may need help to understand that he has not been abandoned and that his father will not suddenly disappear again.

Such separations may also touch our own feelings in a deep place. We need support to look after ourselves, so that we, in turn, have the energy and attention to deal with our child's feelings (see p. 88).

"

I was going back to work and wanted to prepare David for the fact that a childminder would be looking after him during the day. I took him to Judy, the childminder, for a few hours a day before I started back to work and he was distraught each time I left. He would cling to me and he sobbed his heart out. I would give him to Judy, kiss him and say, 'I know you'll have a lovely day. I'll see you tonight, sweetheart'. And when I went downstairs to the car I was the one who cried and felt guilty. But now, three months later, he hardly bothers to say goodbye to me and I am more relaxed too. On reflection I can see that separating was just as hard for me as it was for him."

Janet, a mother

▶ **A patchwork of experiences**
Each transition is both a beginning and an end. It means saying goodbye to what went before and welcoming in the new. There is both sadness for loss of the past and excitement for the future for parents as well as children.

Milestones
Birth
First smile
Weaning
First steps
First words
Playing at a friend's house for the first time
Sleeping in a different house for the first time
Going to a childminder
Pre-school
School

The outside world

When the child goes to pre-school or school, outside factors become more important in both reinforcing what he has learned at home and in offering him new experiences.

At school, the teacher is often a parent figure whose presence enables the child to make the transition between being a member of an intimate family group and finding a place in the outside world. In this wider world the child is directly exposed to others who are different from himself. This may be the first time that children from different ethnic groups, religions, and cultures have mixed and they will show great interest in each other. Not until they are past five years of age do they start picking up the attitudes of the adults around them to "difference" and perhaps begin to repeat some of the prejudiced statements that they may have heard, though probably without fully understanding what they are saying.

A child may want to keep the experience of school to himself. If we say, "What did you do at school today?", he may say, "Nothing". When he says "nothing", he actually means, "This is my world and I don't want you to come in". We need to learn to respect our child's wishes. He has a right to his own world and we need to practise standing back.

The influence of the peer group will show up in the child's behaviour at home. He will start to use new expressions and he may challenge family rules which were not previously questioned. This is a time when we need to be flexible in accommodating the needs of our child who is making a first foray into the wider world. Talking with him about this meeting of two worlds is an important step in helping both him and us on this new journey.

Gender

By three years most children are aware of their own gender. They also have an idea of the different roles of males and females in society, even if their parents do not fit the stereotypes. Thus, the child who sees his father cooking at home may still say that his mother does the cooking.

A very young child will happily take on the roles of the other gender in play. Even though a boy may put on a dress and pretend to feed dolls, he still knows he is a boy. This only becomes a problem if adults are anxious about it. The child needs us to relax and allow him to explore gender differences to satisfy his natural curiosity.

By the age of about four or five, the pressure of their peers forces most boys and girls to play only with others of the same gender and to conform to stereotypical behaviour.

It is important to offer the child choice in his gender role, even though his behaviour is likely to conform to stereotype. He will be able to use this choice when he becomes a young adult and makes decisions about the kind of person he is.

"

I was concerned for my six-year-old son. At school he would sit on his own and hardly play with others. He refused to go to play in other children's homes. I continually tried to encourage him to play with friends because I felt desperate about his apparent lack of companions. But the more I encouraged him the less he seemed to want to. Perhaps he picked up my sense of desperation. To him it seemed that, if I was desperate about him, there must be something wrong with him. Some weeks after I finally gave up, he suddenly asked to visit a friend and gradually 'the problem' disappeared."

Leila, a mother

▲ **New friends**
Going to nursery school or kindergarten may be the first opportunity that the child has to mix with others who are different from himself.

CHAPTER 8

Restoring rhythm

Being parents is one of the most fulfilling tasks we can undertake. It is a joy to see our child growing daily. It is thrilling to see her reach each new milestone and we want to share it with the whole world. But it is not easy being parents. A child will almost certainly upset the order that we have constructed in our lives.

Conflicting needs

There will always be ups and downs in family life. Part of being parents is, at times, putting our child's needs first and giving up for her some of the things that are important to us. But at the same time we must not lose sight of our own needs (see p. 88). Difficulties come when we feel weighed down by the daily stresses and strains of family life, when we seem to be giving all the time and we do not feel that we are getting any-

thing back for ourselves. Then we become irritable and it is all too easy to take our frustrations out on the child, who is so vulnerable to our moods. The more we get angry with her, the more awkward she seems to be. And the more difficult she is, the angrier we become, so that a vicious circle is set up which is hard to break.

A caring atmosphere

In this chapter we will look at ways of dealing with situations in which our needs conflict with our child's. It is important to remember that there are no magic solutions that will solve her difficulties, or our own, with her behaviour. But we can work to create an atmosphere at home in which our child feels that we are available for her when she needs us and we will treat her fairly when there is conflict, while at the same time looking after our own needs.

▲**Testing relationships**
The parent–child relationship can be a testing one. Both parties have needs and both are under pressure.

The needs behind the behaviour

Why do we behave the way we do and why does our child behave the way she does? Let's presume that all behaviour is aimed at meeting needs – ours and our child's. For example, if a small boy likes to wear only blue clothes he may be asserting his need to be independent, and if a father feels warm toward his children when they help with the chores it may be because he feels their behaviour reflects positively on him and meets his need to feel good about himself.

How needs are communicated

The problem comes when our child's behaviour interferes with our needs, or when our behaviour interferes with her needs. Most of the time we react to the surface meaning of our child's behaviour without recognizing, or knowing, how to respond to the need underneath. So, for example, when Jamie calls to his dad for the third time from his bed and asks for a drink, his dad is likely to get irritated rather than recognize that Jamie is trying to convey, through his actions, that he is feeling scared or insecure.

Recognizing needs

A child will communicate her needs through her behaviour, so she is unlikely to say, "I need your attention". She is more likely to shout at us. We must learn to recognize the needs underlying both our own and our child's behaviour, particularly in situations in which needs conflict. Then perhaps we can address them. If we respond only to the surface behaviour then the underlying needs are unlikely to be met.

Problem ownership

Acknowledging who owns the problem offers a way of recognizing the needs behind people's behaviour and helps us in our attempts to respond to them, particularly when two people's needs conflict.

Using the term "misbehaviour" does not help us understand difficult behaviour. What we call "misbehaviour" is a child's attempt to meet her needs in ways that are unacceptable to us.

All needs are valid. The problem arises when our child tries to meet her needs in ways that are unacceptable to us. We can then try to help her meet her needs in acceptable ways. What are the things that your child does that you consider to be unacceptable? Think about the different things that she does and see if you can work out what needs she is trying to meet in each case.

Support where necessary

Parents often take on their child's problems unknowingly (see p. 108). For example, when our child has lost something, it is her problem. By looking for it we have taken it on as our problem and we may unintentionally encourage her to be dependent on us to find her lost things. It is more useful if we take the responsibility for our own problems and leave our child to take responsibility for hers, only supporting her where necessary.

Whose problem is it?

Working out who owns the problem is important because it suggests what to do next. If we decide that our child's needs are to be met first, then we can employ listening and helping skills (see p. 98). If we decide that our needs come first then we can think about ways of getting our child to change her behaviour (see p. 116).

QUESTIONS: ACCEPTABLE AND UNACCEPTABLE BEHAVIOUR

● When, where, and with whom would the following be acceptable?

Eating someone else's leftover food

Being jumped on

Splashing water on the floor

Screaming at the top of one's voice

● When, where, and with whom would the following be unacceptable?

Being hugged and kissed

Being offered money

Playing a game of ball

YOUR CHILD'S BEHAVIOUR
Whether you find behaviour acceptable depends on:
● How you are feeling at the time. If you are relaxed and happy you are less likely to find the child's behaviour unacceptable than if you are tired
● Whose behaviour it is. You are likely to be more patient with a toddler dropping food on the floor than a seven-year-old doing the same thing
● Where the behaviour is taking place. You may be happy for your child to jump on the furniture in your home, but not in your parents' home
● When the behaviour takes place. Loud music during the day may be fine, but not at night

Here are three everyday situations in which you may have difficulty with your child's behaviour:

▲ BEDTIME
Your child never stays in bed in the evening. She keeps calling out, getting out of bed, and coming downstairs

Who has unmet needs?
The parents, who need a quiet evening. And the child, who may need security because she is scared of the dark

Whose needs need meeting first?
Probably the child's. If you can help her meet her need for security, then you are more likely to get some quiet time

▲ MEALTIME
You have prepared a meal and your child says (as she does every day), "It's yucky. I won't eat it!"

Who has unmet needs?
You and the child. Your need is to feel valued by having the child eat the food you have prepared. The child's need is to have her food preferences considered

Whose needs need meeting first?
The child's. It generally does not work to make a child eat food she does not like as it sets up mealtime battles. You need to find alternative ways of feeling valued by your child and encourage her to develop a broader taste in food in her own time

▲ AFTER A BUSY DAY
You have just come home from work and want to relax for a few minutes. Your child insists on playing noisily nearby

Who has unmet needs?
Only you, because you are being disturbed. Your child is meeting her needs by playing

Whose needs need meeting first?
Yours. One way to solve the "problem" is by going to a quieter place to unwind while your child carries on playing

In these difficult situations, where there is conflict between what we want and what our child wants, we tend to react to our child's behaviour rather than respond to her underlying needs. Not only do we overlook her needs, but we are also usually unaware of our own.

Asking ourselves the questions "Who has unmet needs?" and "Whose needs need meeting first?" will help us to understand these situations in new ways and will lead us to more effective strategies for dealing with them.

Challenging behaviour

What is unacceptable behaviour? Each family has its own values that determine what is and what is not acceptable. Some values are shared by most people in society, such as not hurting others, and not breaking valuable possessions. Other values vary between families. For example, saying "please" and "thank you", having good table manners, and helping with the tidying up. It is not for this book to say what is and what is not acceptable. Its purpose is to offer some tools to help us maintain our family values.

In situations in which we decide that we own the problem and that our needs need meeting first, we have to get our child to change her unacceptable behaviour.

If we think back to our own childhoods most of us can remember occasions when our parents scolded us for behaving in unacceptable ways.

When we were scolded we were unlikely to have wanted to change our behaviour. We may have stubbornly continued what we were doing or we may have given in to our parents' wishes out of fear or resignation. In either case, such confrontations damage the relationship between adult and child long term, even if the adult wins in the short term.

So, how can we challenge our children in such a way as to get them willingly to change their behaviour without using our greater size and power and the greater volume of our voices to get our way? (See four-part challenge, right.)

Using the four-part challenge

We need to be prepared to accept solutions which may be radically different from any that we may have thought of. Our challenge may upset our child and we may need to listen to her upset before re-stating our challenge. It may take days or weeks before a resolution appears, but repeatedly stating the challenge at appropriate times and listening to any upset feelings it brings up all help in finding the solution.

There will be times when the child "acts up" because she feels overwhelmed by the raging monster inside. When she is upset in this way, it is she, not us, who owns the problem, and so challenging is inappropriate. She needs us to be with her, to listen to her, and to acknowledge her feelings (see p. 96). At a calmer time we can re-state our challenge.

> **FOUR-PART CHALLENGE EXAMPLE**
> "When you slosh bath water on the floor I feel annoyed because I'm the one who has to clean it up. What's a different game you can play in the bath?"
> Such a message is wordy for very young children. However, what is important about it is the attitude it conveys to the child. In essence, such a message is saying, "I have a problem with your behaviour and I would like your help in solving it." So you can adapt challenging messages to suit the age and understanding of the child. An adaptation of the above message for a very young child might be, "Water belongs in the bath. The floor needs to stay dry. Here's your favourite toy." (while passing the toy)

▼ **Four-part challenging messages**
The purpose of challenging the child is to get her to change her behaviour rather than to let off steam at her (which may make you feel better, but she is unlikely to change her ways). The four-part challenge is respectful of both parent and child and includes the possibility of success.

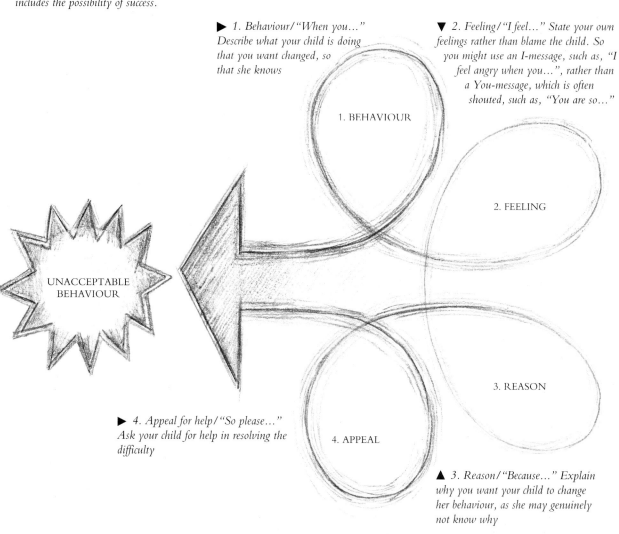

▶ *1. Behaviour/"When you..." Describe what your child is doing that you want changed, so that she knows*

▼ *2. Feeling/"I feel..." State your own feelings rather than blame the child. So you might use an I-message, such as, "I feel angry when you...", rather than a You-message, which is often shouted, such as, "You are so..."*

1. BEHAVIOUR

2. FEELING

UNACCEPTABLE BEHAVIOUR

3. REASON

▶ *4. Appeal for help/"So please..." Ask your child for help in resolving the difficulty*

4. APPEAL

▲ *3. Reason/"Because..." Explain why you want your child to change her behaviour, as she may genuinely not know why*

Gaining our child's co-operation

It is important to challenge our child's behaviour. This helps to create a model of how people can live together in harmony and deal with the difficulties that arise between them. The child then has a picture of assertive behaviour for the future. But there are other ways of getting our child to change her behaviour. These are suggested as additional items to the challenging tool-kit (see p. 116) and not just as alternatives. The examples, right, show a number of situations which often cause tension.

In each example it was the parent who owned the problem and she used an approach that enabled the child to solve her own problem willingly. In none of the cases was the child left with a problem. If she had been, listening skills would have been needed to help resolve the situation (see p. 98).

The power of laughter

Laughter is an effective antidote to stress. One way of enabling a child to laugh off the frustrations of being small and powerless is to swap roles with her in play, so that she takes the powerful role while we, the adults, pretend to be powerless. For example, the child may initiate a play fight in which we feign fear and feebleness while she takes the bossy, tough "adult" role. The aim is to have her laughing hilariously. Through her laughter any inner tensions will dissipate and she will feel more relaxed and confident. However, we need to offer enough resistance to her actions so that she has a sense of being tested, but not overwhelmed.

MAKE A CHART
If you are fed up with having to do all the household chores, call the family together and agree to allocate a task for each day to each person. Make a revolving chart with names, jobs, and days of the week. Once the rota is in full swing, you will find that not only do your children get lots of practice in laying the table, etc, but they will soon also become "watchdogs" and nag those who forget to do their share.

MAKE A GAME OF IT
If your child is reluctant to go to bed you can say, "I'll race you to the bathroom!" The playful element of competition may overcome her reluctance. When your child refuses to put away toys you can say, "How quickly can you put the toys away?" And if she is reluctant to get dressed, "How quickly can you pull your clothes on?" Children love to do things against the clock. It makes boring tasks much more interesting.

PUT IT ON PAPER
One mother was fed up with the fact that her son, Daniel, never put his school lunch box in the kitchen to be washed. At the end of the school holidays she discovered it in his room with fungus growing inside. So she put it on top of his desk with a note on it saying, "Wash me, I stink". Immediately the lunch box appeared in the kitchen ready for washing and Daniel needed few reminders about it in the future.

EFFECTIVE QUESTIONING
Asking a child a question can be more effective than repeated nagging; she can then think of her own answers to problems. For example, how many times do you have to tell a child to hang up her coat? The question, "Where else could you put your coat?" is likely to elicit her thoughtful involvement.

▲ Healing laughter
Laughter is the perfect antidote to stress, especially real belly laughter. And it's even more fun if parent and child can laugh together.

Saying "No" and sticking to it

There are some situations where it is not appropriate to negotiate, for example, if the child is about to cross a busy road without looking. But some of us find it hard to say "No" to our children as it reminds us of the pain of being told "No" when we were young. But the child needs us to set firm limits and, if we don't, she will demand more and more until finally we are forced into saying "No" and perhaps shouting it too. What is not helpful is to punish the child for being upset when we say "No" to her.

We have the right to say "No" at any time. Some of us feel that we have to say "Yes" to our child's every reasonable demand. But we are only human and each of us has only limited time and energy to give our child. Parents, especially mothers, often feel under pressure to put the child first and themselves second (see p. 88). The child needs to see us looking after ourselves as well as looking after her. So it's all right to say "No" to a reasonable request. If we repeatedly say "Yes" when we actually feel "No" then we are very likely to feel resentful and sensing this our child may well feel guilty for imposing on us. It's so much better to say "No" calmly and firmly, have an argument about it, clear the air, and feel close again.

Changing our minds

There will be times when we say "No" only to change our minds later. This is fine as long as it is the exception rather than the rule. So, if we aim to keep our attitudes reasonably consistent and only change our minds when there is a good reason (see quote, facing page), then our child will know where she stands, and will grow to understand that factors influencing our (and her) behaviour can change from day to day.

STRATEGY: SAYING "NO"

● Do you really mean "No"? Your reflex may be to say "No" before you have thought out your reasons properly. You could try saying, "Let me think about it. I'll give you an answer in a moment", to give you the time to think. It's better to say "No" and mean it rather than change your mind once you have said "No"

● When you say "No" the child is likely to get upset. Acknowledge her upset and stay with "No". Say things such as, "You seem disappointed, but I've said no and I mean it". Comfort her through her distress and stick with "No". This is a great help to your child

▲ Expressions of anger
"This drawing shows what I feel like when my mum says I mustn't do something that I want to do."

Tristan, aged 5

"
I took the children to the park. They had fun all day and I promised that they could go again the next day. But the next day I realized that I had to do some pressing household chores and that I would have to change my mind. I said, 'I'm sorry, I can't take you today, I've got too much to do in the house'. The children were upset and complained that I had taken them yesterday, why couldn't I today? I just said, 'Yesterday was yesterday and today is different. I have important things to do here'. The children had to come to terms with their disappointment."

Michael, a father

Family flashpoints

Family life is full of tricky moments that can trigger a set of reactions in us and in our child. Knowing how to handle them can make a world of difference to the quality of our lives.

Smacking and punishment

We are usually at our wits' end when we smack or shout, but a young child (under three) cannot connect a smack with her misdemeanour. Rewarding "bad" behaviour with negative attention such as a smack, may simply encourage further "bad" behaviour. Perhaps most important of all is the damage to a child's feelings. It is humiliating to be smacked or shouted at and it diminishes self-esteem. Other skills, such as recognizing the needs behind the behaviour (see p. 113), may help you deal more effectively with such situations. If we do something that we regret, we can always apologize at a later time.

Night time and mealtime

Young children often postpone bedtime with requests for food, a drink, another story, or a visit to the toilet. They are often scared of the dark, so they don't like being left alone in bed or they may wake up screaming in the middle of the night. The more we want our child in bed asleep so that we can have some time to ourselves, the more determinedly she seems to stay awake.

It's hard not to feel rejected when a child greets the food that we have prepared with "Yuck!", and it's hard to relax at the table when we feel anxious about our child's diet. Many parents become obsessed about how much their child eats. Our child will sense our anxiety and mealtimes can become tense battlegrounds. We need to relax – and help her to trust her own body to know how much food she needs.

SMACKING

There will be times when you feel powerless, when the monster inside rages and you feel like shouting, smacking, or punishing. At times like these, take evasive action (see below) so that you do not take your rage out on your child.

What you can do when you feel like smacking:

● Leave the room for a few minutes to calm down

● Take a deep breath and count to ten

● Go into another room and pound a cushion and scream out your frustration

● Have a change of scenery – take your child out to the park or to a friend's house

BEDTIME PROBLEMS

Establishing bedtime patterns can be difficult, but here are some helpful principles:

● Your child needs to calm down at the end of the day. Establish a slow, relaxing routine such as a bath (with time to talk) and a bedtime story (see p. 241)

● Your child will sense if you are feeling tense and rushed. Start bedtime early so that you can still look forward to a child-free evening

If your child is frightened of the dark:

● A nightlight may be reassuring

● Help her overcome her fears. Telling her about how you overcame your fear of the dark can give her confidence

● If your child calls you after you have settled her, soothe her with gentle words

● When she screams from a nightmare, wake her gently and hold her close to reassure her

MEALTIMES

Mealtimes can become less of a battleground if you help the child deal with the needs underlying her behaviour.

● Make mealtimes an enjoyable social occasion; have good conversations that involve everyone

● Encourage the child to eat a variety of foods by giving her a little to taste rather than forcing her to eat foods she doesn't like. Give small portions and offer second helpings; limit snacks

● Get your child interested in food. Plan meals, shop, and cook together. Try new foods. As you relax about choosing and eating food so will she

● Avoid cooking different meals for different members of the family – unless you want to!

● Let your child know that she needs to eat nourishing food and set firm limits over sweets and sweet drinks

> " Terry is four and until recently the only vegetables he would eat were raw carrots. I went to a clinic and was advised to stop battling with him and just give him the carrots. I found this difficult, but I tried it all the same and after a month Terry was tasting a few vegetables and had started eating them occasionally. I also found I was generally having fewer battles with him and that he was easier to manage."
>
> Judith, a mother

> " Bedtime used to be a tense time of day in our house. It seemed to take hours of cajoling and the children would try every trick in the book to delay going to bed. We found it hard to disguise the fact that we were desperate for a little peace and quiet, and they sensed this. I've found that the only solution is to time the children as they carry out their bedtime routine – music practice, bath, play, read, and bed. They seem to like a fixed regime and comply fairly happily."
>
> Jasmine, mother of two

We were all children once

Life becomes so much more complicated once we become parents. It's not just that our child demands our attention and that our life is fuller. It is also because our child's behaviour triggers all kinds of thoughts and feelings stemming from our own childhoods, whether we are aware of them or not.

Exploring our own childhoods

In this chapter we have been discussing difficult situations that often unconsciously remind us of our own childhoods and where our responses to our child's behaviour are often influenced by what happened to us as children (see left).

We have described and discussed all kinds of skills that we can use to help improve the way we relate to our child. These skills are likely to be able to help us up to the point where the unresolved issues of our own childhoods get in the way. So, as well as using the skills discussed in this section of the book, it is also useful to explore our own childhoods.

Triggers from childhood

Our child can be our guide in this personal exploration. Whenever her behaviour arouses strong feelings in us, we can be sure that memories have been triggered from our own past, particularly if this "re-stimulation" always occurs on particular occasions.

We can use a "listening partnership" with another adult (see Chapter 6) to explore these childhood feelings, or we may decide that we wish to join (or start up) a parents' support group (see pp. 336–40). Organized groups usually run for a number of sessions and parents are encouraged to continue meeting regularly thereafter for support and encouragement.

"
I hated my parents making me eat all the food on my plate. The more they told me to eat up, the more determined I was to leave something. I promised myself that, when I became a parent, I wouldn't make my children eat up all their food. However, Junior is now five, and he picks at his food. It drives me nuts and it takes all my energy not to say anything. Junior is confused by my tenseness at mealtimes and every now and again I just explode at him. I can't help it."

Tony, a father

"
Some five years ago I joined a support and education group for parents. I found out that I could learn some skills to help me choose how to respond to my children's everyday demands rather than be driven by habit. What a radical idea!"

Tom, a father

▶ Mummy and me

"We're standing outside our house, look-ing at the flowers in the garden."

Rowan, aged 4

▼ My family

"Mummy and Alexandra are sitting down, Daniel is playing, and Daddy is carrying me."

David, aged 6

PART 3

PLAY AND CREATIVITY

Mildred Masheder

There have been numerous theories concerning the nature and purpose of play. It is preparation for life, a recapitulation of the development of the human species, activity for fun, the child experimenting and gaining control over his life, and simply, education.

As parents we can see that all of these theories can be identified in our own child's behaviour and that there is considerable overlap between all of them. Play is an overall term, encompassing free-flowing spontaneity as well as more structured approaches, with rules and regulations, which are the essence of games. It is helpful to think of Johan Huizinga's interpretation of play as "doing a thing for the sake of itself".

The main message of this section is that play comes from within the young child and not from the initiative of the parent, though we have a vital role to play as enablers and facilitators. To a certain extent parents should relax and let the child get on with it.

CHAPTER 9

How creative play develops

Childhood is a time of wonder, a time when each child instinctively knows how to create his own development. No one has to teach him what to do. He explores and uses his imagination in play, and we can trust him to follow the same creative development sequence as every other normally healthy child. Given broadly the same set of circumstances, ways of play may vary, but each child plays similarly, with a purpose and for a reason.

Exploring with the senses

Through the baby and toddler phases the creative urge to play centres around the child exploring the world with his senses and by learning to control his body – little by little. From here he gradually transforms his play to take on symbolic and intuitive meaning, and this comes with the blossoming of the consciousness of the Self and the emergence of fluent, free-flowing language. These stages are flexible and different children reach them at different ages.

We do not have to worry about "pushing" our child on to acquire the next skill. The important factor is not how old he is, but whether he is ready to proceed to the next stage in his creative activities. If he begins to take an enthusiastic interest in new skills or pursuits, or if he makes a "leap forward" in terms of body control then we know that he is ready. When the time is ripe we can support and encourage him in the right sort of way, and this comes naturally with experience. This is all we have to do.

Play is the cornerstone of every child's early development. As parents we don't need to teach him how to explore and delight in the world; he already has the gift of awareness and this is the basis of his play, especially in his first two years.

Then comes the stage of imagination: the child engages in role play and weaves a magic web of fantasy around everything in his orbit. Quite spontaneously, he creates a world of his own, which draws from the real world yet is within his active control (see p. 222).

In the years from birth to seven, play is vitally important; it is as much the basis of the child's future wellbeing as it is the foundation of his intellectual, social, and physical development. The child knows instinctively what he needs to develop and he goes about it through play with whole-hearted enthusiasm.

▲ **Our role in the child's play**
If the child can play and develop all by herself, then what do we do? We want so much to give her the best start in life, but aren't we just shadowy figures in the background? Not so – our supportive role really does matter. We provide stimulation when the child needs it; we can broaden her horizons, and above all, we can create an atmosphere of loving approval of her creative efforts.

First play

Exploring through play and discovering the world is what early childhood is all about: it occupies all the child's waking hours. Whether grasping, pulling, throwing, tasting, or looking, the child experiences his senses to the full. In the first months it may seem to us that little is happening. He is already creating a sense of the world. The systematic efforts he makes, he achieves without our help. He perfects every skill by imitating and practising, and he does not need us to "drill" him. All he needs is to be offered a wide range of opportunities. We must be on the alert to know whether he is losing interest in an activity and whether we can provide something fresh to keep the development process going.

Imaginative play

By the time the child is two-and-a-half to three years old, he has come through his sensory-motor years (see p. 31) and his imagination is starting to develop. About this time, many parents begin to worry about whether the child is "just playing" instead of "learning", but they can rest assured that the joyful exploration of the imaginative and fantasy world is the best preparation the child could possibly have for every aspect of his life ahead. The pressure on parents to start the child on abstract learning at the earliest possible age is now stronger than ever, but it is misplaced. All the great educationalists stress that the stage of imaginative, creative play must precede the process of abstract thinking. They make strong pleas for children not to be deprived of the joys of their inner lives by attempting to cram factual knowledge into them too soon. The child benefits by filling his life with fairy tales, fantasy, games, and music.

***ACTIVITY:* SENSE STIMULATION**

Let your child:

● Feel different textures: soft velvet, rough hessian or burlap, silky satin, and fluffy fur fabric

● Try out different smells: roses, fresh herbs, wet leaves in autumn, newly baked bread, or freshly brewed coffee

● Look at brightly coloured fish in an aquarium, mobiles that move in a breeze, colourful wall hangings and collages, and leaves fluttering

● Hear music, bird song, people singing and talking, wind chimes, insects buzzing

● Experience different tastes: natural honey, unsweetened yogurt, lightly spiced foods

PROJECT: A FEELY FAMILY

● Cut out circular pieces of fabric (trace around a saucer). Choose velvet, satin, net, hessian or burlap, corduroy, and flannel to give a good range of textures

● Take the centre of each piece and gather enough to form a head. Stuff with wadding/batting and secure the "neck" with elasticized thread. Draw on features and sew on yarn hair

● Make a wall-hanging house out of firm fabric such as canvas

● Stitch on pockets as windows and doors

PROJECT: A MOBILE

● Cut out tissue-paper circles in contrasting colours and bind several together with coloured pipe-cleaners, to make flowers, butterflies, or angels

● Find three or four flexible twigs and hang one from each end, using coloured threads

● Suspend each twig above the other at the centre

● Hang the mobile above the baby's bed, or in front of an open window, or above a radiator where air movement will cause it to move gently and attract the baby's attention

▲ **Helping the child experience the world**
We need to be involved in the child's physical activity for him to extend himself fully and start finding out about the world. Throwing him up in the air and catching him again brings laughter too.

Play: the instrument of learning

The entire emphasis in a young child's play is first to experience the whole gamut of his senses and body movements, and then to make a joyful exploration of his imaginative and fantasy world. We need to be aware that, in all of this exploration and play, intellectual growth is being built up without any conscious effort on the child's part. Jean Piaget, the eminent Swiss psychologist (see pp. 17, 31, 295), has shown this connection between play and cognitive development in extensive experiments.

Logical thinking

It is true that later research, such as that of Margaret Donaldson, has shown that Piaget's methods do not do justice to the ability of quite young children to think with a devastating logic of their own. This further evidence gives extra proof of the link between children's play activities and the development of logical thinking. But Piaget's basic premise, that only after the stage of intuitive and symbolic thought is the child's mind ready to translate the concrete experience into the abstract, is still absolutely valid and very helpful to us as parents in understanding the importance of our child's play.

The child directs his own play

We now know that at birth the interconnections in the brain between the nerve cells are undeveloped and during the first two years the network of brain patterns will build up as a result of the sensory-motor activity in the physical world. How can parents help the process? As the child is engaged in "do-it-yourself" mode, he initiates and organizes his own play activities, but it is the role of parents to provide a rich environment of resources and not to inhibit natural learning.

"

On holiday at the seaside a father was constructing a sandcastle with his three small children. It was elaborate and perfect and the children were enlisted as carriers of water while he built it. But as the children were soon reproached for spilling the water and sloshing it either too fast, too slow or in the wrong place, their enthusiasm soon waned and they drifted away. The two-year-old began to torment his sleeping grandmother by trickling sand on to her face. He received a "good smack" and was carried off screaming by his exhausted mother. There was another family near by. Two children were happily digging troughs for themselves to lie in, while their parents relaxed in the sun. The children then had the idea of tracing around their outstretched bodies in the sand, negotiating as to who should have the first turn."

A parent

The network of interconnections between the nerve cells continues to be built up during the next five years as one of the major construction programmes of the brain. So the more extensive and complete the child's interaction with the outside world, the greater the development of knowledge within. This physiological explanation helps us to acknowledge the underlying impetus on the part of the child and we can better realize our parental role as a balance between caring bystanders, initiators of resources, and active participants.

▲ **Building a picture of the Self**
When he was asked to draw himself doing the "best thing he'd ever done", James drew himself swimming alone for the first time. As the child grows and experiences such "successes" he creates his self-confidence by constructing his own history and his place in the world.

Self-concept and self-confidence

The child's good self-concept is of paramount importance for his character formation and for creating the basis for good personal relationships. When the child is at ease with himself he can gradually feel kindness and compassion toward others. What can we parents do to promote our child's self-confidence? One answer is to generate a loving atmosphere, showing him that we have absolute faith in his ability. If a child gets the impression that we do not really trust him to regulate his own play, his confidence is bound to take a knock.

So many children become lacking in confidence when they go to school, where they begin to compare their own efforts with other children's. Indeed, far too many adults seem quite unsure of themselves. How many times do we hear older children and adults say, "I can't draw," or "I'm tone deaf"?

The symbolic stage, from about two-and-a-half to three years, is when the child begins to realize his identity and it is from then on that we can give him special help in developing a more positive self-image.

Encouragement and praise

We may already be confident of our role as non-directive parents, but knowing how much our child relies on our whole-hearted support, it is difficult to gauge how much appreciation we should show (see p. 86).

In general, giving encouragement is most in harmony with the non-directive approach, especially if we accompany it with genuine interest and a willingness to listen. Sometimes praise seems to sound judgemental and might well sap the child's initiative in favour of gaining our approval. The process of learning to value our own sense of satisfaction and pleasure in our achievements and not to rely solely on praise from others, is bound up with the development of a secure self-concept.

Early on, we can appreciate our child's efforts at motor-control with our expressions and actions. For example, we can encourage him to take wobbling steps as he aims for our outstretched arms. The imaginative, fantasy stage is more secret for the child and our praise may have little place. Even encouragement needs to be low-key (see also p. 219). But later on, praise is necessary for our child's well-accomplished skill. We can say, "Well done!" if he scores a goal, or "I really enjoyed that!" when he has played a piece of music well (see also p. 87) .

"
Your children are not your children.
They are the sons and daughters of life's longing for itself.
They come through you, but not from you,
And though they are with you, yet they belong not to you.
You may house their bodies, but not their souls,
For their souls dwell in the house of tomorrow
Which you cannot visit,
Not even in your dreams. ...
You may strive to be like them,
But seek not to make them like you."

Kahlil Gibran,
The Prophet

STRATEGY: AVOIDING PITFALLS

● Don't try to take over your child's life – his play

● Don't be tempted into trying to think up ideas for him

● Don't try to "entertain" him

● Don't feel that if he is left to his own devices he will be bored. The child knows what he wants and what is right for him"

Readiness

One of our important jobs as parents is to be aware of what developmental stage our child is at, and to know when he is ready to go on to the next stage (see also p. 128). Every child is unique and develops at his own pace; so it is not helpful to give a rigid guide to the ages for particular stages. Abilities and preferences in different activities also vary wildly from one child to another. We as parents need to think about readiness in terms of it being an extension of our child's previous encounters with the world about him. For example, he may want to know how to write his name because he has seen his older sister labelling her possessions.

Imitation

Imitation is a vital part of the way the child plays and learns (see also pp. 48, 225). So, if we as parents lead active lives and enjoy a range of hobbies and activities, then we can probably count on our child being our enthusiastic follower. If we involve him in household activities, he will want to join in. This can be a mixed blessing when a toddler wants to help mop the kitchen floor but is unable to do the job "properly". This tests our patience. But if we can take extra time to tune in to his level, we can let him do the job in his own way. Then we can both feel pleased: he has completed a "real" job and we have made him part of the real world.

"Pushing"

It is not good to "push" a child into something before he is ready for it. He cannot properly assimilate what is being thrust upon him, and the time spent on the activity keeps him from getting on with his own play, and satisfying his real developmental needs.

"
Whenever the child is given the notion that he needs to be entertained, learning comes almost to a halt."

Polly Berrien Berends,
Whole Child, Whole Parent

Stimulation

The stages of a child's development depend on interaction with his immediate world and the provision of an enriched environment becomes more and more necessary as he grows. Most babies and toddlers will exercise their motor-skills on their own, unless they are restricted in some way, and their sensory experiences will be enough to satisfy their insatiable curiosity. But even at this early stage a diversity of sensations and opportunities for bodily control can be enhancing and invigorating.

The child needs both physical and inner space in which to play. He must feel free to choose his

▲ Space to play
Children like to have their own safe play-space in the home area. They can then concentrate happily on their own activities in their own little patch.

own activity and have, if possible, a back-yard or garden where he can play in safety.

It is between the ages of two-and-a-half and five that parents should supply materials and resources to foster the child's creative and imaginative powers, to sharpen his senses, and to improve his self-controlled movements. Six- and seven-year-olds need more opportunities to explore and play games further afield, as well as support for their ideas and creativity.

"

An elderly relative told my new-born son to 'be a big boy' when he was crying. As he had a high birth weight he was also told that he was a 'big bruiser' by the midwife. In contrast I remember seeing a girl toddler being repeatedly encouraged to clap her hands to the question, 'Who's a pretty girl?'"

Aziz, a father

Gender roles

Many parents are no longer bound by old-fashioned traditions such as "pink for a girl and blue for a boy", but there are still many unconscious ways in which parents react differently toward boys and girls. For example, one recent report showed that people spent twice as much time listening to boys as to girls, and it has also been proved that mothers spend more time bouncing baby boys and more time talking to girls.

It is impossible to unravel the causes of the many differences between boys and girls, which emerge from the earliest days. Some are genetic, but cultural influences are extremely important. This suggests that the environment is a major influence in establishing gender attitudes. For example, adopted children sometimes come to resemble their adoptive parents more closely than their natural parents.

At around the age of two-and-a-half to three years, most children are well aware of what sex they are, and with the build-up of their sense of Self, they begin to have very definite ideas about themselves as boys or girls. They model themselves on people of the same gender and also on the images of that gender generated by the media. So if boys learn that maleness means being fearless, powerful, and aggressive or even violent, this is the path toward which they will gravitate. As parents we have a great influence in countering or reinforcing these concepts by our own behaviour, the toys we introduce (see p. 194), and the stories we tell (see p. 158).

The attitude to gender

Children today are aware of their gender differences at a younger age than ever before. This is partly due to the social differences which focus on sexual and gender issues. It is also true that

▲ The Self, with no gender
We must recognize that in both daughter and son there is an individual who has a part of her or him which has no gender. This is the Self, which cannot be cast in any role. Both sexes are likely to be role-cast, it is just that girls are more likely to be cast in the weaker, less assertive roles.

the attitude to gender is changing. In the past, and still today, parents tend to demand some-what different behaviour from girls than from boys. Expectations may also be different. Girls are generally still expected to become mothers and home-makers and boys to establish full-time careers. Such stereotyping is strongly challenged today, and in homes and playgroups we should avoid imposing role models and keep an open mind about the nature of the child's play. Of course, we can still observe certain characteristics belonging to the genders and it would be wrong to deny them. Different qualities characterize them. Boys may display greater interest in the mechanical and in feats of strength. Girls may be more drawn to living things or the feeling ele-ment in play. Boys may be more inclined to assert the logical, girls the intuitive.

"
One is not born a woman, but, rather, becomes one."

Simone de Beauvoir,
The Second Sex

The challenge of television

Bringing up children in the latter half of the twentieth century is a much greater challenge to parents than it has ever been before and one of the major causes is the ever-increasing lack of safe places to play. This, combined with the dominance of television in many homes, can result in children becoming less active and playful than former generations. As we well know as adults, television can be highly addictive: the more we watch, the less we feel inclined to make the effort to do anything else. And this same inertia affects children, but far more devastatingly.

How tempting it is for we busy parents to settle the child, from a very young age, in front of the television screen, so that we can get on with something else. And if there's nothing suitable on television, why not let him watch the video of *The Jungle Book* for the sixth, seventh, or eighth time? The child is safe, and we have secured some precious peace and quiet.

"
One of my children adores television. He will sit in front of anything at all and it really gets on my nerves. I've decided now to put the television away completely during the summer months and I get it out again for the winter. After a while the children hardly miss it – they spend far more time playing outside."

Dawn, a mother

"
I really couldn't cope without the video. My two toddlers are very demanding and noisy and the only time I can ever get any peace is when I stick them in front of their favourite cartoon. At least I know it's suitable, and they need the opportunity to calm down."

Jennifer, a mother

But watching a good programme together, as a family, can be a valuable experience, especially if we talk about what we have seen afterwards. We can keep an atlas and a dictionary near to the television set to look up new words and places. Television can be a precious tool for family entertainment and education, but it must be kept firmly in its place.

Ground rules and boundaries

We have to make firm decisions and draw up boundaries about television when the child is very young. One idea is to install the set away from the main family room, so that it does not dominate times when the family is together. The first-born child can be kept in blissful ignorance of the television's existence in the early years, but by the time siblings come along, the family must have established well-defined ground rules about what and when they watch.

It is a sad fact that there is very little of quality shown on television that can be enjoyed by the whole family watching together. However, the compulsion in the child to play creatively may be stronger than the compulsion to watch. This all depends on our ability to stimulate him by our own willingness to "play" and be creative in our own activities. Our example serves as a far more powerful model.

The intrusion of television into a child's life can seriously diminish his artistic and dramatic creative impulses. It is not just the time taken up by passive television viewing, but also the quality of the message. The grotesquely distorted faces of cartoon characters, the dubious role models of violent individuals, and all-powerful mechanical robots all have impact. As a born imitator the child mimics all he sees, so we should not be surprised when his "spontaneous" play is closely based on this kind of material.

► **TV choices**

We have to make decisions about the place of the television screen in our lives, because it affects the child dramatically. Here are some discussion points:

Don't have a TV/video/computer

PLUS

● The children are good at motivating themselves and playing imaginatively

● They seem "bright" and do well at school

● They read a lot and have many interests and hobbies

MINUS

● They complain bitterly that they are left out of conversations at school about TV programmes and computer games

● They are reluctant to invite friends home because "everyone" has computer games and they feel ashamed of not having them

Have a TV but limit watching

PLUS

● The child sometimes sees some quite good entertaining and informative programmes

MINUS

● The child is constantly watching unsuitable programmes and it's hard to monitor his viewing. When he can't watch he seems bored and lacking in motivation

● The child wants to watch more and more because he hears about programmes from his friends. It's difficult to mark boundaries

Have a TV but in a special room

PLUS

● We don't have to live with it all the time

MINUS

● The child sneaks off to watch it when he shouldn't

Have a TV in the child's room

PLUS

● It cuts down arguments about who watches what

MINUS

● The child could be watching unsuitable programmes when we think he's asleep

"
My eleven-year-old son was totally obsessed with computer games and with watching television. It was becoming harder and harder to get him to do anything else and I had to nag him all the time to do his homework. Finally, one day I cracked. I decided to get rid of the whole lot. My son missed it at first, but quickly adapted and his school work started to improve. Actually I'm really the one who misses it most now."

Jörg, a father

CHAPTER 10

Play and imagination

The imagination is what lets us try out and possibly fulfil anything we set out to do: imagining the finished task in our mind's eye helps us through each step toward achieving our goal (see also p. 47). If the imagination is well nurtured in its first dawning, it can be a sheet anchor throughout life. Imagination in play provides the basis for the child to grow up and eventually to live in the outside world.

The basis of identity

The flowering of the imagination and the rich world of fantasy is built on the earlier exuberance of body movement and the enjoyment of the ever-changing sensations that pour into the child's consciousness during the first two years of life. Around the child's third year comes the awakening of the Self and she begins to say "I"

(see also pp. 46–7, 219). She becomes increasingly conscious of her own identity. This revelation forms the basis of her imaginary and fantasy play. The child is now mediating her own experiences through role play and the growth in the richness of her language development. From as early as twenty months, her imagination can make a building block into a delicious cake and she starts acting out everyday events such as going to bed. Later, that same brick can become a ship or a horse; a rolled-up handkerchief can be a baby, and she herself can be a train.

Materials for the imagination
To give full scope to her imagination, the child needs only simple things to play with. She does not need toys that are too "perfect" and her creativity can even be hampered by this type of toy, because there is nothing for her imagination to

work on. However, she may push the boundaries of the "perfect" toy and use it for a different purpose to that for which it was designed (see pp. 56, 192). She will want to paint, sculpt, make music, and make models from clay and junk materials. And what she makes she will then use in her creative play. At the beach, large-scale tunnelling, channelling, and castle- and boat-building come into their own and she can "see" the boat she has made sailing down an imaginary river to the sea.

Creative spontaneity

Spontaneity is the keystone of all the young child's explorations and play throughout baby- and toddler-hood, as she reaches out for new horizons. Right up to the ages of six and seven the gift of spontaneous creation is still flourishing and, if it is well grounded, it should provide inspiration throughout adulthood. The child needs to be allowed the freedom to develop this free-flowing spontaneity without being trapped in the "prison house" of the adult world.

PROJECT: A TEN-MINUTE DOLL

● Take a large, square cloth, such as a piece of old sheet. Crease a line along the centre. Roll both sides in to this central creased line

● Tuck a crumpled scrap of cloth inside, about half-way along, fold back, and tie with a loop of elasticized thread to make the head

● Pull out both sides to make arms and tuck flap underneath

● Tie elasticized thread around waist and wrists. Decorate and make clothes out of scraps of patterned fabric or leave plain so that the child can invent her own doll (see also p. 186)

Our role in the child's art

It is important not to impose our adult values on the child's creativity, but how tempting it is to give a hand to a struggling artist or sculptor! Perhaps the child is trying to draw a rabbit and we "help" by sketching in the outline of the body, or she is making a clay sheep which refuses to stand up, so we mould extra-thick legs. This kind of action lets the child feel that her version is inferior to ours and she is undermined. This does not mean that we cannot show the child a variety of processes to choose from. But she must feel free to develop them by herself.

Readiness for art

We can provide stimulating materials, but we must ask ourselves first whether she is ready for them. How do we assess this? For example, should we go out and buy large sheets of coloured paper, paints, or modelling clay? Even a baby will pick up a pencil and scribble on a scrap of paper and expensive materials are wasted on her, so we should go slowly and not allow our enthusiasm to overtake us. It is best to offer one thing at a time and then use our own judgement to decide when she is ready to move on to the next thing (see also p. 128). The child is drawn irresistibly toward anything that she can manipulate. Water, sand, and clay have great possibilities.

"
Very young children are moved to play, experiment with and rearrange the materials of their world. This stage is of the greatest importance, as they are building up understanding of the way in which materials and media behave."

Margaret Morgan (ed), *Art 4–11*

"
Four-year-old Sally was making a clay elephant and she used a carrot as a trunk. I explained that the carrot would be burnt in the kiln, or rot first. Sally acquiesced reluctantly and looked very disappointed. Too late I realized what I had done. Sally was not interested in the finished product so much as the immediate effect, which she had achieved to her immense satisfaction. I had begun to learn the hard way to resist my urges to 'help' and to realize that Sally could find her own rewards for her accomplishments without interference."

June, a mother

ACTIVITY: WATER PLAY

● At home, the child will value playing in the kitchen sink, in a paddling or wading pool, or water-trough with a range of kitchen utensils such as sieves, colanders, and graded measuring jugs. A six- to seven-year-old will experiment with making, floating, and sinking, boats

● When you are out, let your child safely explore puddles, ponds, streams, waterfalls, and the sea

● Bathtime is one of the highlights of the daily rhythm (see also p. 241); the child is back in her pre-natal security of being. She can splash, float, and kick exuberantly; later we can introduce boats, sponges, and squeezy bottles, one at a time, to add to the richness of the experience

▲ **Mud play**

Mud and earth are the young child's first modelling clay. They can be poked, squeezed, squelched, and moulded as his imagination dictates.

Clay and dough

Playing with clay or dough follows naturally from playing with water and sand. Play dough is for the child to handle before she is ready to use real clay. She can squash it, roll it, and pinch it (see right). Modelling comes later.

There is nothing quite like clay; it has a feel and attraction that is unique. Toddlers can pat and prick it, make pretend pastry, and roll it into snakes. From about three years on, the child can press the clay into shapes and make small, simple pots. Six- and seven-year-olds enjoy making coil pots (see below).

Using both hands, the child will push, pull, squeeze, break pieces off, join, knead – before trying to make an object. Then she can start using tools, such as old blunt knives, spoons, and rolling pins.

PROJECT: PLAY DOUGH

● Mix 2 teaspoons of cream of tartar, 1 cup of plain flour, ½ cup of salt, 1 tablespoon of oil, and 1 cup of water to form a smooth paste. Cook slowly in a saucepan, stirring until the dough forms a ball

● Knead for a few minutes, after it has cooled down. Store in the fridge in an airtight container

● Colour the dough by mixing food colouring with the water before adding to the flour and salt. Or knead it into the dough

PROJECT: A COIL POT

Clays are available which don't need firing and which harden naturally.

● Roll out the base with a rolling pin and cut out a circular shape by tracing around a small saucer

● Roll out "sausages" by hand

● Lay the "sausage" on the base and press it down gently. Work round, gently pressing each layer of "sausage" into the coil beneath as you go. Think about the shape of pot you are making

● Blend the coils together to strengthen and create a smooth exterior. Decorate the pot by scoring and making indentations, and paint it when it has dried or been fired

***PROJECT:* BEADS**

● Roll out a long "sausage"

● Using an old, blunt knife, cut the "sausage" into an assortment of small bead shapes

● Using an old knitting needle, pierce a hole through each bead for threading

● Score a pattern on to each bead and leave to dry, or fire in the oven

● Paint the dried beads with brightly coloured paints

● Thread on to coloured string to make necklaces, bracelets, earrings, and belts

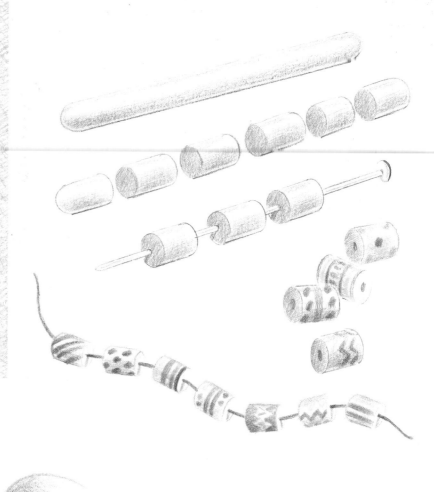

***PROJECT:* MOULDING CLAY ANIMALS**

● Mould the basic body shape from a small ball of clay, shaping the "snout" at one end

● Roll little balls of clay and stick them on to make feet, nose, and ears

● To make a hedgehog or por-cupine, stick in toothpicks. To make a cat, add a small sausage for a tail, add ears, whiskers and mark eyes and mouth, and to make a snail, mould a long shape and add a small coil for the shell

▼ Leaf prints
Collect interesting leaves and make
prints of them. Either paint them first
and press them on to paper, or lay them
on it first and spatter the whole
area with paint.

▲ String printing
Dip string into thick paint and drop it
to one side of a folded sheet of paper.
Press the sides together firmly. Open and
remove the string.

▼ Hand prints
Put thick paint into a paint tray. Cover
the hand with paint and press down on to
a sheet of paper.

▼ Painting and printing on to fabric
Paint directly on to cotton fabric with fabric
paints. To make the dolls and cushions, cut
out a back and a front,
stitch right sides
together, and stuff.

▲ Wax resist
Draw an invisible picture in wax on
white paper. Cover the whole area with
thin paint and the picture will appear.

Paint and print

Here are some easy ideas for painting and printing. Cover the floor, provide unspillable pots of ready-mixed paints, sheets of paper, an apron – and stand back!

▲ Blob and fold

Fold a piece of paper in half, open it and drop blobs of paint down the fold. Press the halves together then open again. Cut the shapes out to make butterflies.

▼ Blow-painting

Drop blobs of runny paint on to paper and, using a straw, blow the paint into different shapes.

▲ Vegetable prints

Cut hard vegetables such as carrots lengthways or slice them, dip them in paint, and print repeat and overlapping designs. To make potato prints, cut the potato in half and carve a raised shape on to the surface. Make patterns on paper and fabric using different colours.

▼ Wet painting

Brush a piece of paper lightly with water, then paint using a very wet brush. Allow the colours to run into each other and blend.

Junk modelling – dolls' house

In the average household it does not take long to collect a large quantity of used cereal boxes, empty plastic containers, wrappers, boxes, plastic bottles and tubes, fabric and yarn scraps, and these are perfect materials for making a dolls' house, plus all the items of furniture to put in it.

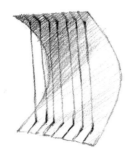

PROJECT: DOLLS' HOUSE FURNITURE

● To make chairs, find some big conkers (horse chestnuts) or halved corks, bead-headed pins, and scraps of brightly coloured yarn. Use four pins for legs and two to construct the chairback – bind them with coloured yarns

● To make tables, stick a plastic lid to a thread spool and cover with brightly coloured sticky-backed plastic

● To make chests of drawers, stick small matchboxes together, and glue on buttons or beads for "handles"

PROJECT: WEAVING

Using yarn scraps and a piece of cardboard from an old cereal box, weave a small piece that could be used as a dolls' house carpet (see facing page) or as part of a larger wall hanging.

● Cut a piece of cardboard about 8x6in (18x15cm). Cut ½ in (1.25cm) slots along each short side

● Bend the cardboard into a bow-shape and bind yarn into the slots using a continuous length. Tie the ends of the yarn at the back

● Using your fingers, weave coloured yarn and fabric scraps in and out of the strands of yarn

● Cut the threads at the back and tie off the ends securely

PROJECT: EASY DOLLS' HOUSE

● Cut the tops from four equal-sized boxes and glue or tape them together to form four rooms. Paint the outside with emulsion paint

● Paper the walls using scraps of wrapping paper, wallpaper, or fabric, or sponge-paint them

● Cut flaps in the sides for doors and window-shutters

● Make curtains from fabric scraps, thread on to elasticized thread and staple in place

● Make beds and chests of drawers from matchboxes

● Make tables from thread spools and plastic lids, and chairs from conkers (horse chestnuts), halved corks, or cardboard tubes and egg cartons

● Use postage stamps as pictures for the walls and cut pictures from magazines of fireplaces and cupboards

● Make carpets out of fabric scraps, or weave your own

Bed

Lampshades

Stove

Chairs   *Table*   *Chest of drawers*   *Woven rug*   *Settee*

Home-made toys

Home-made toys, whether made by the child on her own, by an adult, or by the child and adult together, are a vital ingredient of creative play in childhood. A toy that is a product of the child's imagination, which is made using her own skills, and which is then used as part of her own imaginative play is rich with meaning for her.

Every home generates a vast range of recyclable materials that can be saved and used by the child to make things. Cardboard and plastic packaging, wood, yarn, and fabric scraps, pieces of paper – all have their uses. These pages show a range of toys and objets d'art. Some can be combined with "bought" toys to increase their scope and "play value".

▼ **The world of home-made toys**
1. **Boat** *from plastic margarine tub and cardboard.* 2. **House** *from cardboard and wood (see also p. 303).* 3. **Cars, trucks, and trailers** *from matchboxes, clay, and balsa wood, used with "bought" wooden train track.* 4. **Weaving projects** – *Nature weaving on a twig loom, cards woven on net bags.* 5. **Dolls' school** *with toothpaste-tube box desk (with lift-up top), egg-carton bench.*
6. **"Creations"** *from wood, painted.*
7. **Dog** *from painted boxes, egg cartons, toilet rolls.* 8. **Dinosaur** *from Easter egg carton with ribbon to open and close mouth.* 9. **Plane** *from wood and nails.* 10. **Boats** *from balsa wood, cartons, and paper.*

Dramatic play

Drama is interwoven with symbolic and fantasy play, from which it springs. The child puts herself into someone else's shoes. At first she takes her inspiration from the world she knows; she plays schools, hospitals, or houses. She may favour authority figures such as firefighters or soldiers, or glamour figures such as Robin Hood or Cinderella. Later, at five or six, drama is more structured, and includes complicated plots, adventure, and mystery; her sources of inspiration are the stories she hears and reads.

The dressing-up box is the parents' contribution to this flow of energy. Discarded clothes, especially old, glittery evening dresses, old hats and shoes, and the odd prop, such as a walking stick, are a start, but many "outfits" are easy to make from cereal boxes and unwanted household objects. The overall effect is everything and intricate detail is relatively unimportant.

***PROJECT:* THE ALL-PURPOSE HAT**

This is a basic hat rim, which you can transform into any kind of hat you like.

● Cut a circle from card or an old cereal box by drawing around a large plate

● Cut out a circle in the centre approximately the width of the widest part of the child's head. Alternatively, pierce the centre of the circle and cut "spokes" radiating outward

● Decorate by adding ribbons and tissue-paper flowers, or add a crown to create a stove-pipe hat, or a tall cone for a witch's hat by taping to the rim on the inside

***PROJECT:* THE ALL-PURPOSE MASK**

This is a basic half-mask shape which you can adapt to make any character you choose.

● Cut a basic eye-mask from cardboard (an old cereal box)

● Paint and decorate to suggest the character you are creating. Stick on fabric scraps, sequins, braid, and whatever else you can find to enhance the effect. Staple on protruding pieces such as feathers and whiskers to the "cheek" areas

● Secure with a piece of elastic around the back of the head

▲ **The world of make-believe**
Everyday household objects, such as saucepans, plates, and spoons, are important props in the child's imaginative and dramatic play.

Masks and hats

A hat is a key prop for dressing up and make-believe games. It transforms the wearer in a subtle way. She can "become" her new persona instantly. The addition of a mask can conceal and add a dimension of mystery.

▶ **How the hats and masks were made**

From left to right: a conical cardboard hat taped together with a mouth mask cut from a magazine; a circular hat with slits for the head (see p. 154), hung with corks and sponges; a wide conical hat decorated with tissue-paper flowers; (in front) decorated eye mask; sprayed cardboard centurion helmet stapled together; decorated cardboard pirate hat with an eye mask made from foil dishes and cellophane.

Storytelling

We may have made great efforts not to interfere with our child's creative play, but storytelling needs our active, considered input (see p. 57). Stories can provide rich material for her make-believe and her play-acting. A regular bedtime story provides the opportunity for closeness and intimacy and the security at the end of her day that comes from hearing a rhythm, rhyme, or plot which never changes. It is important for us, as storytellers, particularly if we have invented a story, not to alter the words from day to day. Repeating the correct wording time after time gives the young child the assurance that all is "right" in her world.

In his book, *Steiner Education in Theory and Practice,* Gilbert Childs states, "Steiner insisted that teachers tell stories to the children, and not read them. They should go to the trouble of mastering the details of whatever fairy stories, folk-tales, legends or fables and making them their own, immersing themselves in the pictorial element always present in such narrative material". We may only be able to manage the most well-known stories off the tops our heads, so it is worth reading up on a few forgotten ones to add to the repertoire (see p. 343). *Old Peter's Russian Tales* by Arthur Ransome is an excellent source.

Inventing stories

At first, many of us will feel less than confident about telling a story rather than reading it, but the child's rapt attention to our every word can give us great encouragement and we may find that we are better at it than we thought. Toddlers enjoy a disguised account of what they have done during the day. We can stop from time to time to ask questions such as, "And what do you think happened next?".

ACTIVITY: **FEELY-BAG STORIES**

If you want to tell spontaneous stories, but are stuck for ideas, try using a "feely-bag".

● Make a drawstring bag out of a fabric remnant and keep in it a collection of "mystery objects" such as small wooden ornaments, marbles, toys, conkers (horse chestnuts), dolls, and pine cones

● At story time, give your child the bag and let her feel the objects without opening it. Then let her put her hand into the bag and, without looking, take out one object

● Let her hold the object and look at it while you start to make up a story. Stop from time to time to let her make her own suggestions

▲ Telling, listening, imagining
The gentle rhythms of the voice, clearly articulating the words, help the child picture the story in his imagination. Physical closeness offers reassurance.

The world of books

A baby explores books with her senses. She will bite, taste, twist, and tear, given the chance. But it is not a waste of time giving her books to handle, and eventually to look at under supervision, though it is wise to provide her with tough board or cloth books. Soon she will start to look at the pictures and realize that she cannot pick the objects out of the pages. The toddler loves to sit on her parent's lap and look at the pictures in a book while the words are read to her. She will soon want her favourite stories read to her time and time again (with no changes to the wording). She will take a dim view if we skip pages. When she has absorbed all she can from one story, she will want to discover and explore new ones, and will usually prefer those that are firmly connected with her everyday life.

Which stories for which age groups?

The three- to four-year-old enjoys more adventurous stories, still based on her own life, but with a more imaginative turn. She begins to relate to the simplest fairy story such as Tom Thumb, and from the age of five she will like Hansel and Gretel, Rumpelstiltskin, Jack and the Beanstalk, and The Sleeping Beauty. In these stories a variety of life situations are described, with conflict between good and evil, and good triumphing in the end. There are strong feelings of love, jealousy, and hatred portrayed in an adventurous way so that the child can relate to these emotions indirectly, but deeply. By the age of six or seven, the child may be interested in myths, legends, and fables, such as the tales of King Arthur and Greek myths and legends. These stories penetrate the depths of the human psyche and this is conveyed to the child in a symbolic form which she understands.

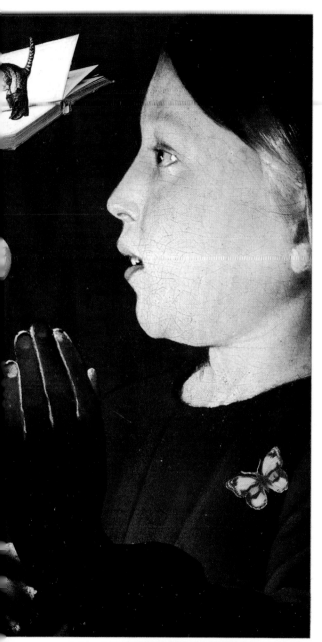

▲ The gift of a book

A volume that is well-produced, well-written, with good-quality pictures, will be treasured for life. The child will own a particular "window on the world" which will have a lasting effect.

Subtle influences in stories

Young children take in their experiences uncritically, including what they hear in stories and read in books. Most of the hidden messages in these stories are positive, showing that the deeds of good people can triumph over the wicked. However, more subtle influences can be repeated and reinforced over and over again until they become fixed as unalterable truths in the child's mind. Until recently it was difficult to find books in which black children were the main protagonists. Sometimes, their only roles were as the "clowns" of the story. But with growing awareness, this stereotyping is gradually diminishing.

Stereotyping

Gender stereotyping (see also pp. 138-9), where boys are already on their way to becoming "macho" and aggressive, and girls "feminine" and passive, abounds in children's literature, although contemporary children's fiction is far more anti-sexist. But a book which consciously attempts to give a less-than-traditional image of what women and men do may seem contrived. However, it is vital to seek out these titles as we realize that boys are gentle and caring and that girls have initiative and courage.

People first and foremost

We have it in our power to start our child on a path that is far less "gender-fixed" than in previous generations, remembering that all children have a part of them that is neither male nor female (see also p. 139). They are just themselves, and they are people first and foremost. We may have the experience, when thinking about a son or daughter, of receiving a picture of them that is neither male nor female. Then we are truly focused on the individuality and personality of the child: her Self.

Singing

The baby's first attempts at song come from trying to imitate the sounds from the parents' songs. So it is vital for us to sing! The radio or the tape-recorder is just not the same. Traditional well known nursery rhymes are a good starting point, and babies love songs such as *Rock-a-bye Baby*, which have a surprise element at the end. Babies from only a few months of age love being bounced on the parent's knee in accompaniment to these songs. Rhythmic games which involve actions, such as *Pat-a-cake,* will soon inspire the baby to try to clap in imitation.

The symbolic stage is a time that is full of song and movement. Three- and four-year-olds sing dolls and soft toys to sleep, and singing games, such as *Nuts in May*, have long been popular for groups of children.

Ride a Cock-horse
Ride a Cock-horse
To Banbury Cross
To see a fine lady
Ride on a white horse.

Rings on her fingers
And bells on her toes
She shall have music
Wherever she goes.

Actions
Bounce the baby on your knee and point to her fingers and toes as you sing.

Jack and Jill
Jack and Jill
Went up the hill
To fetch a pail of water;
Jack fell down
And broke his crown,
And Jill came tumbling after.

Up Jack got
And home did trot
As fast as he could caper.
He went to bed
To mend his head
With vinegar and brown paper.

Actions
With two children on your lap, gently let them tumble to the ground in turn.

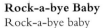

Rock-a-bye Baby
Rock-a-bye baby
On the tree top
When the wind blows
The cradle will rock

When the bough breaks
The cradle will fall
Down will come baby
Cradle and all.

Actions
*Hold the baby on your knee and sway
backward and forward. When the cradle
falls, let the baby gradually slide between
your knees.*

Pussycat, Pussycat
"Pussycat, pussycat, where have you been?"
"I've been up to London, to visit the Queen."
"Pussycat, pussycat, what did you there?"
"I frightened a little mouse under her chair."

Actions
*Sit opposite the child and take turns to be the pussy-
cat. Act out frightening the mouse under the chair.*

Music-making

If music is already an important, celebrated part of the home, then the child will want to make her own. The baby will shake a rattle and, later, use a wooden spoon to drum on an upturned saucepan. An older child will enjoy filling jars to different heights with water to make a "xylophone", or filling plastic containers with dried beans or sand to make shakers.

PROJECT: BELLS

Make several bells from different-sized flower pots and suspend them from a broom handle. Use wooden beads as the clappers and/or strike with a beater.

● Thread one bead on to a piece of string and make a knot

● Make another knot to hold the second bead about 1in (2.5cm) shorter than the height of the pot

● Thread the string through the flower pot hole and make a loop

● Hang all the pots on a string or broom handle and suspend between two firm objects such as upturned buckets. Strike with a beater made from a piece of garden dowelling bound with large elastic bands

PROJECT: MUSICAL INSTRUMENTS

● Stretch elastic bands around a shoe box. Use bands in a variety of thicknesses, and make sure that they do not touch each other. Pluck the bands. Thin ones will produce high notes, thick ones, low notes

● Save an old coffee tin and two plastic lids. Remove the bottom from the tin. Pierce a hole in each lid and put one on each end of the tin. Thread a string through the "drum" and tie to form a neck-loop

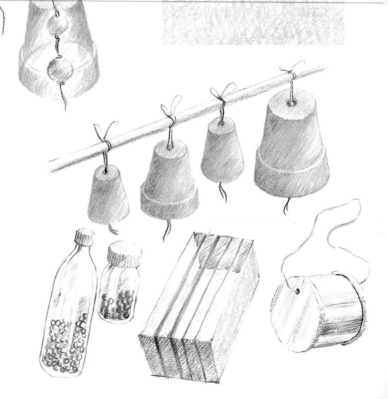

Dance and movement

Babies love to "go dancing" in their parent's arms and as soon as they can toddle they "dance" whenever they hear music. Rudolf Steiner developed the art of movement, called Eurythmy. He found that every sound can be portrayed by a movement of the body. It is a perfect way of introducing children to movement and letting them respond naturally and freely to what they hear, in a physical way. Steiner's idea is that movement springs from a response to the sound itself, whether it is played or sung, and not as a response to interpreting what the sound is trying to convey. So Eurythmy can connect sound and colour, for example.

▼ Dark colours
The child can interpret his feeling of "dark" colours, such as blue and purple, which he pictures in the music, by moving his arms downward, with his hands rounded inward.

▼ Light colours
If the child feels the colours of light and energy, such as red, yellow, and orange in the music, then he can express them by stretching his arms and hands upward.

Spirituality and creative energy

The creativity of the child is the inner driving force for spiritual realization: a seeking for wholeness. Wordsworth describes young children as "trailing clouds of glory" as they come into the world and there is something quite ethereal in their sense of wonder at the world around them. Our hope as parents is to help the child preserve that inner spirit of creation which is manifested in all of her imaginative spontaneity. The child is closer to the spiritual than the adult tends to be. The spiritual is an integral part of her life and she may seem quite matter-of-fact about it. In families who practise a religion, prayers, or a time for quiet thoughts together at night can be a reassuring ritual. All families, whatever their personal beliefs, can share some thoughts for others and some thanksgiving at the end of the day. A child can derive much comfort and security from her intuitive sense of a strong spiritual force in her Self.

Working together in fun
The inner spirit of childhood can be nourished in an atmosphere of love and security, which is the most important single factor in being able to grow up as a complete human being. The parent and the child can participate together in spiritual awareness through such practices as relaxation, guided fantasy, meditation, and yoga, and some exercises to try are introduced on the following pages. Provided that these are always considered by both to be fun and an extension of play, they can enhance the child's feelings of peace of mind and a deep sense of communion between them. As adults we have to be careful that we do not force our ideas about spirituality on to our child – she already has her own, which we must recognize and nurture.

John, my five-year-old, told me that he was talking to God in his tummy when I came into his room in the morning."

A mother

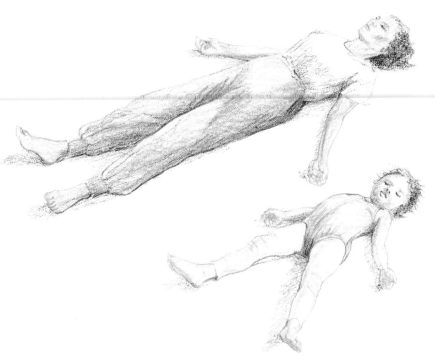

Relaxation and guided imagery

We can try some exercises to relax ourselves, and our child may naturally imitate us and want to join in. So the exercises on this page are for adults, and for the child to do in imitation. It is important not to instruct or "teach" the child, but to do them together, in a spirit of fun.

The purpose of introducing a child to guided imagery is to take her "out of herself" for a few moments. It should be done in a relaxed and informal way – as an extension of play – and should not suggest that there are "right" and "wrong" methods. If the child can imagine her own "special place" this can become a place of solace and comfort for her to return to whenever she wants. Guided imagery can open the doors of the imagination and release creative energies. From age three onward, the child can be more attentive and enhance her learning ability, since she can focus on her inner strength.

Relaxing together
Try some of the ideas on pages 166–9 together, in the spirit of fun. Start by lying on your back on the floor, arms slightly out, and palms facing upward.

EXERCISE: SIMPLE GUIDED
IMAGERY

Don't make suggestions: the child should invent her own ideas.

● Lie down on the floor, side by side

● Think of your own special place (a beautiful garden, a secret cave, a sandy shore)

● Walk around and explore

● Find something special

● Come back to the present

Meditation and yoga

The benefits of meditation and yoga are well known for adults and it is now being realized that quite young children can participate and share the experience of peace and inner rest. They can gain in concentration and therefore learn more easily. However, the exercises should not be presented to the child as anything more than fun activities to try – there should be no success rate or pressure for her to "achieve" or "experience" anything.

EXERCISE: SIMPLE MEDITATION

Talk the child through the meditation while doing it yourself.

● First, dance or sing energetically to release excess energy, then do a simple relaxation exercise (see p. 167)

● Sit cross-legged and with eyes closed. Imagine you are in a peaceful place

● Make up a word and repeat it silently. Breathe deeply and rhythmically

● If thoughts pop up, just return to your special word and carry on repeating it

● After a few minutes, come back to the present moment

▲ **Frog squat and frog sit**
Crouch down and lean forward with hands on the floor between the knees (above). Sit upright, open the knees, and straighten the back (above right).

▶ **Ostrich**
Put your head and hands on the floor and straighten your legs.

▲ **Bear sit and bear stretch**
Sit down and open your legs in front of you as wide as they will go. Lean forward and put your head on the ground between your knees.

Beginning yoga

Young children can benefit from one of the most effective forms of exercise, yoga. It is believed that the exercises affect the internal organs of the body, especially the endocrine glands, and this is important, as over- or under-secretion of these glands is believed to cause mental disturbances and negative emotions, threatening peace of mind. The exercises are non-competitive and help the child to channel restless energy and become calmer and better able to concentrate. However, yoga must be presented as fun – a game – and not as a strict regime. One way to approach it is for the child to imitate animal poses and to make up a story as she goes along.

▶ Stork stand
Standing up, lift one foot and try to stand on one leg.

▲ Snake stretch and snake curl
Lie on your front, putting your hands on the floor in front of you (above). Lift your head, chest, and shoulders high in the air. Take some deep breaths. Lift your feet (right) and try to scratch the back of your head with your toes.

▲ Lion pose
Sit on your heels, palms on knees. Breathe in through your nose, lean forward, breathe out through your mouth, making an "Aaaah" sound. At the same time, stretch your tongue and fingers and look up. Hold, then close your mouth and breathe in through your nose.

CHAPTER 11

Play and learning

From his very earliest days, the young child tries to make sense of the real world. Whether this process is explorative and imitative, or based on fantasy and the imagination, it is all "learning". Whatever the kind of play the child is engaged in, he learns best and most easily through his active participation: he must do it himself and it is his "work" (see p. 133).

Fantasy and imagination

Today it is thought by some that play which develops the cognitive skills is more "productive" in terms of learning. There is but a thin line between this kind of play and imaginative or fantasy play and there is growing acceptance that using the imagination freely in play brings greater benefits, such as better concentration, improved language development, and most important of all, an inspired and enlightened approach to problem solving.

It is vital that we acknowledge and encourage the precious gift of fantasy and imagination in our child (see Chapter 10). This is his natural heritage and we now know that if he is deprived of it he may be not only emotionally hurt but his learning ability can be permanently damaged. We should be aware that schooling, which comes later, may be overly concerned with cramming "facts", and information masquerading as knowledge, into the child's head, without any "thinking" taking place (see Chapter 21). If he is forced too early into intellectual and abstract thinking rather than being allowed to let his powers of fantasy and imagination flourish and to get on with his own "work", he may be turned off at the prospect of formal school learning. He may, literally, be disenchanted.

Outside pressures

Most parents have a far clearer picture of their child's needs than anyone else, but we are constantly bombarded with messages and pressures on how to hasten his progress. It sometimes feels, both to us and to him, as if he is involved in a race and it is hard for us to know what is best for him (see p. 74). We should be careful not to fall into the trap of feeling that he should learn as early and as rapidly as possible. For what is the rush in the long term?

This chapter attempts to offer some guidance on how we can work alongside our child, as well as allowing him unquestioned freedom to get on by himself with his "workplay".

Understanding the world through play

During the first two years it may not be obvious to us that our child is building up his intellectual powers in his insatiable zest for play. But it is happening below his awareness, as unconsciously as the growth of the hairs on his head. This should bring a message of great reassurance to us parents. Our child is doing the right thing, and we must trust him. Our best efforts should be to understand that his imaginative world is also his real world and that we should nurture it. We may be tempted to tell our three-year-old that the sun doesn't come out specially to wake us in the morning. But this rational approach might dampen his incessant flow of ideas, which can have the richness of poetry and the flair of inspiration (see also pp. 38, 247).

Later, when he is four or five, we can introduce humorous games which "have a laugh" at the natural world (see above right) and heal any tension in our relationship (see also p. 118). Games that introduce the concept of time, space, and number such as *Hopscotch* and *Grandmother's Footsteps* can promote a solid basis for learning.

Activity: "Giraffes fly!"

● The children form a circle, and one is chosen to stand in the centre

● The other children take it in turns to call out the names of animals

● The child in the centre flaps his arms when the name of a creature that flies is called out, but not if, for example, "giraffe" is called out

▼ **Giraffes fly!**
Children's artwork of giraffes "flying" and other fantastical animals. Such ideas appeal to the child's imagination and sense of humour.

Learning from the senses

From birth, the child explores his physical world through his senses (see also pp. 128–31). He "tastes" things that are far from edible, such as mud. He smells and feels, he listens to every sound and looks at everyone and everything with an intent gaze (see also pp. 34–5).

The home itself is a haven for exploring with the senses. Cooking smells come from the kitchen, food is tasted, footsteps come and go, there is music and singing, the door bell rings, people greet each other and talk.

During the first two years parents play a background role. We supply the loving ambience, the food for the senses, and we talk reassuringly to our child when he needs us to. The next stage can demand our initiative and we can devise games and activities to highlight the experience of the senses.

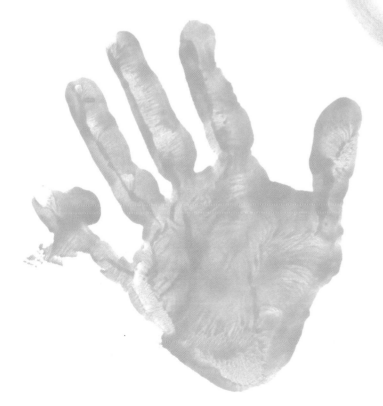

ACTIVITY: "KIM'S GAME" VARIATIONS

● Let the child examine a tray full of different small objects. Remove one object. What is missing?

● Add some different objects and remove others. What is missing? What has been added?

● Sit facing each other and look carefully at each other's appearance. Then, without looking, take it in turns to change a small detail and see if the other can guess what it is

"

When a child was shown a special object but was not allowed to touch it she cried out, 'Let me see it with my hands!'. Feeling is as important as seeing".

A parent

ACTIVITY: SENSE GAMES
The child is blindfolded.

● "What are these sounds?" Ring a bicycle bell, munch an apple, pour water from a jug, turn the pages of a book, rustle cooking foil or silver paper

● "What are these tastes?" Let him guess the tastes of apple juice, cocoa, honey, peanut butter, a piece of orange

● "What are these smells?" Let him smell a rose, a piece of chocolate, some soap, a clove of garlic, a sprig of mint

▶ **Exploring slime**
This wonderful sensory experience lets the child enjoy the feel of something that is runny but has body to it; not quite clay and not quite paint.

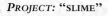

PROJECT: "SLIME"

● Mix 2 cups of water and a little food colouring with 6 cups of cornflour/cornstarch to create a nice, thick "slime"

● If possible, arrange this activity outdoors on a plastic-covered surface. Dress the child in a plastic apron, roll his sleeves up and let him plunge his arms into the slime and enjoy letting it run through his fingers and making patterns with it

Imitation: learning by example

The young child learns through imitation, instinctively and without any conscious effort (see also p. 48). His first models are his parents, so the patterns that we lay down at this stage are the ones that he absorbs most deeply.

The right tools for the job

At the toddler stage, the child can start to mirror our activities (see also p. 136). If we cook, type, or dig the garden he wants to do exactly the same too, for real, and not "pretend", even though we see him incorporating what he has learned into his private, imaginative play. He must use proper tools for the job, even if they are scaled down, and not toy plastic ones. He can then feel that he is carrying out a real task which matters and counts for something. There are many "real" activities we can set up such as cutting slices of bread for sandwiches or using a real mop to wash the floor. If we cannot tolerate his "help" at this early stage, then we forfeit our chances of bringing him up to share the daily tasks of the household later on.

Warning: parents should teach children to use dangerous tools safely and should stay nearby when they are in use.

"
*As every mother knows, he will stop
playing with the most elaborate toy to
ask, 'What you doing?' and will follow
that up promptly with, 'I want to do it
too'. And while sometimes this expresses
a desire for companionship, it also reveals
the child's desire to 'be in on things'. So
he wants to learn to cut with scissors, roll
out pastry, vacuum the floor, wash the
cabbage, strike matches – in short to enter
actively into the life about him."*

Phyllis Hostler,
The Child's World

"
*Children, seeing others pitching a tent, or
constructing a house in a neighbouring
garden, will quickly start making a house
or tent themselves."*

Susanna Millar,
The Psychology of Play

▲ Real tools: real creativity
If the child can use real tools from an early age he knows that his play is really his work and that he is taken seriously. True creativity comes from this feeling.

fiona

Hannah

Markus

James

Letters through play

The motivation of the child to write is all-important, based on gradual preparation through experience with words, whether heard or seen. Vygotsky (see pp. 18–19) maintained that the origins of writing lie in the child's imaginative and symbolic play, which helps him to replace an object with a symbol. This creates an early disposition toward actual writing, although it might take time to manifest itself.

Writing for a reason

A wide range of experiences help to facilitate this predisposition. Children today are surrounded by the written word: on shop fronts, advertising hoardings, on the sides of lorries. Most children will begin to reproduce these letter shapes in their own writing. When we write a shopping list, he can do the same and we can ask him to read it to us when he is finished. He may start to write by wanting to write his own name, or his initials. This is a mark of his individuality and he can use it for a purpose: to show that something belongs to him, whether it is a pencil case or a lunch box. His signature on a holiday postcard to a grandparent can be a source of great pride. This is writing for a reason and out of good motivation: his desire to communicate.

In Steiner schools, children are not rushed into writing. Much preparation takes place first. Some teachers use the method of choosing familiar words and taking the first letter, "f" in fish, for example, and weaving an imaginary story around it and using the letter in a pictorial way. A number of "f's" drawn on a page could represent a shoal of fish. An "m" could be drawn to represent a mountain. This approach gives meaning to the letter being learned by letting the child's imagination work on it.

ACTIVITY: **LETTER GAMES**

● As a group, combine bodies to form letters and words

● Put the letters of the alphabet (on cards) into a bag, take it in turns to pull one out and mime the letter for others to guess

● Take it in turns to "write" letters in the air for the others to guess

● "Draw" letters on the floor with the feet or toes. Or write large letters in sand

▲ **First "writing"**

The child will begin to reproduce letter shapes he has seen in his own "writing", without prompting or help from adults.

le serpent

Schlange

Snake

◄ **S is for snake**

Snakes hold a particular fascination for many children, so the snake-like letter S allows the child to make a strong connection between the word and the letter in his imagination.

Counting and numbers

In Steiner education the importance of numbers and counting is the rhythm that they bring to life (see p. 59) and the child is taught to grasp this concept first of all. There are many ways we can engage the child in learning about numbers: we can count heaps of nuts or apples; we can share things out, and the child becomes involved in the reality of what numbers mean in real life. At the beginning of the symbolic stage (around the age of three) the child can think of numbers pictorially. For example, three knives, forks, and spoons to lay the table. He must spend as much time as he wants in this stage before he has to start thinking about numbers in an abstract way.

"

Now we explain to the child: I have a heap of beans – and I have three children of different ages who eat different amounts… The heap represents the sum and the children can see it is the same as the three parts. In this way, we get the child to enter life with the ability to grasp the whole and not always proceed from the less to the greater."

Rudolf Steiner,
in M. C. Allen,
Teaching Children to Write

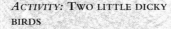

ACTIVITY: ONE TWO, BUCKLE MY SHOE

Mime the actions with the child as you chant the rhyme.

One two, buckle my shoe
Three four, knock at the door
Five six, pick up sticks
Seven eight, lay them straight
Nine ten, a big fat hen
Eleven twelve, dig and delve
Thirteen fourteen, maids a-courting
Fifteen sixteen, maids in the kitchen
Seventeen eighteen, maids in waiting
Nineteen twenty, my plate's empty!

ACTIVITY: TWO LITTLE DICKY BIRDS

Stick a piece of scrap paper on each index finger and rest them on a table edge. When they "fly away" over your shoulder replace them with your second fingers (without paper), then let them "come back" again.

Two little dicky birds
Sitting on a wall
One named Peter
One named Paul
Fly away Peter
Fly away Paul
Come back Peter
Come back Paul

▼ Natural counting

Objects and creatures the child sees in Nature have great scope for counting games for the child in the symbolic stage of number awareness.

ACTIVITY: ONE-TWO-THREE-FOUR-FIVE

Mime the actions as you sing together. This song is useful for learning the difference between left and right as well as counting.

One two three four five
Once I caught a fish alive
Six seven eight nine ten
Then I put it back again
Why did you let him go?
Because he bit my finger so
Which finger did he bite?
This little finger on the right

ACTIVITY: NUMBERS IN NATURE

Ask the child to count the features on natural objects.

● How many legs does a beetle have?

● How many legs does a spider have?

● How many legs does a cat have?

● How many petals does a daffodil have?

● How many wings does a bird have?

● How many ears do we have?

A sense of time

Today, in the industrialized world, we are obsessed with clock time and it tends to dominate our lives. We think of it as a controlling factor in our lives, and this has a major effect on children. David Elkind, in his book *The Hurried Child*, writes, "We do our children harm when we hurry them through childhood". He illustrates this by talking of how we can be so caught up by the apparently imperious demands of passing time that we try to push our child to achieve things before he is ready to, and this means hustling him through the various stages of play.

It is vital for his creative development that the child can have continual moments, full of vivid experiences, when he is not pressurized to hurry. On a social level it is good to create opportunities for the child to develop a more profound sense of time. For example, he should be able to enjoy playing with people older and younger than himself so that he can see a continuity in terms of years.

Ages of awareness

At about three years of age, the child will be able to talk in the past, present, and future tenses, and know how old he is and at what time he goes to bed. At five, he will be aware of the days of the week. At six, he will know the four seasons and at seven he will probably be able to tell the time. He gradually absorbs these simple concepts of time in his imaginative play and games such as *What's the time Mr Wolf?* may help this process. As parents, we can reinforce the concept of time by involving our child in planning future events, and by talking over shared memories such as past family holidays and birthdays, to give a sense of the passing of time and of continuity through the years (see also pp. 242–4).

ACTIVITY: **HOW LONG IS MY SHADOW?**

Let your child witness how time passes throughout the day by showing him the sun's effect on shadow-length. Let different-sized children participate.

● On a sunny day, choose a spot away from buildings

● Mark where the child is standing and where the end of his shadow falls

● Repeat this at different times of the day: early morning, mid-morning, noon, mid-afternoon, and evening. If possible, put pegs into the ground at the various points with the times written on them

ACTIVITY: A WEATHER CHART

This encourages the child to observe changes between one day and the next.

● Make a chart (see right) of the days of the week. This could be on a blackboard, slate, wipe-clean note board, or large piece of paper

● Draw pictures each day to describe the weather (sun, cloud, rain, snow, thunder and lightning, rainbow) and add comments about temperature, types of cloud, etc. Record the times of the observations

● To record temperature, place a thermometer in a shaded place, 3ft (1m) from the ground. Record at the same time each morning, midday, and evening

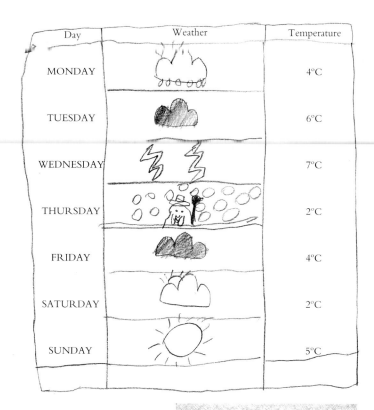

Day	Weather	Temperature
MONDAY		4°C
TUESDAY		6°C
WEDNESDAY		7°C
THURSDAY		2°C
FRIDAY		4°C
SATURDAY		2°C
SUNDAY		5°C

PROJECT: CLOCKS

These simple projects will help your child to understand how we measure time.

● Candle clock – take 2 household candles 6in (15cm) long. Light one and time it, marking off its height on the other every quarter of an hour, with felt pens. A candle of this size takes approximately three hours to burn down

● Water clock – prick a small hole in the bottom of a plastic bowl. Stand it on top of a large jar. Fill the bowl with water and mark the passage of time every five minutes by scratching marks on the falling water line inside the bowl. Stick scraps of tape on the rising water line on the outside of the jar

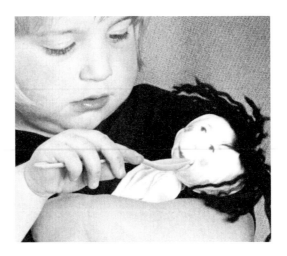

CHAPTER 12

The world of toys

Toys are an important part of childhood. In the early years they are mainly chosen by adults, who are often at a loss to know what makes a "good" toy. Should it be made of plastic or wood, be educational or just fun? Giving a toy to a child should be a spontaneous joy, not thwarted by uneasy feelings of obligation, pressure, and inadequacy.

Giving from the heart

If the present is to be prized then it must come from the heart of the giver, as a symbol of love. The child will respond with equal feeling, knowing that the message coming with the toy is one of loving care. Giving a present that is just what the child wants at that time is an equal pleasure for both parties, and the light in her eyes as she receives it shows that another bond of under-standing has been forged between the two. There is also a message of trust in the transaction: that you have confidence in her ability to use it and care for it.

The young child can be overwhelmed by the plethora of presents that arrive on birthdays, and she can easily get the idea that quantity is what really matters rather than quality. Later, she may become overly concerned about how much the toy cost. At this age, it is not necessary to even discuss such things with her. Later, when she can manage her own pocket money, she can decide how best to spend it, with the wisdom accrued from years of using toys she really appreciates. Our attitude is all-important here.

So many people give several presents when one would have done. Somehow the number of presents detracts from the "specialness" of just one well-chosen gift. So we should try to choose

▶ **"Small is beautiful"**
*The young child may get far more plea-
sure from a small, simple, well-chosen gift
than from a large, elaborate one.*

a toy that will maintain the child's interest over a
long period of time rather than flooding her with
a quantity of ephemeral playthings. Some people
like to give "big" presents, but this may plant in
the mind of the child the idea that big is somehow better. Sometimes the contents of a large,
interesting-looking box are disappointing in
their play value; something small and perfect
would have been so much more appropriate.

Why we give toys

Sometimes, we might feel compelled to buy our
child a really "wonderful" toy. Guilt is often
responsible on these occasions. Perhaps we have
been rushed and distracted and hope that a "big
surprise" will compensate for the attention she
has missed. Are we providing sufficiently educational material for her intellectual progress?
Perhaps we did not have the same opportunities
when we were young and we want to give her
the toys that we would have liked ourselves
when we were children.

The important concept to focus on is that
virtually all our child's play is part of a learning
process (see pp. 170–81); all we have to ask ourselves is "Does she need this toy at this stage in
her development?". As the years go by it
becomes ever clearer that her need is really for
tools, not toys at all. So if we can watch carefully
enough when she plays, we will be guided by
her, and know what to give. Then we will be
doing her a real service, by providing something
for creation; an "open-ended toy" for the imagination to work on (see also p. 192).

Making toys

The emphasis of this chapter is on creativity, and this means making toys wherever possible rather than buying them. Another important point is that toys should be as simple as possible; the less sophisticated the toy is, the more imaginatively it will be used by the child. Our attitude toward our efforts to make toys is all-important. If we can pass on a message of satisfaction and encouragement, then our child will be less likely to sneer at home-made toys. It is a shame that there is sometimes a negative attitude toward home-made things, particularly amongst older children, who may consider them second best.

Shared creativity

Many children have never experienced the glow of pleasure that accompanies the completion of a home-made toy. One way of enhancing our child's sense of achievement is not to interfere in the making process, except to help when we are asked. If our child regularly sees us making things, whether a simple woollen ball (see right), or a boat, she will start to imitate us and derive great satisfaction from the creative process. Perhaps the best way to start is to share the project as equal partners, then neither the adult nor the child is the "expert": both can learn together.

PROJECT: **A SIMPLE WOOLLEN BALL**

Use the woollen ball as the basis for making a variety of toys and animals.

● Cut out two cardboard rings. Cut a hole in the middle of each and put the two together

● Wind the wool through the hole, until it is tightly packed

● Slide a scissor blade between the two cardboard circles and cut the wool

● Thread a piece of wool between the two circles and tie firmly. Pull the circles off. Trim any long ends

PROJECT: VERY SIMPLE DOLL

This doll can be made very quickly from a square of soft fabric such as flannel.

● Fold the fabric square in half, crosswise, to form a triangle

● To make the head, bunch the fabric in the centre of the long, folded side and stuff with wadding, holding it in place with elasticized thread. Sew, or draw on features, if any, and sew on wool for hair

● Tie off the "wrists" with elasticized thread to make the hands

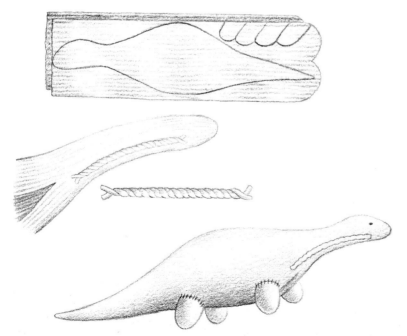

PROJECT: SOCK BRONTOSAURUS

Use a pair of men's towelling tube socks.

● Cut open both socks and lay them out flat

● Cut out two bodies and eight legs

● Sew the body pieces right sides together. Turn and stuff with wadding (batting)

● Stuff and sew on the legs

● Insert twisted pipe cleaners to stiffen the neck. Blind stitch them into position. Sew up turning slit

Dolls and puppets to make

An important part of the child's imaginative play, a family of dolls and puppets can be vivid characters in her life. They become doubly significant if the child has made, or helped to make, the character herself.

▶ **1. Dog:** old sock, felt and sequin eyes, tinsel scraps.
2. Ghost: scarf body, coat hanger, tied "wrists", thin card head.
3. Pig: painted yogurt pot, two holes for "trotters", coloured paper, felt pen features.
4. Mophead: washing-up mop, felt face drawn with felt pens, paper bag dress.
5. Spoonhead: wooden spoon, wool hair, coloured paper face.
6. Flatface: paper plate, stick, curled-paper for hair, cotton wool and glitter features.
7. Cat paper bag: little finger and thumb fill out ears.
8. Woollies: wool wound around card, separated, tied, trimmed.
9. Fir cones: fir cones and nuts, fabric scraps.
10. Pipe cleanies: (see p. 188).
11. Paper dolls: crêpe and tissue paper.
12. Mitts (see p. 188).
13. Fingers: old glove, felt scraps.
14. Ten-minute dolls (see p. 143).
15. Doll family: stuffed towelling and stockinette, wool hair.
16. Dolls' house dolls: fabric scraps.
17. Clothes pegs: wooden clothes pegs, fabric scraps.

The world of puppets

Translating a story into a puppet show and performing it for children, or helping children to create their own plays, theatre, scenery, and characters can be very rewarding for everyone. As Steiner said, "We must do everything in our power to help children to develop fantasy".

PROJECT: **THEATRE CHARACTERS**

● Cut out characters from a magazine, or draw and colour them yourself, and paste them on to thin card. If you want to manipulate them from the top of the theatre, attach a stick (garden dowel) to the head. This is appropriate for flying characters such as angels, birds, or insects

● If you want to manipulate the characters from the wings, stick them to folded strips of card on one side. They will then stand up by themselves, leaving your hands free

PROJECT: PIPE-CLEANIES

These can be dolls in their own right (see also p. 186) or you can make them into puppets to use in the toy theatre by attaching them to rods or stands.

● Twist two pipe-cleaners together to make the body. Twist a third around to make the arms and bend the ends to make hands and feet

● Wind scraps of wool around the pipe cleaners. Sew in ends. Make clothes out of fabric scraps and slip them on to the body before you put on the head

● Make a head out of a circle of stretchy fabric. Stuff with wadding and sew the neck tightly on to the body. Sew on features and hair, using wool

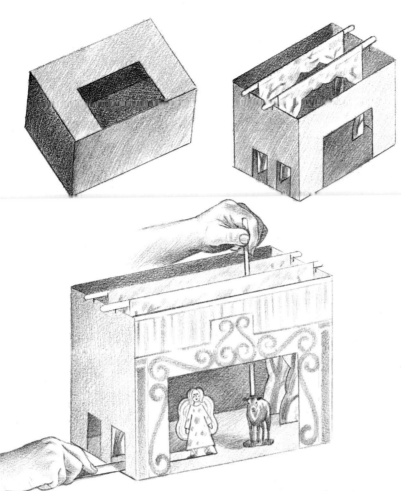

PROJECT: TOY THEATRE

● Find two similar-sized boxes. Cut an arch in the front of one, leaving the open end at the top

● Paint the whole box, inside and out, in colours of your choice

● Cut a matching pair of slots in the top of each side of the box to hold the scenery

● Make scenery from the other box and suspend it from thin dowelling rods

● Cut openings in each side of the theatre to slide the characters in and out

PROJECT: MITTS

● Draw a mitten shape around the hand on to a double thickness of sturdy cotton

● Draw a face on to one side, using felt pens or fabric paints

● Stitch the pieces right sides together

● Turn right way out, and sew on wool or string hair and any other features such as buttons for eyes (see also p. 186)

Toys for the wind

There are many toys that we and our children can make to enjoy out of doors (see also p. 250). We can choose from a whole range of recycled materials including fabric scraps (decorated with fabric paints), pieces of garden dowel, discarded packaging of all kinds, and plastic bags .

Warning: young children should be carefully supervised when using plastic bags.

▶ **Kites, flags, and banners**
Windmills: coloured paper pinned to garden canes (p. 260). **Kites:** tissue paper on a cardboard frame, with tissue paper tied to string for a tail. **Banner:** (below) painted on an old sheet, fringed with tassels made from torn fabric and sewn on to garden canes. **Flags:** paper decorated with stickers and drawings, and fabric painted with fabric paints, sewn or stapled on to garden canes. **Windsocks:** fabric and paper strips stapled to rims of plastic cups and plates, attached to garden canes. **Fish windsock:** cellophane stapled on to the rim of a plastic plate, with shredded polythene bags for fins and tail, attached to a garden cane. **Small fish:** shape cut from paper glued into a tube shape, paper strips added for tail, attached to a garden cane.

◀ **The simple life**
The young child needs simplicity in her toys; she can bestow the utmost loving care on a folded cloth doll. It is as though child and doll were at one with the world.

"
When two young girls aged two and four were given an electric train set they took all the carriages apart, wrapped them up in dolls' bedding and rocked them to 'sleep'. Such is the ingenuity of children! Their active imaginations let them find a use for an inappropriate present."

A parent

Using and choosing toys

In her play, the child must experiment and do her own research and she needs "open-ended" toys. Those that are "finished" or "perfect", such as the doll that wets itself, leave little room for her imagination to get to work. The baby starts her imaginative play by building with small bricks, and the toddler constructs with larger bricks and cardboard boxes. These become, in her imagination, castles, shops, farms, railway systems, and moonscapes. They must be built by the child herself and we should not "help" or impose our own ideas. If we are asked to help, we can, but we should let the child lead the way (see also p. 78). The real reward comes from doing it herself.

Getting the timing right

If the toy comes into your child's life too early or too late then she has little use for it. For example, a battery-operated car skidding about the floor might attract the baby's fleeting attention, as would anything that moves. But this does not mean anything more than that. A toddler might show more interest, but would become frustrated at not being able to "work" it herself, whereas a simple wooden toy on wheels would fit the bill far better. In any event toys made from natural materials are usually more satisfying than metal or plastic ones, particularly for very young children.

Pandering to crazes, or not

The commercial world now has the advantage of advertising goods right in our homes, on the television screen, and it is hard to stay immune from this pressure. The child automatically wants the toy, especially if she is influenced by her friends. There have always been crazes for certain toys, and when the media generate even more interest, the child who does not have the toy can easily feel under pressure. Peer pressure is particularly hard to resist and we have to make up our minds, as parents, where we stand. We may fear that our child will be ostracized by her friends if she doesn't have the toy. If we want to "go with the flow" and buy her the latest toy, then we have to be prepared to see it discarded as soon as the next craze has taken a hold. Fashions for toys change rapidly.

If we decide to "ride over" the craze culture our child will, in time, respect this and understand our view. She needs us to take the lead and sooner or later we have to draw boundaries on every aspect of her life, including this one. It is a sad truth that the more the child can persuade us to buy, the less satisfied she will be and the more she will want.

> **TOYS FOR LEARNING**
> We do not have to look far to find "educational" toys for our child. Old kitchen utensils, broken typewriters and telephones are all tools for learning. The child uses them to make sense of her world and to store away knowledge for the future. There is little need to buy specially designed educational toys, but later on, a magnifying glass, a torch, and a simple microscope could add a different dimension to the child's play.

▼ **The Ninja craze**
This craze swept the four- to eight-year-old age group and was all-pervading for two or three years during the early 1990s. Parents found themselves not only buying Ninja toys and merchandise such as bags, lunch boxes, and pencil cases but also ready-made birthday cakes and track suits.

Toys and gender

The pressure of the hard advertising sell has widened the gap between toys for boys and toys for girls, despite encouraging changes in society (see also p. 138). There has been progress in good uni-gender toys, such as Lego; it is not long since construction sets, such as Meccano, were considered suitable only for boys.

It is good to encourage a small boy to have dolls or toy animals to care for. By the time he is five or six he may well have been pressurized out of doll play by his peers, but he will have bene-fitted already from the earlier years, and this early influence will stay with him.

It is unfortunate that recognition, in the com-mercial world, of the fact that boys do play with dolls has manifested itself in the sale of unappeal-ing futuristic and militaristic robots and soldier dolls. The influence of this kind of toy concerns many parents, for playing with something that carries with it a mood of violence and aggression can seduce the child into thinking that this is an acceptable way of being.

Mercifully, girls have been left out of this sce-nario, but the commercial drive for a grip on their play has been for sophisticated "women-dolls" which carry their own insidious message. They seem to be saying to young girls, "This is the way to be when you are grown up". If we give our daughter one of these dolls then we are really passing her a message that says that we approve of this self-image.

Violent and militaristic toys

Violence seems to be the main ingredient in commercial toys for boys. We may feel that until the age of seven, we can protect our child from this influence, but we find that even "mild" toys such as Transformers are aimed at children as

▲ Sticks as guns

The guns our child invents have a differ-ent meaning for him than toy guns. They are the products of his imagination and so are less insidious.

young as four or five. These militaristic toys can be "transformed" by the dexterous child from a robot to a war plane, to a helicopter, and back again. Some educationalists feel that these toys can be used imaginatively, but with only two changes possible (and these the product of adults' minds), this benefit is debatable.

It is true that we have always had traditional toy soldiers, tanks, and guns, but the new, more pervasive, style of violence embodied in so many toys gives children more opportunities to engage in this type of play. It gives the message that it is fun, to be expected, and that there is always a need for an enemy.

The gun debate

There is an on-going debate about whether to allow children to play with toy guns. Some say we should give toy guns to children because, if we don't, they will simply use sticks or their fin-gers. Others say that to give a toy gun is to con-done real guns, and what they can do, in the eyes of the child. Whatever our standpoint, it is inter-esting to note that children who make their own swords and guns are far less bullying and violent in their play. They can play on a make-believe wavelength rather than on a "reality" one. Snowballs become hand grenades and lorries become tanks, in their minds.

Equipment

Many parents fall into the trap of thinking that they need to buy an endless supply of expensive equipment to keep their child occupied and help her develop. In fact, the child needs only a few essentials, and these can often be bought cheaply second-hand, or borrowed.

Motor-development is all-important for small children, from toddler age onward, and a piece of equipment with wheels, such as a small sit-on vehicle without pedals or a push-along cart, is well worth acquiring to help encourage this. The baby loves being given rides and the toddler enjoys propelling herself along using her feet. She can soon manage a simple wooden tricycle, without pedals, and, by around the age of three, can pedal by herself. By about six or seven, or earlier, her mastery of balance will enable her to ride a two-wheeler.

▲ **Using wheels**
The crawling baby pushes a wheeled toy and then a trolley when she can walk. Soon, she can pull along a toy on a string, or propel herself on a pedal-less tricycle. Later, she can pedal by herself, ride a scooter, and enjoy converting an old pushchair into a "rattletrap". The five-, six-, or seven-year-old masters the two-wheeled bicycle.

"
The first time Mummy took the stabilizers off my bike I couldn't balance at all. She ran along holding the bike while I pedalled and every time she let go I fell off. I got fed up and I started crying, 'I can't do this!' Then Mummy shouted, 'You are doing it!' and I realized I was riding on my own. It was brilliant."

Daniel, aged 7

Sports equipment

Under-sevens are not ready to use proper adult sports equipment, but small, lightweight equipment, especially designed for children, such as tennis racquets, hockey sticks, and cricket bats are available. It is better to buy the scaled-down "real" versions, rather than toy, plastic ones as they "work" better and last longer. If the child is enthusiastic about a sport, it is tempting to kit her out with proper clothes and equipment at the outset to "encourage" her. This might prove to be too great a challenge for her to live up to and her enjoyment of the sport may be marred with anxiety about whether she is doing well enough. She may lose interest after a few weeks, or develop a fascination for the clothes and the equipment rather than for the sport itself. It is better to borrow, or buy second-hand equipment until it becomes apparent whether or not she has a long-term commitment.

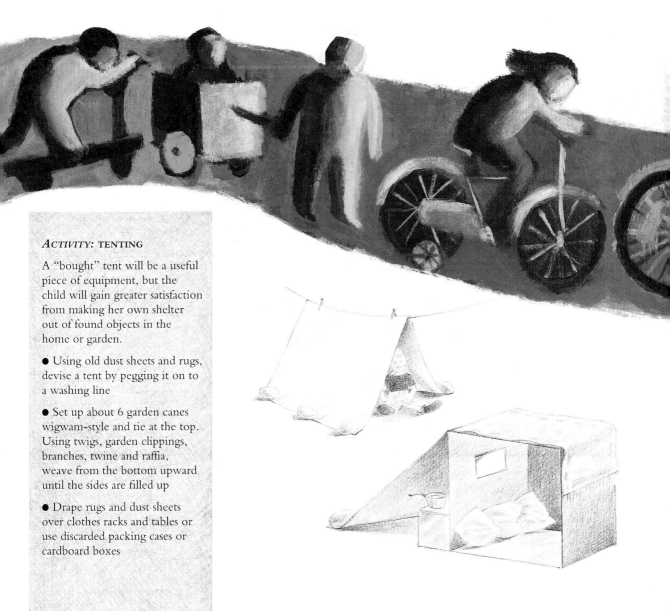

ACTIVITY: **TENTING**

A "bought" tent will be a useful piece of equipment, but the child will gain greater satisfaction from making her own shelter out of found objects in the home or garden.

● Using old dust sheets and rugs, devise a tent by pegging it on to a washing line

● Set up about 6 garden canes wigwam-style and tie at the top. Using twigs, garden clippings, branches, twine and raffia, weave from the bottom upward until the sides are filled up

● Drape rugs and dust sheets over clothes racks and tables or use discarded packing cases or cardboard boxes

Organizing and storing toys

Maria Montessori always stressed the importance of storing toys and household things in such a way that children can find and use them easily, then put them away afterwards. During the first few years, "out of sight" usually means "out of mind", so we can help the child to concentrate on one thing by only letting her have access to a few toys at a time. A jumble of miscellaneous playthings can be very confusing, particularly if toy "sets" are incomplete and muddled. It is a good idea to present only a small number of toys in a basket to the toddler. For storage, we can arrange toys in baskets or boxes on low shelves, and we should encourage the child to share the daily job of putting things away together (see also p. 88). Since all learning is concerned with sorting and storing information, the young child has a natural bent toward this task and finds it truly enjoyable.

As she grows older, the child can gradually cope with more choice, though we should continue to avoid the possibility of her having access to a vast accumulation of playthings at any one time. Periodic clearing out is the long-term answer to storage problems and, with the help of our child, we should weed out toys that are no longer valued and used. We can encourage the child to think of giving some old toys away, but we should not apply any pressure.

Work and play spaces

For the early years, play space needs to be near where the parent spends most time, either in the living room or in a corner of the kitchen, if it does not expose the child to any dangers. The play area should be kept as uncluttered as possible. If weather permits use outdoor space, especially if part of it is under cover, such as a porch.

IDEAS: TOY STORAGE AND PLAY SPACE

● Arrange objects by type and size, such as farm animals and toy cars, in baskets on low shelves, or improvize with old cartons. Ensure that they are easy to remove and replace. Put the most-used items in the most accessible places

● Make draw-string bags from scraps of fabric for storing small items such as marbles, conkers (horse chestnuts), and beads

● Keep small, miscellaneous items in several small baskets, not in one large box

● Set up the child's own low-level table and chair so that she can paint or model in comfort. Or arrange a flat surface over two small drawer units which can be used for storing art and craft equipment

◀ **Sorting**
The child will enjoy deciding how things should be sorted and where they should be stored. We can reinforce this activity by letting her share in other sorting tasks, which have the added attraction of being "adult work".

◀ **Play and put it away**
Improvize a work surface and seat with a large box and bucket. Store toys in bags, stacked boxes, baskets, and on low shelves (near left).

CHAPTER 13

Games and activities

Playing games is a vital part of every child's development and the child will play them whatever we provide for him, and even if we don't.

Disappearing playfulness

Play is an instinctive need and one fully recognized by the United Nations Declaration of Human Rights. In industrial societies we face problems of decreasing motivation and performance amongst school children. Some of the contributing factors to this are the decreasing involvement of adults, in terms of support and backup, and the deterioration of the environment in which children can play. The lack of safe space in the streets and countryside has curtailed much of the traditional lore, handed down by the children themselves, and the invasion of the media in the form of television and computer games (see also pp. 140 and 207) lessens the time available and the motivation for playing games. These factors all play their part in robbing many children of their own playfulness and the essential experience of enjoying and sharing in games. We should, if possible, aim to restore to them what is their natural birthright.

Until the ages of six or seven, exploratory, free-flowing play takes precedence over more organized games. But this does not mean that more structured games are unimportant. The emphasis is on the child's own control of his play, but perhaps with adult support. The imposition of rules by an outsider could inhibit the child's confidence in his own imaginative ability.

Rules exist, to some extent, in all play, but they are spontaneous and flexible in free play, not least because of the need to adjust to the ideas of

▶ **Chasing and catching**
*The game of chase and catch ("tig, "tag",
"it", or "he") has many forms and variations and is played by children everywhere
(see also p. 208).*

other players. "I'll be the doctor and you be the nurse", "No! I want to be the doctor." So the process of taking turns and co-operating is set in motion and this is an essential part of social development (see also p. 106). Games can be flexible too, especially the ones that are derived from the lore of children's traditional play. Here the players may have fixed rules to begin with, but they are continually being altered by consensus amongst the players.

Physical development and games

Today's children need all the physical exercise they can get because of the necessity to be driven everywhere in cars rather than to walk and because of the time spent in passive activities.

Since walking alone to school or playing in the woods, or even visiting the nearest playground can be fraught with hazards, we find it difficult to enable children to exercise their bodies to the full. Babies and toddlers need less space and, in any case, have to be supervised. Three- and four-year-olds need more space, but a backyard or small garden is enough for them to carry out their adventurous initiatives, practise their skills, and play their games.

Children of all ages need to play out in the fresh air, even in bad weather, provided that they are warmly wrapped up (see p. 284). Perhaps the garden can be adapted for the children's use for a few years, to be reclaimed by the adults when the children are older.

▲ **World Cup 2014?**
Even a child as young as two will look
the part when practising kicking a ball.

Body skills

Skills are developed in every aspect of exploration and play in the birth-to-seven age group.
From the time the baby endlessly tries to sit up
and then to stand, right through to the efforts of
the seven-year-old to aim the ball into the net,
there is a self-imposed effort to learn a skill.

This applies to all of the activities the child
performs: he repeats the same process time and
time again until he is satisfied that he has learned
it. In a broad sense it is the exercising of a skill
that makes the child assimilate each process at an
inner level.

When we are thinking about skills, we tend
to think generally about bodily achievements,
but the innate propensity to practise is just as

valid when applied to cognitive development. For example, multiplication tables and spelling tend to be learned superficially while the real integration of the concepts goes on subconsciously. However, when it comes to skill in games and sport, the child's motivation is usually much stronger and more self-regulated.

The parental role

Our role as parents is to provide safe challenges and also to admire the child's tenacity and final success. From the time that the toddler insists on balancing along a low, narrow wall, to the everlasting ball catching, bouncing, throwing, and aiming, the process is one of repetition. It is a source of wonder to us to watch this intense concentration and meticulous rehearsal, knowing that we do not need to coach or coax. Our child will achieve his goals himself, if he has the inner motivation.

A place for sport

The child may become involved in a sport from quite an early age and there is no harm in this as long as he is not pushed further than his capabilities, or allowed to spend long periods doing it in place of other activities. Such sports include: ice skating, rock climbing, trampolining, skate boarding, cycling, judo, tai chi, gymnastics, dancing, and all the different ball sports.

It may help the child who shows an interest to focus on one activity so that he can start to find his niche in it and feel confident. Swimming is a special activity because all children have to learn to swim at some point for their own safety and the sooner they are introduced to water the better. Babies are ready to get used to being in and around water before they can crawl and toddlers can become quite efficient swimmers (with the aid of arm bands).

ACTIVITIES: GAMES TO ENHANCE SKILLS

● "Snake rope" – hold a rope between two, ripple it along the ground, getting higher and higher while others jump over it in ones, twos, threes, and so on

● "Co-operative frisbee" – in a group throw a frisbee to each other, but the catcher has to be touching another player or be touched by one. How many co-operative catches can be made in a sequence?

● "Co-operative balloons" – in pairs (each with a balloon and two thin cardboard strips) try to get the balloon into each of four baskets placed at four corners

Social development and fair play

Games and free play call for co-operation and this is an important part of social development. Fortunately humans are co-operative beings and it is in our nature to practise this quality of good-will. Co-operation begins at the toddler stage, but three- and four-year-olds often experience difficulty. Parents are very aware of the many conflicts that arise, but we can be reassured that, if possible, it is better to allow children to resolve them without intervention, unless there is risk of danger or violence.

Winning and losing

Our society puts great emphasis on competition and this extends into children's games (see also pp. 106–7). Some people say that, since we live in a competitive world, the sooner the child gets used to it the better. A child as young as two can be expected to put on a "brave face" on losing, though right up to the age of seven and beyond it is hard for him not to feel he is a failure. For the child, games and play are life-blood and the basis on which he learns about the real world, so the message can come across that the world does not think too highly of him. He suffers loss of self-confidence.

The best we can do is to watch and see when our child might be prepared to risk losing in games of chance or skill. Until then it is best to rely on co-operative games (see also pp. 210–11) so that the emphasis in all game-playing is on fun and not on winning or losing.

There is a still a strong case for playing competitive games, but with a structure of agreed rules and regulations. Fair play can then come into its own. It is all a question of not pushing the child into premature exposure to failure. We can also encourage the idea of competing against himself, where competence and progress are rewards in themselves.

ACTIVITY: CO-OPERATIVE FOOTBALL

● There are three players in each goal and the other players try to score as many goals as possible, first in one goal and then the other

● Scorers change places with one of the goal keepers when a goal is scored

ACTIVITIES: GUESSING GAMES

● In pairs, one asks the questions and the other must reply truthfully, but without using the words "yes" or "no" and without nodding or shaking the head. When one makes a mistake it is the other's turn

● The players sit in a circle and are alternately "deaf" and "dumb". The deaf ones ask questions of the dumb ones, who can only reply by miming or gestures. Then they reverse roles

ACTIVITY: DRAMA GAME – THE MAGIC BROOM

● Everyone has to think of a job that he or she wants to mime. The broom is the only prop and can be used for any purpose, except as a broom

● The one who guesses the job is the next one to mime

Indoor games

There is nothing more consolidating than a game enjoyed by the whole family, but it must be handled carefully. As family relationships have many emotional undertones, games must be appropriate for the development stage of the youngest child. The reverse may be disastrous. The youngest of a large family forced to be "dummy" in, say, whist or bridge may be put off card games for life.

As adults, we should be aware of what we are doing when we play games with children (see also p. 106-7). If we always let the child lose, he may feel that he is somehow destined always to be the loser. We should make allowances and surreptitiously let him win on occasions. It takes a long time for a young child to realize that games of chance depend on luck rather than skill – for him, losing at such games can be just more proof of his inadequacy.

PROJECT: MAKE YOUR OWN BOARD GAMES

There are now many co-operative board games on the market; no one loses and everyone wins. Or make your own board games using a large sheet of cardboard and brightly coloured felt pens. If you need counters, make them from self-hardening clay and paint them in appropriate colours. The two games (see right) are suggested themes for home-made board games.

IDEA: "ADVENTURE ISLAND"

Four children arrive at an island and decide to build a cabin but they need twenty logs to build it and there are none on the island. Each player will have to get five logs from the mainland. The players can help each other: they can go in twos to get the logs, they can give each other points which enable them to get the logs more quickly. Everything is going well until the sea starts to swell and it becomes more and more difficult to bring back the logs. What can they do?

IDEA: "SLEEPING GRUMP"

Grump has taken the villagers' treasures and is now asleep at the top of the beanstalk. Together players climb the beanstalk and recover their treasures, but Grump must not be wakened or he will take everything back. The players share the treasures and leave some behind for Grump. Their kindness will help to change him.

Inside the board image: START, START, and various hand-written labels including "Super...", "Maze with Magic healing herb at centre!", "are you scared?", "Avoid the center of the planet we're on!", "dath water", "Two species", "stake", "ptatod Nice melt", "R", "B".

PROJECT: **HOW TO PLAY EARTHQUAKERS**

● Make up a board to represent a map, with twenty locations and connecting red and green squares (see picture left)

● Each player invents a character with special strengths and weaknesses

● An "arbitrator" distributes Dilemma, Accident, and Good Fortune cards depending on where the characters land

● Each player shakes a dice and visits each location in turn, facing and solving problems on the way. The game finishes when a player has reached all the locations and solved the Dilemmas

▲ **Earthquakers: an idea for a home-made board game**

Earthquakers was invented by a group of children aged 5–14. The basic idea: a board with pieces to move around, locations and problems to solve can be adapted to suit any theme.

In Earthquakers a team of explorers is sent to a new planet by the League of Worlds to make contact with the native species and try to persuade the people to join without using force of any kind. All they can do is persuade peacefully. Problems are faced together and solutions arrived at. Players progress around the board and the game ends when they have solved all the dilemmas peacefully.

COMPUTER GAMES
Parents must think carefully about whether or not to allow children to play computer games. There are claims that these games develop dexterity and quick thinking, but there are also claims that it is better for children to develop these abilities through sport and exercise. In addition, many computer games are high in violent and sexist content. In a study conducted in the United States, it was found that 72 per cent of Nintendo games were in the violent category. Even the sports games surveyed were found to have a certain vitriolic quality.

Outdoor games

Outdoor games and activities are vital in order to counteract the attractions of passive entertainment, such as the television, video, and computer games, in the cosy confines of the home. Once children have enjoyed a good game in the open air, they return exhilarated, exhausted, and satisfied. This is what they really need.

In the lively game of tag the children can be more proficient than the adults. Children are so often affected by the apparent superiority of their elders that it builds up their self-concept to realize that they can beat them. "Nature games" out of doors are also a delight (see below).

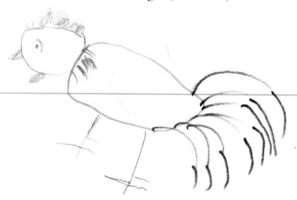

ACTIVITIES: TAG GAMES

● **"STATUE TAG"**

One or two chasers chase the others. Those who are caught must keep the position they were in at that moment. Their fellows can rescue them by taking their places in exactly the same positions

● **"MAZE TAG"**

All except two players join hands to form a maze. The chaser and the runner cannot cross under the joined arms of the maze, which should be open-ended. Both the chaser and the runner can touch maze players on their backs and change places with them

● **"CHINESE TOUCH"**

One player stands on a mat in the centre and must not step off it. The others try to touch the mat without being tagged by the one in the centre

ACTIVITIES: NATURE GAMES

● **"GUESS MY TREE"**

In a wood or park, players spend time looking at the shapes of the trees. They then each choose a tree and take turns to "mime" its shape for the others to guess

● **"MAKE AN ANIMAL"**

In groups of three or four, choose an animal and "make" it with your bodies. The others have to guess what you are. Make sounds too

▲ An ideal den
This imaginary treehouse has a rocket-powered lift, a direct route from the child's bedroom, a rope to climb, and a ladder.

Co-operative games

The essential spirit of co-operative games is the idea of playing solely for the fun of it; so the challenge comes from the process itself rather than from striving to be the winner. These games can take many forms. Some are based on traditional games that have been adapted so that those players eliminated from the game can start a new game of their own rather than being "out". In this way all sorts of games can be adjusted to put co-operation before competition.

▼ **Parachute fun**
Using a parachute with a group of children can be great fun – it hovers magically in the air, giving time for games beneath, before it descends gracefully again. The players must co-operate to manipulate the parachute.

ACTIVITIES: **PARACHUTE GAMES**

● **"PASS BALL"**

A number of small balls is passed around the players, who are holding the parachute at waist height. When the leader calls out "Pass ball!" everyone inflates the parachute and those holding balls have to exchange places with someone else

● **"CROSS-OVER"**

When the parachute is inflated on a count of "1, 2, 3, parachute!" the leader calls out instructions for players to cross beneath it, for example, "Everyone wearing yellow"

GAME: **THREE-LEGGED FOOTBALL**

Two teams are formed by pairs of players, the two children in each pair tied together at the ankles. The aim is to kick a balloon or light-weight ball into the opponents' goal

GAME: **CIRCLE PING-PONG**

● As many as possible get around a ping-pong table

● A bat is placed on each side of the net and as they run round, players take it in turns to hit the ball over the net and leave the bat on the table ready for the next player

● The ball must only bounce once, but the new serve is taken by the next player on whichever side the ball landed

GAME: **CO-OPERATIVE DODGE BALL**

● Divide into two teams, one making a large circle around the other

● With large, light-weight balls, those in the outer circle try to hit those in the inner circle below the waist

● Anyone who is hit then joins the outer circle

GAME: **BALLOON PUSH**

● Divide into two teams and have two goals, one at each end of the area

● Distribute as many balloons as possible between the two teams

● At the word "Go!" each player tries to pat a balloon into their opponents' goal, where it must remain. Only hands are allowed to touch the balloons, and the aim is to score as many goals as possible without bursting any balloons

● Goal keepers change each time they let a balloon through

Parties

Although they are eagerly anticipated, parties can be a major disappointment to small children, so it is no mean feat to organize a successful one. However, by following a few basic guidelines, the children can all be happily engaged and the experience can be a step forward in their social development. For some parents, the current trend is to hire an entertainer such as a conjuror or clown, or a children's video, but this is not as challenging, invigorating, enjoyable, or as memorable as playing some good games.

One good guideline is to keep numbers of guests small for the very young: one guest for babies, two for toddlers, three for three-year-olds, and so on. Party time can be kept fairly short, say one and a half hours for the toddlers, who will probably like a parent to stay at the party with them. This age-group will be happy exploring their host's toys, so precious or delicate toys should be hidden away. It is also a good idea to play a few action games.

IDEAS: TODDLERS' PARTY

● Traditional circle games such as *Squeak piggy squeak*

● Nursery rhymes with actions such as *Ring a ring a roses, Round and round the garden, Jack and Jill, Ding dong bell*

GENERAL TIPS
Draw up a list of games and activities, timed approximately. Follow the plan as far as possible. If guests bring birthday presents, it is a good idea to save them and open them after the party so that those who have brought modest presents do not feel "small" and the group does not become overexcited. Don't have tea too early – it takes up less time than you think and will increase the children's energy.

IDEAS: SIX- TO SEVEN-YEAR-OLDS' PARTY

● Treasure hunt – lay a trail of rhyming clues around the house and/or garden. Leave one small, named prize for each child at the final destination

● Quiz – divide the children into small groups and ask each team in turn a question on a theme. The team members may confer with each other

● Themes for fancy dress – pirates, cowboys, dragons, fairy stories, firefighters

IDEAS: THREE- TO FIVE-YEAR-OLDS' PARTY

● Traditional circle games such as *Pass the parcel*

● Nursery rhymes with actions such as *The farmer's in his den, Sally go round the moon, Oranges and lemons*

● Action games such as *Blind man's buff, Musical chairs,* and laughing games such as *Poor pussy* – blindfold pussy sits on someone's lap and meows. If that player can say "Poor pussy" three times without laughing, pussy goes on to the next lap. The one who laughs becomes pussy

PART 4

THE UNFOLDING
WORLD

Lynne Oldfield

*W*orking outward from the family unit, where respect and care for Mother Earth and for our fellow human beings are manifested in simple but imaginative ways, we can give new meaning to the phrase "small is beautiful". We then acknowledge the power of the family as a forum for change.

The young child is deeply affected by all that surrounds him and spontaneously imitates the actions of his companions. Imitation is a fundamental aspect of his development – it is how he learns and practises new skills. The behaviour of others also affects him and the way he goes out to meet the world is shaped by these early influences. Observing the adults' gesture of reverence toward Gaia, both inwardly and outwardly, children come naturally to respect Nature and to acknowledge Spirit in Matter. As he grows up with the reassurance of a steady, rhythmical existence, living close to the seasons, and filled with wonder at the annual celebrations of the year's festivals, Earth becomes the child's Mater, truly his Earth-Mother.

CHAPTER 14

The child's world

As the new-born child gradually "awakens" to her world what she perceives there is the model for her own future thinking and behaviour as an adult. We, as parents, must ensure that she is surrounded not only by our love and care but also by images of love and care for her fellow humans and for the planet that is her home. Perhaps in this way we can help to secure a positive future for our children.

Inner changes

Observing the changes that occur in the child from year to year is one of the great joys of being a parent. We see many changes. The child sits, crawls, then stands, and takes her first, long-awaited step. She grows taller and loses some of the "chubbiness" of babyhood, and she imitates the language of her community.

There are, however, inner, less visible, changes which make their contribution toward her development. These changes also determine her experience of the environment and her responses to it. Embracing these inner realities in our understanding of our child allows her to grow holistically and brings empathy into parenthood. We then begin to accept our child not only as a physical body but as a unity of body, soul, and spirit. Parents and teachers work in harmony with the spiritual worlds and the child's true nature when they address all three. In this way we form our own personal defence against the movement toward a totally materialistic interpretation of what it is to be human. We may inwardly ask of our child: "Who are you? What do you need to do?" The patient listening for answers to these profound questions lies at the very heart of being a parent.

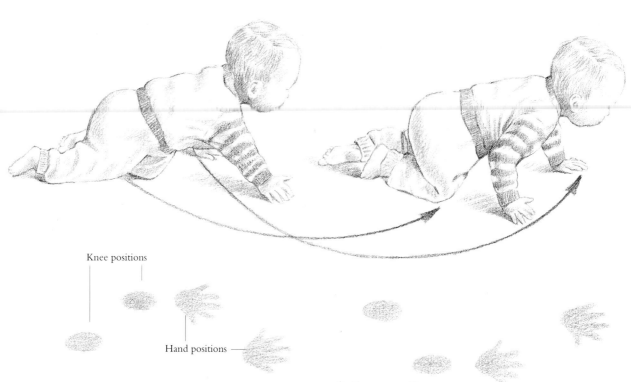

Knee positions

Hand positions

▲ Cross crawling
The opposite arm and leg are thrust forward simultaneously, and the child begins to learn co-ordination. Some children may omit the crawling stage altogether or find mobility by "bottom-shuffling" instead.

Natural development

Within the "house" of the body of the newborn individuality certain potentials for human activity are sleeping. They are the capacities for Thinking, Feeling, and Willing (see also p. 20), which reveal themselves gradually and rhythmically. The healthy child will progressively take control of her body from the head downward (see also p. 29). Each child does this in her own way and we support this activity when we resist the modern inclination to hasten all development. At around three months she will be able to lift her head. This control, centring on the natural strengthening of muscles, will then extend to the torso, enabling her to sit up. Crawling frequently acts as an intermediate stage between sitting and the miraculous moment when the child rises fully into the vertical.

"
The rhythmical pattern of cross crawling (opposite arm and leg being thrust forward) is significant not only for the development of proper physical co-ordination, but also aspects of the development of the brain and how a child learns."

Rahima Baldwin,
You are Your Child's First Teacher

"
To watch the child unfold through this great evolutionary panorama, seeing the ego express itself by pulling the body upwards, defying the law of gravity as the blood flows upwards to the head, is to be filled with humility and wonder, for here in the child, we most truly witness the handwork of the Gods."

Joan Salter,
The Incarnating Child

Hastened development

Many of the developmental aids such as baby-walkers, bouncers, and some babycarriers and car seats which have recently become so popular are designed to encourage the child prematurely into an upright position. This can cause her to strain unready muscles, and the crawling phase, which is important for her mental as well as her physical development, may be undermined.

Unnatural acceleration

To allow our child to experience the freedom and benefits of a natural childhood we need to question the usefulness of these many "aids". Frequently, the intention is to give unnatural acceleration to the child's physical development and she is increasingly denied the opportunity to make her own individual inner efforts toward these accomplishments. All development, spiritual, emotional, and physical, rests, to some extent, on personal effort.

Supporting physical development

We can offer practical support toward our child's physical development in other ways too. At no other time, except in old age, is physical warmth as important as it is during this time when the forces of growth are so active in forming and strengthening the child's physical body. The head, where this activity begins, is particularly vulnerable and hats that cover the ears are necessary. We should keep the child's limbs warm too and use soft woollen tights if possible, beneath the often flimsy garments so common these days (see also p. 284). A rhythmical, steady existence, the security of a regular routine, and a healthy, natural, balanced diet also give essential support to this important work of the child's physical development (see also p. 282).

The unfolding soul

This work on the physical body continues and, at the same time, the inner life of the child begins to stir. As an adult she will require the means, and confidence, to reveal her inner nature, the "who-I-truly-am", to her companions. In this way, she becomes not only a human being, but a social being.

Thinking hearts and heart-filled thinking

The inability to form a bridge between the "who-I-truly-am" and others, to express Self in a flowing, comfortable way can be the cause of great suffering in adulthood. The modern trend toward early intellectuality, particularly at the expense of an expressive, flowing, intelligent, feeling life, freezes the flow between "I" and "you". The future calls for thinking hearts and heart-filled thinking.

With sensitive observation we shall see the growing child seek to express herself through her unfolding capacities for Thinking, Feeling, and Willing. We watch, listen, guide, encourage, and give a great deal to our child when we are able to maintain a true interest in her efforts to discover her own identity.

The phases of childhood

In her first seven years, if not inhibited or redirected by, for example, early intellectuality, the child is most inclined to explore and respond to her world through movement and activity. In middle childhood, seven to fourteen years, she reaches out and is most affected by all that arises in her feelings. In adolescence, between fourteen and twenty-one (the threshold of adulthood), she strives to make sense of her situation through her developing ability to think logically as well as in an increasingly abstract way.

"
The soul walks not upon a line, neither does it grow like a reed. The soul unfolds itself, like a lotus of countless petals."

Kahlil Gibran,
The Prophet

Parental support

One of our greatest and most fulfilling tasks as parents is to give our child the support she needs to help her achieve a vital balance between Thinking, Feeling, and Willing. We can view education and being a parent in the broadest sense as a striving to help our child to clarify Thinking, deepen Feeling, and strengthen the Will. In time, the awakening Self will be able to take hold of each of these means of expression and in so doing will be able to reveal itself more fully as the child grows toward adulthood.

"

At two-and-a-half, the child has an increasing sense of 'I' but he does not have himself well in hand. He is impetuous, defiant, unreasonable and contrary, but also hesitant and dawdling. He is just discovering a new realm of opposites. He has to learn to choose between alternatives – between giving and taking, between mine and thine, between 'I want' and 'I don't want'. There are frequent tantrums."

A. Gesell

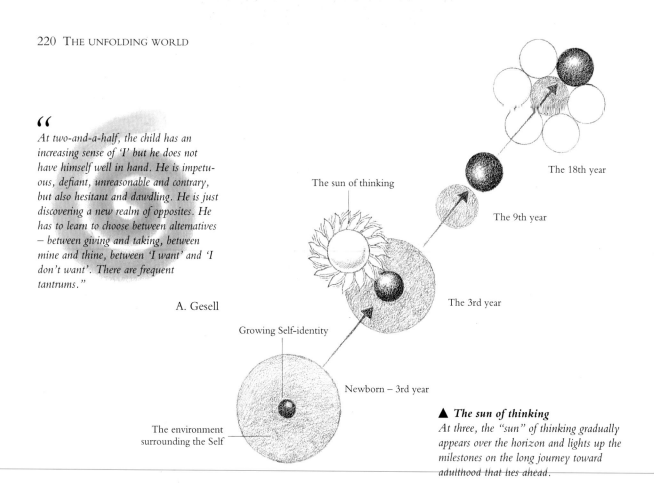

The sun of thinking

The 18th year

The 9th year

The 3rd year

Growing Self-identity

Newborn – 3rd year

The environment surrounding the Self

▲ *The sun of thinking*
At three, the "sun" of thinking gradually appears over the horizon and lights up the milestones on the long journey toward adulthood that lies ahead.

The awakening of self-awareness

The newborn baby is at first totally "asleep" to any sense of Self, with only a dreamlike awareness of her environment. As she moves toward adulthood she experiences a slow awakening to herself as an independent "I", a separate identity capable of self-determination and self-control. This arises out of an expanding sense of herself as "other than" her surroundings.

As the awakening process continues, we can be aware of certain milestones in self-awareness, particularly in the third, ninth, and eighteenth years. In the early weeks the child is, in a sense, "at one" with the world. A dawning sense of separation and differentiation, at first dimly felt, arises in the first three years.

In the third year the "sun" of thinking, born out of the acquisition of memory and speech, begins to light up her inner world. Thinking will lead her to awaken to her own inner activity and an experience of enhanced separate identity. She becomes more assertive and needs to demonstrate her newly conscious Self-ness by opposing the world. She frequently uses the word "No" to display this opposition.

This necessary and totally positive phase has great significance for her future wellbeing. She has begun the journey toward self-realization. In one way she is only now "on earth, fully born". She stands in the world by calling herself "I". This may be a challenging time for parents. We can try to distract the child, or avoid situations which trigger this opposition.

▲ *Me, myself, I*
By studying her own reflection in the mirror, the child discovers how "Self" appears to others.

In the ninth year self-awareness is again deepened and the child responds from her feelings. She may experience painful sensations of loneliness and become critical of the significant adults in her world. The paradise of childhood, when all seemed possible, is lost with this separateness, but a new pleasure awaits. With increasing sense-of-self, an ego-sense, she now has the ability to truly recognize Self in the other and the world of relationships beckons her onward.

The adolescent strives to move from the self-experience of the ninth year to self-expression. Self longs to bear fruit. This longing is the true foundation for the idealism of the adolescent and the many questions that arise at this time: "What work should I do?" and "How should I dress?", all of which are variations of "Who am I?"

"

In your longing for your giant self lies your goodness and that longing is in all of you. But in some of you that longing is a torrent rushing with might to the sea, carrying the secrets of the hillsides and the songs of the forest. And in others it is a flat stream that loses itself in angles and bends and lingers before it reaches the shore."

Kahlil Gibran,
The Prophet

The child's view of the world

Does the world appear differently to the young child than it does to us? At certain times in her development this is most certainly so. The understanding of this difference, and the appropriate handling of the situations that arise from it, present a great challenge to parents. At-oneness with the environment and the unawakened Self (see p. 220) produce in the child what may be called a participating, or dreamlike, consciousness. This unselfconscious state of being allows the child to "dream" into her activity and surroundings becoming, at times, "within" the situation, with no sense of separation.

Imagination

How can we come to understand this type of consciousness? Watch how intensely the child is involved in play. If she is in a sandbox she is totally absorbed in the simple movements of filling and refilling a pot of sand.

Or she may drape some cloths about her body, becoming a pirate. Entering into fantasy she is the pirate. We constantly hear, "Let's pretend..." (see also p. 154). Walking behind her parent, a two-year-old may stop to look at a leaf and the purpose of the outing is forgotten. Only the "here-and-now" of the leaf exists. These moments often bring us frustrations, but it is important to understand that this is natural behaviour for under-sevens.

Transforming the world

What are the qualities of this way of viewing the world? How do we embrace and protect them? In this condition there are no boundaries. Everything is possible and the child demonstrates a wonderful creative mobility which most adults, except creative artists, have lost. No object is totally inanimate or one-dimensional and objects

IDEAS: LETTING YOUR CHILD PLAY

● Leave your child to play undisturbed. Avoid interrupting her or rushing her to finish. She needs time

● If you watch her, don't let her know you are doing so. It will destroy her concentration and make her self-conscious. Never discuss her fantasy games within her hearing. She may feel she is being spied upon and mocked

● Avoid bringing her back to self-awareness with questions such as: "What are you pretending to be?"

ACTIVITY: GATHERING TOYS FROM NATURE

● With your child, collect a variety of "toys" to use in imaginative play from Nature, such as feathers, stones, shells, bark, and pinecones

● Put each different type of item into a small basket so that she can arrange and rearrange them as she chooses

● Give her some non-toxic glue, and pieces of coloured paper, ribbon, and fabric scraps and let her make "pictures" with the "toys"

assume an almost symbolic quality. If given the right conditions, the child displays enormous imagination: a stick is a sword at one moment, a doll or a flute the next (see also p. 142).

This "dream consciousness" of the early years is imbued with the magical quality of metamorphosis. The child's world is constantly re-shaped, transformed. This type of consciousness is most clearly visible when we see the child at play. Early learning, and constant intellectual explanations weaken the child's ability to enter her "dreaming" space. Television, video, and over-stimulation in general also undermine this phase. Sympathetic play environments that provide sufficient time and space, and toys that have the possibility for transformation, give support.

The impact of sense-impressions

As adults we are able to form concepts with our awakened capacity for thinking. We form judgements and make decisions about what we include in our environment, which allows us to filter the impressions and to distance ourselves from them. The young child cannot do this and so is totally exposed to all that takes place in her environment. The behaviour of others, images on television, conversations held in her presence, the content of stories, the form of her toys, all affect the vulnerable, developing individual. Formed in this way, either positively or negatively, the child goes out to meet the world and shapes it according to these early influences.

Parental responsibility

The future of our planet may depend on parents taking responsibility for choosing what streams toward the child. We stand as guardians on the threshold between child and environment. Today much emphasis is placed on intellectual development at the expense of emotional and moral growth. Our world is full of violent images, and humankind seems indifferent to the destruction of natural resources. The invasion of the soul of our child by sensory "junk" calls for us to be awake and courageous. We may need to make independent decisions as to what influences our child (see also pp. 140–1).

What can we do? We must look at the amount and pace of the sensory impressions that we offer the child. Sense-deprivation can result in soul impoverishment or an over-stimulated, nervous system. Morality, the sense for the distinction between good and evil, finds its roots in early childhood and is shaped through imitation of the adult world. From her innocence, the child looks to us for guidance.

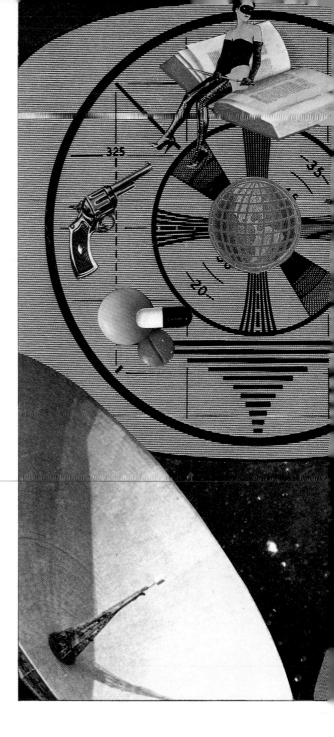

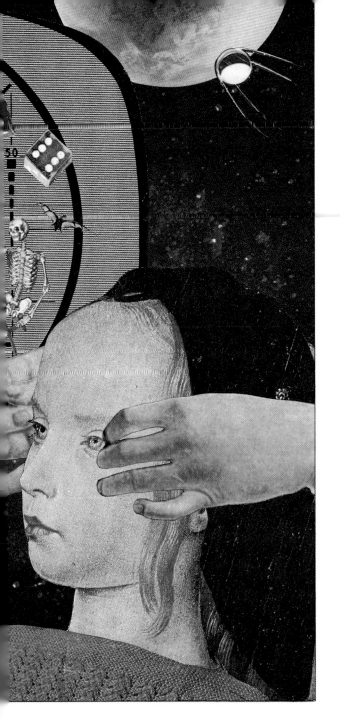

▲ Imitation, trust, and openness
*By protecting our child from media vio-
lence and sensory "junk", we demonstrate
not only our love for her, but also our
concern for the future of our world.
Imitation, activity, trust, and openness –
these are the natural ways of the child.*

Imitation

In contrast to the adult's reflective, cognitive approach, which may lead to action, the child is driven to grasp new situations with activity.

One of the most significant characteristics of the child's development during this time is imitation. The child is in a condition of total openness toward her surroundings. She is, at the same time, wholly movement. This openness, and the drive toward activity lead her to respond with imitation. A three-year-old cannot remain detached from the sight of her mother baking. She is impressed by her movements kneading the dough, rolling out the pastry, and pressing out shapes. She must imitate, and the mother needs to meet this with sympathy (see also p. 136). What is happening in the environment enters through the senses, is then grasped by will forces, and is expressed in the act of imitation.

Setting a good example

Imitation in the child arises out of a deep trust and love for the world. It needs to be met with responsibility and reciprocal love on the part of the adult. A natural childhood must encompass an understanding of how a child is most naturally inclined to respond to her unfolding world. Not only does she imitate visible activity but she also imitates less visible behaviour. If anger, hypocrisy, and dishonesty exist continually in her surroundings then she will imitate these also. So she will absorb positive activity and attitudes which influence her development. The child may observe adults treating each other with respect, tending the environment with care, confronting work with enthusiasm. These actions impress her and help to form her values. Using imitation works far more effectively than explanation, criticism, or punishment.

CHAPTER 15

Living in activity

By understanding the different stages of development of the Will, we can accept our child's need for constant activity and his early inability to control that activity. One of the secrets of being a successful parent lies in the readiness to adapt our responses and expectations to meet the changing needs of our child and to ensure that, with our help, he reaches adulthood with strong and healthy Will forces.

The nature of Will

The awakening of the child's Will forces is a most important factor in his development because with this awakening comes the potential for humankind to build a better world.

Watch the breathtaking energy of a child "at work", digging, moving, filling, breaking down, building up, tirelessly and relentlessly.

The potential for the adult's purposeful action has its roots in early childhood. The vibrancy of the young child's activity, if nurtured and guided with love and understanding, can lay a firm foundation for his ability for self-discipline and his willingness to take the initiative in the future.

Self-control

In the early years, a child's movements have a chaotic quality. He cannot exercise self-control because he is not yet conscious of Self. As he becomes more self-aware, and can take control of his Will, his movements will become more directed and purposeful, but, as yet, such control is far beyond his reach.

The sleeping Will is first aroused by the presence of others nearby. When the child sees his parent's face above his cot, he responds by lifting his head and turning and moving his arms and

legs about wildly. Other activity around him, such as noise, movement, and touch, has the same effect. These are involuntary, reflex movements over which he has no control. He is, at this stage, "wholly movement".

"Physical religion"

Rudolf Steiner described this aspect of early childhood development as a type of "physical religion". Certainly, the whole of the first seven-year phase of development is almost entirely devoted to movement.

The child's impulse to stand and walk arises out of his need to imitate what he sees around him. He unconsciously draws on his will-power to achieve this motion. In his second year he is rarely still. With great determination he moves, takes, lifts, and runs. The healthy child must, and will, move. He cannot do otherwise and all efforts to restrain him are unnatural even if, at times, they are absolutely necessary for his well-being or for the wellbeing of those around him.

Parents often describe their children of this age as "strong-willed". It is more accurate to say that their children have "strong impulses". A strong Will is, as yet, something that is far into the future, when the Self has developed the ability to direct the Will. This development requires a considerable awakening of consciousness.

The second and third years

In his second and third years the child may display explosive expressions of Will. This is the
stage of development so frequently termed "the
terrible twos and threes". His frequent tantrums
are caused by his growing self-awareness, which
leads him to experience himself as a separate
being. There is now himself, and others, who are
"over there" and somewhat threatening. He is
also becoming aware of a conflict between his
Will and the Will of others; hence the threat.
Often, at this stage, his vocabulary seems to
shrink to only two words: "I" for himself, and

"No" for others! This phase will continue until
he discovers that his Will can, and must, learn to
live in harmony with other people's.

The sheer energy of the child's will-forces
can leave even the most patient and sympathetic
parents exhausted to the point of despair. We can
deal more easily with this important phase in the
child's development by remembering that it is
temporary. He needs a great deal of love and
support at this time. Directing his energy into
activity and a regular daily routine will help harmonize the chaos (see also p. 115).

The fourth and fifth years

The fourth and fifth birthdays can bring a welcome release from the traumas of the twos and threes as the Will finds new expression in the outlet of creative play. Happily engaged in play, the child is far easier for us to live with. Having passed through the transitional "I" experience, the Will now gradually connects to the awakening imagination and manifests itself in fantasy.

Activity and imagination

This may be seen as the second phase of the first seven years. In the first phase, the incoming sense impressions are met by the child's Will and re-emerge in the act of imitating. Now, however, the child sees everyday things such as cardboard boxes and planks of wood around him and, with his imagination, draws upon his Will forces and transforms them into boats, tables, or houses. His creativity at this time is astounding and, given space, time, and suitable toys and materials, he will endlessly, joyfully, exercise his Will to transform his world (see also p. 144).

Sometimes, the child can be slow to develop his creativity, and may, for a time, become listless and discontented. We can help him through this phase by involving him in our own day-to-day activities. There are many simple but meaningful ways to make him feel he is helping in a real way. For example, he could sort the sewing basket, where he may discover a "treasure chest" of coloured ribbons and spools of thread, or he could help to build a compost heap in the garden, where a whole world of tiny creatures will fascinate him. He will feel secure and contented in our company and will very soon move on to imaginative, creative play.

Children are free, safe, and at peace when they play. This is the heart of natural childhood.

IDEAS: DIRECTING ENERGY

● Let him use his hands, arms, and legs in a positive way by giving him access to sand and water to play in

● Take him to the park where he can roll down hills and tumble on the grass

● Dress him in boots and a raincoat and take him out after the rain to jump in puddles

"
I remember a four-year-old girl who had become disruptive as a result of disturbances at home. One morning, after days of unpleasant interruptions to the play of other children, I led her to the task of washing up the paint jars in a sink of warm sudsy water. For most of the morning she presented a picture of deep peace as she was drawn into this work. She asked to continue this activity for each of the next two mornings and toward the end of the week had rejoined the group in a game of make believe with her old harmony."

A teacher

Five years plus

The child now moves into a third phase, the end of which will be marked by the change of teeth (see also p. 32). A crisis may occur at this time. Some children, frequently those who have been the most active and imaginative, may begin to say, "What can I do? I'm bored!" For the moment, the fertile well of imagination has dried up. The child is pausing between one phase and the next, unknowingly waiting for ideas to arise. When they do, he will again be motivated to activity, but from a new source, his awakening ability to think.

Activity aroused by thinking

Before the age of five, the child's activity and fantasy were stimulated from the outside. For example, the four-year-old saw a log and, with his power of fantasy, transformed it into a train. Now play activity will be generated from within, with the Will needing to make an inner effort. An idea, a mental "picture" rather than a visible object, will stir the child to action. The six-year-old begins with, for example, the idea of a train. He looks around for the means to make it, finds a log and adapts it to his needs. At this stage he also discovers the need for friends who will join him in his games, and friendship will become increasingly important. There is no need for parents to be concerned about "sociability" before this time. It is quite natural for under-fives to be content with their own company.

Rest and replenishment

If the child seems to lack ideas we may need to help him to find his way forward. We should resist the temptation to encourage him to re-enter his world of fantasy with suggestions such as: "Why don't you pretend to be Peter Pan?"

▲ **Real responsibility**
Your child can now be led to the idea of taking responsibility for simple tasks. He should feel that these are real and necessary and within his ability.

IDEAS: GIVING YOUR CHILD RESPONSIBILITIES

● He could feed the family pets each day

● He could water the houseplants every week

● He could put food and water out for the birds

● He could do simple dusting

● He could polish

● He could wash the dishes or load the dishwasher

The stages of Will development

In the first seven years the broad stages of Will development may be summarized as follows:

0-3 years	The presence of the other awakens activity (Will) through imitation. The child is all movement
3-4 years	Will-forces meet the Will of the other and conflicts arise
4-5 years	Awakening imagination allows the Will to flow out through the activity of play
5-6 years	The activity of thinking leads the Will into directed activity

What he needs now is physical activity such as woodwork, sewing, simple craft projects, gardening, or baking (see also Chapter 10). This allows for constructive activity until he is ready to move on to the next phase. After this "rest and replenishment", he will again be moved to take action in order to give expression to a specific idea he has had.

Purpose and direction

We now begin to see a specific purpose in what the child sets out to do. He will often say: "I am going to..." or "Let's pretend to...". By having a plan of action, he is less flexible than before and, therefore, open to frustration and disappointment. When he was four, his play was more spontaneous. For example, he could set off on an imaginary train journey on a log and return on an imaginary horse. Now that he is six, he sets out with the specific intention of transforming the log into a train, often with quite definite ideas as to how it should be and, inevitably, because he lacks the necessary skills, he encounters difficulties. He will be grateful if we are willing to help him over these difficulties and by doing so we build a bond of closeness and trust and lay the foundations for his respect toward the adult world (see also p. 83). After the age of five the child has more self-control and self-direction. We can now begin to guide him away from what he thinks he wants to what is actually right or good for both himself and others.

Future Will development

The Will undergoes considerable transformation as the child grows and it can make its own significant contribution toward the potential for human development. Let us imagine Will as a strong force, a possibility for action. Without consciousness, unharnessed by Self, it is chaotic and undisciplined as in early childhood. Its full potential as the force behind purposeful activity is achieved with the transformation brought about by expanding consciousness as the child crosses the threshold into adulthood. The Will may eventually come under the direction of "I", rather than "I" being at the mercy of Will.

A warming "furnace"

Rudolf Steiner described Will as having a sleeping quality, with Feeling having a dreaming nature and Thinking being the waking aspect of our Soul life. In this sense, Willing and Thinking are opposites, with Feeling the warming "furnace" in the middle.

In the beginning, human beings respond to the world partly from an instinct for survival. Hunger leads us to seek food, fear makes us hide. This is an entirely natural, unconscious, force for life. At another level, movement arises out of impulse and desire – the impulse to defy gravity and to stand upright, the desire to eat the cake on the plate. Only during the sixth year, when movement begins to be controlled by consciousness, does it now become appropriate to use the word Will in the sense of conscious Will.

The breakthrough of motivation

The essential factor in this transformation of the Will is the awakening of consciousness. As this consciousness develops a moment will come when the young adult is able to ask himself the

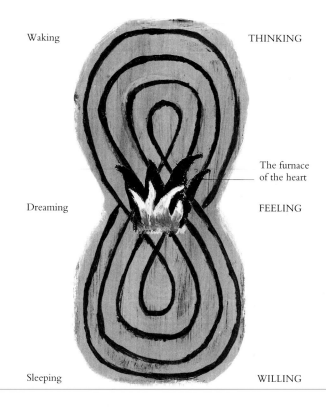

Waking · THINKING

Dreaming · FEELING

The furnace of the heart

Sleeping · WILLING

▲ **The sleeping aspect of the soul**
Willing can be seen as the sleeping aspect of the Soul, opposite a wakeful Thinking, with dreaming Feeling being the central warming "furnace" of the heart.

"
Something which should always stand in front of the soul of (Man) as if in golden letters – that initiative is enshrined in his karma and that much of what meets him in his life depends on the degree to which he is able and willing to become conscious of the power of initiative."

Rudolf Steiner

question, "Why did I do that?" He enters the realm of motive, becoming conscious not only of his activity but of his responsibility for it. He can now choose to take the development of consciousness further. His questions may be followed by a statement of intent, "I wish to do better than this". The next stage is encompassed in the statement, "I shall!"

The potential for change

The willingness and ability to take action, to carry out a conscious act of Will, is linked with the enormous dimensions of karma, for the young adult gradually becomes aware that out of his own Will he can give direction to his life. Perhaps the most useful thing that we can give to our child as he leaves home to make his way in the world is an understanding of cause and effect, of his freedom to make his own judgements and decisions, and his responsibility for his actions. If today's children reach adulthood with strong, healthy Wills, their foundations strengthened in the free activity of early childhood, there is then a prospect for change, a possibility that humankind may turn away from a destructive path and begin to put right the wrongs done to the world. What arises in our thinking, all that stirs in the life of feeling – here then is the possibility for them actually to bear fruit.

The way forward

The wish to build a better world must be met with a firm sense of morality. Our children will need dynamic will-power to shape the world in a positive way. The contemporary inclination toward intellectual advancement at the expense of other aspects of human development, which leads to cold, detached, immoral activity, needs to be softened and warmed with a true education of feelings (see Chapters 20–22).

▼ **The developing Will**
As the Will develops it progresses from instinct, the force for survival, through impulse and desire, motive and choice, and onward toward decision and purpose-filled action.

PURPOSE-FILLED ACTION "I WILL"

WISH
△
CHOOSE
△
MOTIVE
△
DESIRE
△
IMPULSE
△
INSTINCT

Right behaviour

Teaching the child "good" behaviour should be a gradual process. If we begin early enough, in his second year, we can take advantage of his natural inclination to imitate. For example, if we always take care not to leave litter and to close gates behind us in the countryside, these practices will soon become habit in the child too. We should always be aware that the way we speak and what we say will also be imitated, as will our attitude to others and the environment.

When the child reaches adolescence, we can help him to become more conscious of morality by encouraging him to discuss the many issues, such as AIDS and drug-taking, which he will face at that age. All that he has learned since his early childhood will still influence his behaviour, but now he needs to understand the conflict between good and evil.

Responsibility

As a young adult, he will also need to understand the principle of cause and effect in relation to his own free action, and that adulthood calls for responsibility. A true "moral" life comes about when we begin to direct Will from out of thinking; when we are no longer pushed along into mindless activity by our drives and impulses, but take conscious, self-directed action.

Strengthening the Will

By understanding the long-term implications of our will-forces it is natural for us, as parents, to try to ensure that our child grows healthily in this aspect. Some children appear to be born with a particular strength in this direction. Others seem naturally beset by great difficulties. The Will is like a muscle that can be exercised and strengthened even well into adulthood.

▲ **The moral maze**
Developing a moral code to live by – an inbuilt sense of right and wrong – comes from within the child himself and from having imitated and learned from his parents' example.

Positive activity

Since movement is the predominant feature of the child's first seven years, it makes sense to explore all the ways of introducing our children to natural and positive activity.

Within the home parents can explore ways of adapting normal household activity – washing up, polishing, laying the table, and tidying away toys – to include the child, not as chores but as play. Imaginative play, with the right toys, also draws them into positive activity (see p. 253), while outdoors the whole world of Nature calls forth activity (see pp. 256–65).

However the most significant factor in early childhood, from the point of Will development, is the presence of clear rhythms in the life of the child (see p. 237). Everything in the nature of rhythm and repetition strengthens the Will.

A natural childhood provides the foundation needed for movement toward self-realization. A healthy sense-of-self enables each child to eventually sing his own song and to join in the chorus of his fellow beings.

"
You direct the impulse of the Will ... not by telling a child once what the right thing is, but by getting him to do something to-day, and to-morrow and again the day after! The first five years he is not yet 'awake' enough, conscious enough, to be lastingly affected by verbal pleas to do a particular thing – he can't 'hold' on to it. With rhythm and repetition we can gradually work into his consciousness, leading him sympathetically to self-mastery."

Rudolf Steiner,
Waking

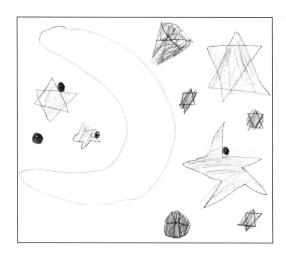

CHAPTER 16

Rhythms in the life of a child

Rhythm and life cannot be separated. Plants, animals, and human beings all reveal rhythmical qualities in form, movement, and growth patterns. Humankind moves through life embraced by great, rhythmical "tides" – the cosmic rhythms of the planets, Nature's rhythms of day, night, and seasons, and the biological rhythms of heart and lungs (see also Chapter 3).

The nature of rhythm

Rhythm is the regular movement between two contrasting, often complementary, states. Rudolf Steiner described learning to "breathe" as one of life's fundamental tasks; not the essential physical task of breathing but the need to live as we breathe, to move rhythmically between contraction and expansion, to find a balance between solitude and companionship.

As parents, we may find it difficult to take time for ourselves, but doing so is far from being a selfish act because, unless we can sometimes draw into ourselves and be refreshed, we cannot do the best for our child (see also p. 88). When, for example, we rest, meditate, read, or walk alone, we contract. We return to ourselves and gather strength. We touch Self and experience our essence, our centre. We gather ourselves in and reach toward our spiritual nature to be refreshed and revitalized. When we expand we go out to meet the world, become social, interacting beings and, by truly knowing ourselves, we more easily relate to others. The understanding of the significance of this activity leads to an important question. How can we go out to meet our companions, give support to our families, if we don't take the time to "fill up"? Then we truly have something to give – a little of ourselves, our stillness. We can then give out a mood of "I am here. Children in particular are reassured by this quality in us.

Stability

Our physical and emotional wellbeing depends upon a balanced interplay between contraction and expansion, between rest and activity, incoming and outgoing. If we remain too long in a state of introspection, we become isolated and self-absorbed, removed from reality. This can cause tension and may eventually lead to emotional and physical disorders. Likewise, if we dwell too long in the "out there" we become formless, removed from our centre, far from "I". We unravel.

Introvert or extrovert

It is important that the child also develops a balance between rest and activity, so that she is always able to face the world with vitality and enthusiasm. But some children do not flow naturally between these two states. We may find that a child is shy and reserved and rarely inclined to be outgoing, or she may be almost breathtaking in her energy and confidence. Until the child is at least seven years old, a rhythmical pattern in her life is essential for her wellbeing. After this age she can begin to adapt to the rhythm imposed by the culture into which she was born, but it is still important for us to help her to achieve and maintain a balance between rest and activity. Establishing a regular routine will help us to lead her toward the necessary balance in a natural, unforced way.

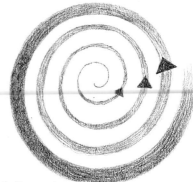

▲ Expansion
As we expand we turn outward to meet the world and become social, interacting, communal beings.

◀ Constant rhythmical exchange
Our physical and emotional wellbeing depends on the constant, rhythmical exchange between contraction and expansion, the steady ebb and flow into and out of ourselves. In this way we truly "live as we breathe".

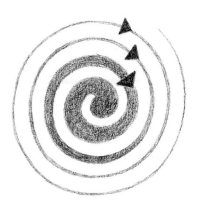

▼ Contraction
In contracting, we turn inward, toward our spiritual nature and gather strength.

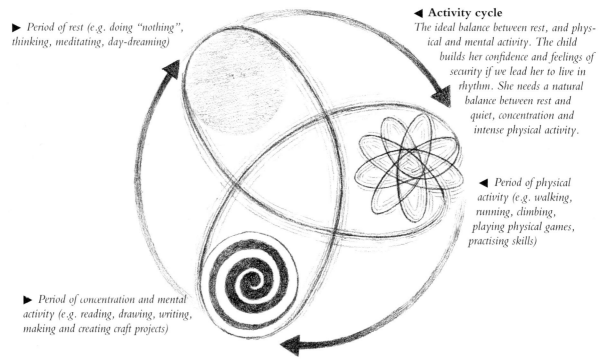

▶ *Period of rest (e.g. doing "nothing", thinking, meditating, day-dreaming)*

◀ **Activity cycle**
The ideal balance between rest, and physical and mental activity. The child builds her confidence and feelings of security if we lead her to live in rhythm. She needs a natural balance between rest and quiet, concentration and intense physical activity.

◀ *Period of physical activity (e.g. walking, running, climbing, playing physical games, practising skills)*

▶ *Period of concentration and mental activity (e.g. reading, drawing, writing, making and creating craft projects)*

The effect of healthy rhythms

Today it is common for children to be involved in a busy timetable of planned activities. Often they are left with little time to "dream" into their surroundings, neither time to linger, nor space for wonder. They quickly lose the ability to be by themselves.

As adults, we know the effects of insufficient sleep, irregular meals, and too much activity. A young child is even more sensitive to such disruptions and can be upset by only very slight alterations to her routine. We need to develop a sense of timing when dealing with young children – for the time to "gather them in" and the time to "let them out" – so that vitality and resistance to illness are strengthened.

Consistency gives a child a comforting sense of security and if we establish a regular rhythm in her life she will learn that there is a right place, a right time, and a right way for everything. Exhausting negotiation between parent and child begins to disappear. But she will not become unimaginative or inflexible. Teachers find that children who have a stable and consistent home-life are the most secure and can deal confidently with the unexpected. By creating parameters, parents allow their children to move happily and freely within safe boundaries.

Building confidence
If the child is nervous and insecure we can help to strengthen her confidence by being consistent. Her trust in the world will deepen with the knowledge that certain things will be the same tomorrow as they were yesterday and today. If, for example, she knows that her father will come up and read her a story every night, she will gradually lose her anxieties and will step out into the world with confidence. As the world

▲ Periods of rest

It is important for the young child to get sufficient sleep, but it is also equally important that she rests from her life of ceaseless activity. She needs to be well-rooted in her daily routine.

"

I well remember when my daughter Sophia spent a day with her much-loved godmother. It was a happy time, filled with activity and fun, thoughtfully provided by the godmother, but five o'clock brought an embarrassing tantrum, simply because she had been allowed to stay too long. The time for my daughter's 'incoming' had been miscalculated."

A parent

becomes familiar to her, and the adults around her reveal themselves to be dependable, her feelings of insecurity will begin to disappear. The principle of keeping the home routine consistent can be applied in the single-parent situation, where it may be of even greater significance.

Without an established balance between rest and activity, a child who is naturally outgoing and energetic can become overtired, and this can often leading to tantrums, hyperactivity, and disturbed sleep. By giving her the security of a regular routine that encourages her to share her time between energetic and more restful activities we prevent the emotional and physical exhaustion that is often at the root of her anti-social behaviour. She will become happier, more contented, and will sleep more peacefully. A rhythmical and secure lifestyle strengthens a child's Will and lays the foundation for her to become a reliable and self-disciplined adult.

Day and night

When the sun has set we turn to sleep and the world of dreams. We turn away from the pull of the outside world and return to ourselves. In the morning, with the return of the sun, we re-enter the world with our day-time consciousness. The moon also casts a spell on the Earth and its inhabitants, through the rhythm of its waxing and waning, the ebb and flow of the sea, and changing weather patterns. In ancient times, people sowed and harvested according to the phases of the moon.

Daily rhythms

Early morning and early evening affect children in different ways. Each part of the day has a particular mood. Morning is more wakeful and a good time for the more energetic activities such as visiting friends or trips to the supermarket. We should devote the afternoon to more restful activity as vitality begins to wane. This is particularly so for the child of school age. Sometimes it may be wiser to have a birthday party at a weekend instead of after school, when there may be little energy left to deal with the excitement.

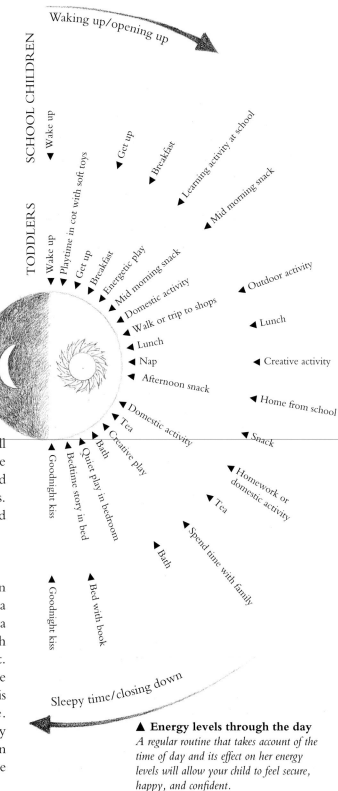

Waking up/opening up

SCHOOL CHILDREN

Wake up
Get up
Breakfast
Learning activity at school
Mid morning snack
Outdoor activity
Lunch
Creative activity
Home from school
Snack
Homework or domestic activity
Tea
Spend time with family
Bath
Bed with book
Goodnight kiss

TODDLERS

Wake up
Playtime in cot with soft toys
Get up
Breakfast
Energetic play
Mid morning snack
Domestic activity
Walk or trip to shops
Lunch
Nap
Afternoon snack
Domestic activity
Tea
Creative play
Bath
Quiet play in bedroom
Bedtime story in bed
Goodnight kiss

Sleepy time/closing down

▲ Energy levels through the day
A regular routine that takes account of the time of day and its effect on her energy levels will allow your child to feel secure, happy, and confident.

The child is particularly sensitive to the thresholds between sleep and waking. As adults, we can choose our bedtime routines. We may, for example, enjoy a warm bath followed by a little reading. In the morning, we may jump straight out of bed on waking, or we may prefer to linger under the warm covers. As parents, we should find ways of ensuring that these times are pleasant experiences for our child too. Transition times, recognized and handled in the right way, can make life run more smoothly.

Familiarity

It is a popular belief that a child needs constant fresh stimulation. The result is a generation of children who need always to be entertained and appear to have few inner resources of their own. In fact, the under-sevens have the ability to make much of little. If we make a habit of taking the child for a walk along the same route every day she will feel happy in the security of familiar surroundings and be fascinated by the subtle changes within the same environment. For example, she might splash in a puddle today and slide on its icy surface tomorrow, or discover the first snowdrop on a familiar piece of ground.

Weekly rhythms

There was a time when every day of the week had its own allocated routine. Monday was washday, the ironing was done on Tuesday, and so on. Today, for most of us, such routines are impossible, but with a little thought we can establish routines to fit with our own lifestyles. For example, if there is only one day in the week when there is time for a leisurely family breakfast, we can make it a special occasion by, perhaps, serving food that the family does not have during the rest of the week. These special family rhythms are welcomed by the child.

IDEAS: **BEDTIME ROUTINES**

A regular routine will make bedtime an enjoyable experience for you and your child and she will make the transition to sleep more easily. You can decide on the sequence of events that most suits your circumstances, and repeat them in the same way each night. For example:

● A warm bath with lots of bubbles, some toys and, perhaps, time to chat

● Into pyjamas, bathrobe, and slippers

● A free time to play quietly in the bedroom

● Into bed with a soft toy for story-time and, perhaps, a prayer or shared thoughts for others

● A goodnight kiss

Seasons and festivals

The whole world is subject to Nature's own wise rhythms. The ever-renewing cycle of the sun's ascent and descent is echoed in the rhythm of sprouting, blossoming, fruiting, and decay. In the seasons we have the contraction of autumn and winter followed by the expansion of spring and summer, and by understanding the seasons' different moods we can learn to live in harmony with them. For the child, these ever-recurring seasonal changes are full of magic and wonder.

Through technology, we can live outside of Nature, no longer subject to her rhythms as we once were. But somewhere within us there continues a deep longing for the peace that arises when we are "in tune" with natural rhythms. We are still deeply affected by the moon's phases and the presence, or absence, of the sun affects our sense of wellbeing. We need now consciously to re-form our connections with Nature in a new way.

The origin of festivals

Since ancient times Nature's rhythms have been the signals for celebration, helping people to deal with their fear of Nature's powers and to express their gratitude for her generosity. At the same time, they established their own personal relationships with Nature and their spiritual selves. Today, these two aspects of festivals have sunk beneath the weight of materialism, so that a modern Christmas can leave us disappointed and cynical. But we can learn to celebrate in a new, conscious way and to re-create beautiful festivals that are full of meaning. Our children can then begin to know the seasons and the rhythmical qualities in Nature, and to respect the hidden side of existence. Festivals raise us above the daily grind, revitalize us, and strengthen communities.

▼ Morning
In spring Nature reawakens. All is fluid, rain falls, streams flow, and outward movement begins.

Spring

EXPANDING

BREATHING IN

Winter

▲ Night
Winter pulls us further inward, back to Self and introspection. Outwardly all is still, but beneath the surface much stirs.

▼ Afternoon

Summer is the time of "letting go". The whole world beckons us away from Self and out into the world of Nature.

Summer

BREATHING OUT

CONTRACTING

Autumn

▲ Evening

Autumn is crisp, alert, and calls for action. This is the time to harvest, store, and prepare for winter.

ACTIVITIES: SEASONAL IDEAS

In every family certain activities can be repeated at the same time each year. The child is reassured by this repetition and enjoys being involved in the tasks. For example:

● Springtime means spring cleaning, planting seeds, storing winter clothes

● Summer calls for outdoor activities such as picnics, trips to the beach, and barbecues

● Autumn and winter are times to gather logs, make jams and preserves, sweep up leaves, stock the bird table, clear the snow, and build snowmen

"

Every year we approach Christmas with the same sequence. The first Advent Sunday sees the arrival of the Advent calendar and the Advent wreath with its four red candles. The second Sunday brings the decoration of an archway with greenery, the third Sunday is dedicated to baking Christmas biscuits and icing the cake, and on the fourth Sunday we collect the Christmas tree, which we decorate on Christmas Eve. Every year there is one new decoration. As the older decorations are lifted out of their boxes, great delight is expressed at discovering old friends. These family traditions may well be re-enacted in the future with grandchildren, and so the rhythm of reassuring family rituals will go on."

A parent

▲ Animal births
Children can witness and accept the birth of animals and birds more easily than they can the birth of a sibling. Or if they visit farms and zoos where new animals are born, they can be aware of the beginnings of life for all the earth's creatures.

Birth and birthdays

The child needs to know the facts about how babies are conceived and born at the right time in her life, but she also needs to know about the spiritual beginnings of life. When a new sibling is expected, she is bound to ask questions about where the baby comes from. We should give her as much information as she needs at the time, but no more. We must know the child and be sufficiently tuned in to her to be aware of what this is (see p. 80). The spiritual aspects of birth can be put across in stories.

People disagree about whether the child should be present at the birth of a brother or sister. But given that the child experiences all

(see p. 80)

IDEAS: SEASONAL BIRTHDAYS

SPRING BIRTHDAYS

● Give bouquets of spring flowers or decorate birthday presents with tiny posies

● Make a birthday cake in the shape of a bird's nest with small sugar eggs in the centre

● Have a kite-flying party

SUMMER BIRTHDAYS

● Give a flower press, or rose or lavender water in coloured glass bottles

● Make a "maypole" birthday cake

● Have a "pizza picnic" party

AUTUMN BIRTHDAYS

● Make a birthday card decorated with leaf stencils and give bowls of bulbs that will flower in spring

● Make a birthday cake with seasonal fruits such as apples or blackberries

● Have a bonfire party and make pumpkin lanterns

WINTER BIRTHDAYS

● Decorate parcels and birthday cards with sprigs of holly

● Make a "snowman" birthday cake

● Play party games such as *Here We Go Round the Mulberry Bush*, and serve hot mincemeat pies and fruit punch

events out of a different consciousness than ours, the birth experience is very likely to be far too intense for her. The normal sights and sounds of birth may be misinterpreted by her. And if we want her to have a spiritual view of the world, this very physical experience may weaken it.

A positive experience

There are other ways we can make the child feel included in the arrival of a new sibling. For example, she can help in the preparation of the clothes and the cradle, and perhaps find one of her old baby toys to give to the baby. She can be brought in to see the new baby just after the birth, and perhaps she can find a gift "from the baby" in the cradle. All these things will make birth a positive experience for her.

"

… in a family of five children the grand-mother had died…. The difference in each child's attitude could be seen clearly, showing what stage of maturity the soul life of each had reached. While the four year old was soon back in the sandpit and lost in play, the nine year old took every-thing in very attentively and clearly real-ized that she could not be sad in the same way as the adults. Deep inside, she knew that Grandmother would not come back and had died but she could give very little expression to this feeling. The reaction of the twelve year old was different… she remembered her last meeting with her grandmother… her eyes filled with tears… The inexorability and yet also exaltedness of death remained in her soul for days."

Dr. Michaela Glöckler,
A Guide to Child Health

Death

It is inevitable that, at some time, the child will experience the death of others, and we need to be aware that she does not think and feel as we do. She will, of course, be affected by the absence of the one who has died, but before the age of seven, death itself will not cause the concern that it does in older children. "Forever" has no real meaning for the young child. Before the ninth birthday she is quite likely to view death as a type of sleeping or "somewhere else", where normal activity, such as playing, continues. In general, she will respond to a death differently, according to her stage of development and, depending on our personal beliefs, it can be an opportunity to bring the spiritual and physical levels of existence together for her. The child can readily accept, "He is with the angels", as the picture comes within her view of reality. She will also accept an honest, "I don't know".

Acknowledging feelings

The child may need to be assured that she is not in any way at fault. It is also important to accept any fears or sadness that may be expressed. We should not try to talk her out of these expressions, but nor should we attempt to force such expressions if she does not show them. If you feel strongly that your child should attend a funeral, make sure that an adult is asked to look after her if, for example, she wishes to leave. An alternative is a special commemoration at home with a sharing of positive memories.

When burying pets, our own behaviour is important. The child can help in the preparation of a special box for the dead pet and, in choosing a song or prayer for the burial, she can witness our respectful attitude and take comfort in putting flowers on the grave.

CHAPTER 17

Sharing Nature with children

"The child is soft, his flesh is tender. Sun, moon, rain, wind and silence all descend upon him. The child devours the world greedily, assimilates it and turns it into a child. I remember sitting on the doorstep of our home when the Greek sun was blazing, the world fragrant with basil and lemon. Shutting my eyes I would hold out my palms and wait. God always came – as long as I remained a child. He never deceived me – he always came, a child like myself, and deposited his toys in my hands – sun, moon, wind, silence. Though I did not know this I possessed the Lord's omnipotence: I created the world as I wanted it. I was soft dough: so was the world." Nikos Kazantzakis, *Report to Greco*

Wonder and reverence

In this statement Kazantzakis beautifully describes the child's relationship to Nature. His openness to all that surrounds him allows him to be deeply impressed by his experiences. He has no need to approach Nature intellectually, but stands comfortably at the centre of the experience. He is spared the unsettling experience of being "other than" the natural world and so can live within it without question. Because of his sensitivity to sensory impressions, he is richly nourished by Nature's sounds, smells, and forms.

To a young child the world of Nature is truly magical. He is filled with wonder at the power of the wind, the sight of the reappearing sun, the sighting of the first snowdrop. By cherishing and nurturing the child's ability to experience wonder we are laying a foundation for his spirituality as an adult. Wonder leads us to consider our spiritual nature and allows us to be astounded by what we may meet in that spiritual search. Without it we fall into cynicism and materialism.

Respect for the earth

The child can learn to love and respect the earth by following our example. We need not go into lengthy explanations about why we build a compost heap or recycle paper. By seeing us do these things, he will know instinctively that it is right.

Picture-filled language

The child's sense of wonder and reverence toward Nature will be greatly enhanced if we use imaginative, pictorial language. For the under-sevens scientific explanations mean far less than a language filled with "pictures".

We can tell the child that he mustn't walk on the grass because the "seed babies" are "sleeping", or explain that Jack Frost can't harm the bulbs he has just planted because they are safely tucked up in their earthy "beds" for winter. This type of response works in harmony with his consciousness and will nourish his imagination. For example, a young girl was delighted by the suggestion that the stars were holes left in the sky by God's walking stick while, for another, the rain was "angels' tears" and thunder and lightning were "King Winter's" temper tantrum.

"

Three-year-old Oliver was sitting on the sofa while I busied myself with the washing up. Suddenly he asked dreamily: 'Why does the sun go away sometimes?' I replied: "At the end of the day he goes to sleep, and so do we. In the morning he comes to shine on us again and then we wake up". Oliver nodded contentedly with this explanation and then added: 'Sometimes he plays peek-a-boo behind the clouds. He's not sleeping then, just playing about!"'

A teacher

"

The kindergarten group was having a snack. Not far away was a seasonal display. A King Winter figure, with four 'seed baby' figures at his feet, was arranged in the alcove. Hannah suddenly noticed all this. 'Who's that?' I replied; 'That's King Winter'. 'What's he doing?' 'He's taking care of the seed babies.' A draught came down the chimney and created movement in the backdrop to this scene. 'What's that then?' asked Lana. Hannah replied: 'Oh that's Brother Wind. He's come to chat to King Winter. They're good friends.'"

A teacher

IDEAS: **THE EXPERIENCE OF NATURE**

● In spring, make kites (p. 250) and Chinese lanterns (p. 257). Sing songs and read poems about rain, cuckoos, and daffodils

● In summer, collect shells and driftwood. Gather lavender and rose petals to make herb pillows

● In autumn, collect leaves to make leaf prints (see p. 249). Make corn dollies. Sing songs about harvest and falling leaves

● In winter, make a bird table and bird-box. Read stories about Jack Frost and the Snow Queen

The four elements

Nowhere does Mother Nature reveal herself more clearly to a young child than through the elements – earth, wind, water, and fire. To the child these four expressions of Nature come alive as "Mother Earth", "Brother Wind", "Sister Rain", and the fiery "King Sun". With careful adult supervision there are many ways in which the child can safely experience the four elements and enjoy positive activity within Nature throughout the year.

▼ Earth

The earth yields many secrets. It holds the seed world and cradles spring bulbs. It hides fossils, offers shelter to insects and worms, and provides homes for a whole world of creatures. Mud dams rivers, makes "pies", and squishes exquisitely between the toes. Dry sand trickles, and tells the time in egg-timers. Wet sand makes castles, fortresses, moats, bridges, and tunnels. The child "at work" in mud and sand is naturally an architect, effortlessly a sculptor.

ACTIVITIES: MUD AND SAND

- Dress your child according to the season. He needs a warm coat, hat, and boots in winter; cool clothes, a sun hat, and sun screen in summer (see p. 284)

- Let him dig in the garden, discovering the creatures that live in the soil, and making mud cakes and pies

- Pieces of rope, logs, planks, and old wooden boxes have endless possibilities

- Give him old saucepans, spoons, and plastic jugs and pots for play in the sandbox

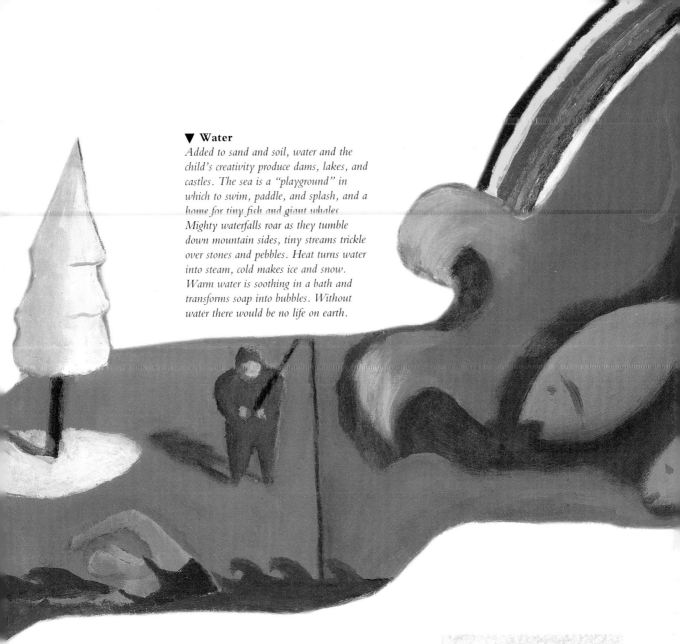

▼ Water

Added to sand and soil, water and the child's creativity produce dams, lakes, and castles. The sea is a "playground" in which to swim, paddle, and splash, and a home for tiny fish and giant whales. Mighty waterfalls roar as they tumble down mountain sides, tiny streams trickle over stones and pebbles. Heat turns water into steam, cold makes ice and snow. Warm water is soothing in a bath and transforms soap into bubbles. Without water there would be no life on earth.

PROJECT: WATER WORLD

● Put a few rocks and large pebbles in an old basin

● Collect some moss and pat it firmly on to the rocks to form islands

● Add water to come halfway up the rocks. Sail boats made from walnut shells or pieces of bark (see right)

PROJECT: WALNUT AND BARK BOATS

● Choose a perfect half shell and cut a sail from thin card. Pierce it through with a toothpick and stick it into the bottom of the shell with modelling clay

● Find a suitable piece of bark, a small twig for a mast and a large leaf. Pierce the leaf with the twig and stick it to the bark with modelling clay (see also p. 253)

▲ Air

Children are fascinated by the power of the wind, and thrilled by the sensation of flying through the air on a swing. The wind can strip the leaves from the trees and blow them along like crowds of twirling dancers, or take balloons and delicate bubbles on a gentle, bobbing flight. Sometimes it whistles through keyholes, moans in chimneys, and slams doors. At other times it is playful and takes kites high up into the sky only to drop them again without warning.

PROJECT: SIMPLE KITE

● Take two pieces of thin dowel, one about two-thirds the length of the other. Form a cross; bind together with string

● Cut notches in the ends of the dowels. Stretch string around the frame, through all the notches

● Draw around the frame on to a piece of paper or plastic and cut round, leaving a border

● Fold in the borders and tape them down. Tape the dowels to the kite

● Add a tail of twists of paper tied to string. Make a string loop between the top and bottom of the long dowel and tie the flying string a third of the way down it

"
Mother Earth Mother Earth
Take our seed and give it birth
Father Sun gleam and glow
Until the roots begin to grow
Sister Rain Sister Rain
Shed thy tears to swell the grain
Brother Wind breathe and blow
Then the blade so green will grow
Earth and Sun and Wind and Rain
Turn to gold the living grain
The Wind will blow
The Rain will flow
The Sun will glow
Mother Earth Mother Earth
Take our seed and give it birth."

Adapted from a poem by
E. Hutchins

ACTIVITY: **FUN WITH FIRE**
Warning: *ajlways supervise your*
child wherever there is fire.
● With extra-long matches she
can safely learn to light candles
or fires by herself

● Organize a family gathering
around a campfire or barbecue.
Cook potatoes in foil, chestnuts,
corn-on-the-cob, and marsh-
mallows on sticks

● Make a lantern from a
hollowed-out pumpkin

▲ Fire
Humankind has long considered the
hearth to be the heart of the home. In
many cultures people give gifts of coal or
wood to symbolize prosperity. Fireworks,
lanterns, and bonfires feature in celebra-
tions and festivals around the world and
candles are an essential part of countless
religious ceremonies. Fire lights our way
in the dark, protects us from the cold, and
cooks our food. When primitive people
harnessed the fiery element they took their
first step toward civilization.

The seasonal table

Making a seasonal table will help the child to become aware of changes that take place in Nature from one season to another. On a small table, a shelf, or a window ledge, we can create a scene which changes slowly throughout the year.

In winter, for example, a King Winter figure can sit on a "throne" with crystals at his feet and some jars of winter flowers. A few weeks later he makes way for Lady Spring, surrounded by paper butterflies and fluffy woollen "chicks".

The summer scene might have a paper sun and handmade bees on bunches of fresh herbs and bright flowers. This is followed by bowls of nuts, dried beans, and grains alongside rosehips, dried seed heads, and branches of colourful leaves to represent autumn and the harvest.

▲ **A spring tableau**
Choose fabrics in yellows, greens, and violets. Add decorated eggs – symbols of rebirth – fresh spring flowers, and moss.

◄ **A winter tableau**
Decorate with fabrics in cool, winter colours. Light candles at special times and arrange evergreen branches all around.

PROJECT: SEASONAL TABLE

You will need:
● A background cloth for each season: deep blue for winter, yellow for spring, rose-pink for summer, orange for autumn

● A candle to light on birthdays

● Bare branches in winter, flowers in summer, coloured eggs in spring, and berries in autumn

● A seasonal picture: a snow scene in winter, chicks in spring, the beach in summer, an autumn woodland scene

● Dolls dressed as King Winter and Lady Spring

Toys from Nature

If the child's imagination is not thwarted by early intellectuality and materialism he will use it to transform the ordinary into the extraordinary. He will find endless possibilities for shells, smooth pebbles, driftwood, or autumn leaves. These "treasures" from Nature will be transformed again and again by his powers of fantasy. Today, he may make chestnuts into a necklace, and tomorrow they may appear as money in a game of shopping, or potatoes in a pot. Soil and sand are moved, dug, remoulded by the child and bakeries and rivers miraculously appear. He will move logs with great determination and lay planks in a certain way so that a "ship" can set sail. These activities make sense to the child, and are deeply satisfying (see also p. 142).

▲ Treasures
Children will transform simple, natural things such as leaves, bark, shells, weeds, and seeds into a multitude of functional and decorative objects.

IDEAS: NATURAL TOYS

● Strips of bark, leaves, and twigs make boats (see p. 249)

● Sea shells make dolls' cups, sand-cake decorations, and mosaics

● Daisy-like flowers make neck-laces and posies (see p. 258)

● Non-poisonous petals in water make soups and perfumes

● Honesty (*Lunaria*) seed heads become money, fairy wings, dolls' plates, mirrors, or even rafts or earrings (see p. 263)

Preparing for festivals

In the past when we were much closer to Nature and the heavens than we are now, people could enter into the celebration of their festivals in an unconscious, almost childlike, way. Today, we need to understand the meaning behind each festival in order to be nourished by the experience. Out of this understanding, we can find the right symbols to express our feelings and show our understanding in a creative way. We must realize that the young child, certainly up to the age of nine, does not need to understand the festival, but needs only to experience it. It is enough that he is active in its celebration. He needs a doing/experiencing entry into each festival.

(N.B. All seasons relate to the northern hemisphere, so festivals take place in the opposite season in the southern hemisphere.)

QUESTIONS: FESTIVALS

Finding anwers to these questions will help you and your family enjoy festivals to the full.

● What does this festival mean? What are its origins and what does it celebrate? How can my family relate to it?

● What is happening in Nature at this festival time and how do our celebrations reflect this?

● What symbols are appropriate to this festival and how can I help my family display them to the best advantage?

Spring festivals

Spring festivals celebrate victory and rebirth: the victory of the light and goodness of spring over the darkness and evil of winter, and the rebirth of Nature. Teng Chieh, the Chinese Lantern Festival, marks the beginning of spring, and at Holi, the Hindu Festival of Colours, a bonfire celebrates the triumph of good Prince Prahlad over evil Princess Holika. For Jews around the world Purim, the March Festival of Lots, celebrates their victory over the villainous Haman, and Buddhists in Thailand greet the May full moon with garlands of lotus flowers symbolizing purity and truth. The Christian Easter Festival, celebrating the resurrection of Christ, has its roots in ancient celebrations of rebirth and fertility.

Summer festivals

Summer is the time for celebrating the fullness of life and the power of the sun. Since the times of the Ancient Incas, Peruvians have lit bonfires to honour the sun at the festival of Inti Raymi. In Britain, Morris Dancers dress in white and dance the "union of sky and earth" in honour of the White Goddess. The July Tanabata festival in Japan celebrates the reunion of separated lovers, with paper decorations and fireworks. In August, Sikhs and Hindus reaffirm love between brothers and sisters at Raksha Bandhan, and Muslims celebrate the birthday of the Prophet Muhammad. This is the season for Christian pilgrimages to the shrine of St Bernadette at Lourdes and for the midsummer Festival of St John.

▲ **The Advent wreath**
Christians light one candle in the Advent wreath on each of the four Sundays before Christmas to herald the birth of Christ on Christmas Day.

Autumn festivals

Autumn thanksgiving celebrations and festivals of light have their roots in ancient times. In the USA Thanksgiving celebrates harvest and also a new beginning in a new land. During Succot, the Jewish Harvest Festival, a special shelter is built (see p. 261) and fruit and vegetables are hung from the walls. In Britain, the Christian All Hallows began as a Celtic bonfire festival to the sun god and later incorporated the Roman celebration of Pomona, the goddess of fruit. A model of a Viking ship is burned in Up-Helly-Aa, the fire festival of the Shetland islanders, and in India, Hindus celebrate Divali by lighting Diva lamps in every window and praying to Lakshmi, the goddess of wealth.

Winter festivals

The tradition of a god born in the middle of winter is an ancient belief based on the returning power of the sun and the lighting of candles is an important ritual. When the Ancient Romans celebrated the birth of the Time Lord Saturn, at Saturnalia, candles were lit to keep evil spirits at bay. Hanukkah, the Jewish Festival of Lights, centres around a nine-branched candlestick, and Christmas celebrations begin in early December with the lighting of the first Advent candle. In many cultures, the New Year is celebrated in winter and wishes of good fortune are expressed. In China, pictures of fat babies and carp signify wealth and abundance and in Scotland lumps of coal symbolize comfort and plenty.

Spring

As the sun slowly begins its upward journey after the darkness of winter we enter the ascending cycle of the seasons. Spring is the morning of the year, when Nature awakens from her winter sleep and greets the returning sun with green shoots and the first spring flowers. It is the season of expansion and outflowing from the inward-ness of winter. This is the time to take the child out into Nature to witness the resurrection of the autumn-planted bulbs. It is the time for him to sow seeds and to see for himself the miracle of germination and growth.

▲ Involved in planting
A young child plants seed potatoes with her parent's help. In doing so she witnesses Nature in activity.

***PROJECT*: GERMINATING SEEDS**

● A few seeds of mustard and cress or alfalfa will quickly ger-minate on a piece of wet cloth on a sunny window ledge

● Sow some large seeds, such as runner beans, singly in small fibre pots. When the seeds have germinated their roots will grad-ually penetrate the damp fibre

● Grow a variety of seeds in a window box and observe varia-tions in the plants' growth rates

● With a small plot of his own the child will learn about planting, weeding, watering, composting, and the vital role of insects in the growth cycle

● If he saves some seeds from his flowers, he can plant them next spring and begin again

▲ Waking up
Bulbs and seeds planted in autumn are resurrected from their earthy beds by the ever-increasing warmth of the spring sun.

***PROJECT*: SPRING CLEANING**

Teach your child to care for the environment by involving him in spring cleaning.

● Clear the kitchen cupboards of all out-of-date foodstuffs. Empty jars, bottles, and packets on to the compost heap. Save tins and glass for recycling

● Remove buttons and zippers from unwanted clothing made from natural fibres such as wool or cotton. Tear the clothing into small pieces, add to the compost. Reuse the buttons and zippers

● Collect old newspapers and magazines for your compost heap or for recycling

PROJECT: DECORATED EGGS

● Dye eggs by boiling them in water and vinegar with natural dyes such as onion skins, turmeric (yellow), spinach (green), or beetroot (red)

● Decorate blown eggs with acrylic paint by dabbing on different colours with a small, damp sponge

● For a pretty marbled effect, stick tiny pieces of wet, coloured tissue to the shell. Peel it off when dry

● Paint blown eggs with enamel paint. When dry, glue a sprig of fennel or other fine-leaved herb to the shell with PVA adhesive

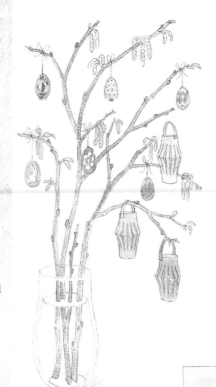

PROJECT: PAPER LANTERNS

As used at Teng Chieh, the Chinese lantern festival.

● Decorate a rectangular piece of paper with crayons and fold it in half lengthways

● Cut straight or wavy lines from the folded edge half-way to the opening

● Unfold the paper and glue the two short edges together

● Attach a narrow strip of paper to make a handle

Summer

Summer is Nature's season of growth. Flowers bloom, nestlings fly, and fruits swell on the trees. It is the season for visits to the beach to hear the sound of the waves, to watch the sun dance on the water, and to gather shells. In the countryside everything is green and hedgerows teem with bees and butterflies. Sweetly scented herbs fill the air and can be gathered and dried to preserve the memory of summer. At the height of summer, the child will enjoy camping out under the stars. He will be fascinated by the sky and the sounds of Nature's night creatures.

**"
July**

The earth no longer laboured; shaded lay
The sweet-breathed kine, across the sunny vale,
From hill to hill the wandering rook did sail,
Lazily croaking, amidst his dreams of spring,
Nor more awake the pink-foot dove did cling
Unto the beech-bough, murmuring now and then;
All rested but the restless sons of men,
And the great sun that wrought this happiness,
And all the vale with fruitful hopes did bless.

William Morris

A time to open out

The days start to lengthen and sleeping winter gives way to waking spring. The world begins to expand and stretch itself. Colour begins to enliven the outdoor world and all living things unfold and unfurl. The air is full of promise, hope, and new life.

▼ Nature's jewels
The delicate flowers of spring come early, before the leaves appear to shade the woodland floor. Subtle blues, pinks, and yellows are the jewels of the natural world. We can gather a basketful and transform the flower heads into garlands.

▲ **Breathing out**
*Sap rises in the trees, feeding the buds,
which swell, become fat, and burst to
reveal their colourful riches. In the soil
seeds germinate, push down, then up.*

▼ **New life**
*Eggs, the symbol of life, hope, and a fresh
start can be decorated for Easter celebrations. We can boil them in onion skins to
give a lovely ochre colour or wrap them
in wet tissue paper to give a marbled
effect (see also p. 257).*

▶ **A time for summer**
*Warm weather and free time give children
the chance to be close to water, pebbles,
rocks, and shells.*

PROJECT: WINDMILL

● Make a 4in (10cm) cut from
each corner toward the centre of
an 8in (20cm) square card

● Decorate the four sections and
fold every other corner into the
middle

● Push a tack through the centre
of the card and hold it in place
with a small cork

● Press the point of the tack into
a length of thin dowel, about
1in (2.5cm) from the top

PROJECT: POT POURRI

● Mix 1pt (½ litre) dried, scented rose petals and herbs such as
lavender and rosemary, ½ tsp
each of ground lemon peel, cin-
namon, and cloves, and 3 bay
leaves

● Sprinkle one tablespoon of
uniodized salt over a 1in (2cm)
layer of the mixture in an
airtight container

● Repeat to fill the container.
Leave in a warm dark place for
about a month

Autumn

As the year begins its descent toward winter it is time for all Nature's creatures to prepare for the lean times ahead. We can watch small animals gathering provisions for their winter larder, and flocks of migrating birds hurrying away in pursuit of the sun. We can collect dead wood and branches for the winter fire or for a bonfire, and leaves, nuts, pinecones, and seed heads for decorations. At home it is time to plant the bulbs that will announce Nature's awakening in spring.

▲ A time for autumn
When days shorten and Nature starts to prepare for winter, children enjoy playing in fallen leaves.

PROJECT: A HARVEST HOUSE

As used at Succot, the Jewish harvest festival.

● Cut one long side from an empty cardboard box

● Decorate the box, inside and out, with pictures of vegetables and fruit

● Put in a table and chairs from a dolls' house (see p. 151)

● Spread twigs and leaves on the top of the box to form a roof

● Hang small bunches of fruit, such as grapes or redcurrants, from the "ceiling"

PROJECT: HIBERNATION BOX

● Cut a hole 5in (12cm) square in one side of an old wooden box. Make a wooden lid

● Fill the box with dried leaves, grass, or straw and put it in a sheltered corner

● Occasionally, in mild, dry weather, lift the lid to see if a small animal has taken up residence for hibernation

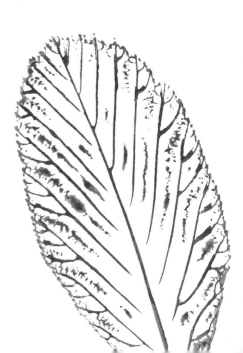

A time to gather in

As summer gives way to autumn, Nature provides for the dark winter days ahead with grapes and rosehips for wines and cordials to comfort us in the cold, and holly and mistletoe to brighten our homes.

▼ Winter preparations

In a pageant of russets and gold, Nature bids farewell to summer and turns to nurturing the new life that sleeps beneath the soil. With a carpet of fallen leaves she provides warmth and shelter for her "seed babies", and replenishes her "larder" of leaf mould that will feed the young plants as they emerge in spring. Gather the prettiest leaves and preserve the glory of autumn in leaf prints and stencils (see also p. 149).

▶ The vital larder

Seed heads and nuts sustain birds and animals through the lean times of winter and hold the promise of continuing life on earth. Gather Honesty (Lunaria) seeds to make fairies and festive angels, dried grasses and poppy seed heads for winter bouquets, and sweet chestnuts to roast on winter evenings.

▲ The winter "waiting room"

As the year draws to a close, Nature's promise of spring is carried in pod and bud. Winter blossom brightens the bare landscape, new leaves and flowers wait to burst forth to welcome the first life-giving rays of sunshine, and the unchanging cycle of life continues.

PROJECT: LAMP

As used at Divali, the Hindu festival of lights.

● Roll out a small ball of clay and smooth out a hole big enough to take a small candle

● Leave the clay to dry, then decorate with coloured paints

Winter

On cold winter days, when outdoors seems uninviting, there are many indoor craft projects for the child to enjoy. With adult help he can make scented candles to light on special family occasions, or cut pretty snowflakes from silver foil to hang in the window. This is the time of year to spare a thought for the birds, and put out a few scraps of food to sustain them through the bitter weather. In return, they will provide hours of entertainment for the whole family.

PROJECT: POTATO LATKES

Pancakes, as eaten at Hanukkah.

● Grate 3 large potatoes and a small onion into a bowl. Add 2 eggs, 2 tablespoons of flour, and 1 teaspoon of salt and mix

● Fry spoonsful of the mixture on both sides in a little hot oil in a frying pan

● Serve hot with apple sauce

PROJECT: CHRISTINGLE

A Christian custom ("Christ-light") to celebrate God's gifts at any time of year.

● Cut a small cross in the top of an orange. Cover the cut with a 3in (7cm) square of aluminum-foil. Push a candle into the cut

● Push dried fruits and nuts on to 4 cocktail sticks and insert them into the orange. Tie a ribbon around the orange

PROJECT: WINTER BOUQUET

● With silver paint, spray 3, 24in (60cm) branches of blue pine, and some twigs (with cones attached)

● Tie the branches and twigs together at one end

● Using three lengths of narrow ribbon in pink, red, and silver, make a long-tailed bow and attach it to cover the join

● Decorate the branches with small bunches of red and pink Helichrysum (everlasting)

▲ **A time for winter**
Wrapped up warmly, children enjoy all the activities associated with snow and ice.

PROJECT: WINDOW LEDGE BIRD TABLE

● Offer different foods and scraps to attract a variety of birds and always provide water

● Always include foods with a high fat content such as bacon rinds or cheese

● Make a "bird cake" by mixing kitchen scraps, peanuts, and bird seed with melted fat. Pour into half a coconut shell threaded with string and leave to solidify

● Never serve stale peanuts. They can prove fatal to birds. Make sure your bird table is kept well stocked in winter

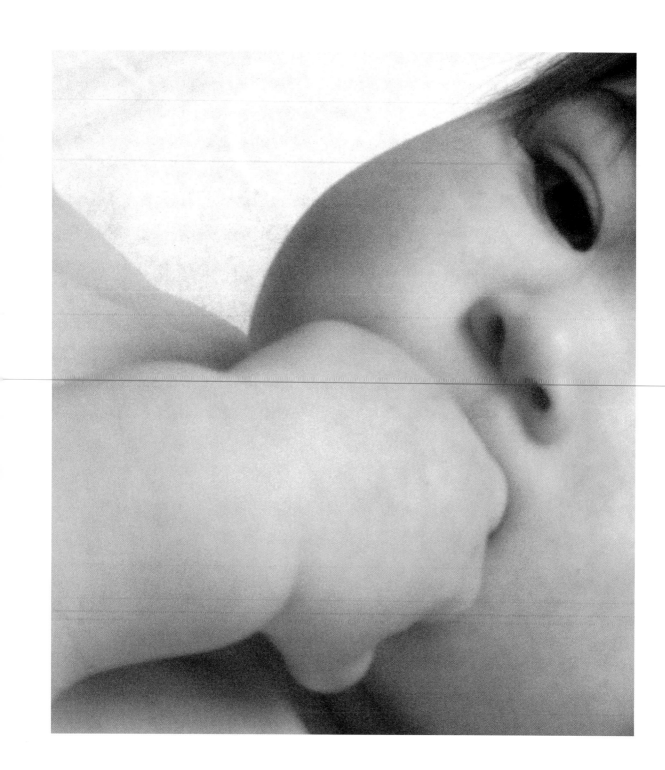

PART 5

HEALTH AND HEALING

Dr Michaela Glöckler

*A*s human beings we are all engaged in the process of ongoing physical, psychological, and emotional development. Childhood constitutes only the first, but certainly the most dramatic, of these stages.

How can we gain meaningful insight into those early stages in their varied aspects, and what role do, for instance, childhood illnesses play? Considering immunization, what is help and what is more of a hindrance for the developing child? When is fever our friend and when does it turn out to be our enemy? How should we deal with sleep problems? How do we ensure our child has a nutritionally balanced diet? How can we accompany a child on his way to becoming a free individual with a free relationship to his possible constitutional one-sidedness? How can medical insight support a natural education?

In this section these and other questions are explored and discussed, to enable parents to find their own relationship to these issues, and to find their own solutions to the many practical problems they are faced with in real life.

CHAPTER 18

Illnesses of childhood

It is only since the 19th and 20th centuries that Western medical practice has been based on a knowledge of the physical body, gained by observation and experimentation. Before this time, healing took into account the soul and the spirit, too. Today, this disregard is increasingly recognized as being to the detriment of health and healing and there is a revival of ancient medical traditions such as acupuncture, herbalism, and ayurveda. But there are also new ways to integrate the spiritual being of man into medicine, for example anthroposophical medicine, which was developed by Rudolf Steiner and Ita Wegman in the 1920s.

Gradual recognition

The multiplicity of medical traditions being revived today reflects our multicultural society and the general quest in society for a "better way". Many leading representatives of orthodox medicine recognize this trend and state-funded scientific research programmes are investigating so-called alternative or complementary medical therapies. Hence contemporary medicine stands at the threshold of a major process of integration in a now pluralistic medical science.

The concern of anthroposophical medicine is to achieve such an integrated medical science. It does not reject other methods of treatment but attempts to show their value and where they are placed in the overall context of a truly human-centred medical science. Orthodox medicine, in particular, is fully recognized as a science of the physical body. And when it is complemented by Rudolf Steiner's research in the field of life functions, the Soul, and the Spirit (see chart opposite), it provides a good starting point for an integrated medical science.

The four constituent levels

Anthroposophic medicine describes four constituent levels of the human being: the physical body, the etheric body, the astral body, and the "I". In healthy people, these levels interact more or less harmoniously in delicate equilibrium. In illness, this equilibrium is disturbed and needs to be re-established. The level from which the healing process is initiated will determine the range of therapeutic possibilities.

> *… the Vital Force is working in the plant, in the animal, in the human body, and produces the phenomena of life, just as the magnetic force is present in the magnet producing the phenomena of attraction."*
>
> Rudolf Steiner,
> *The Education of the Child*

> *… only the physical body becomes completely independent at birth and there is a kind of birth of the etheric body around seven, of the astral body around 14 and the ego at about 21."*
>
> Dr Michael Evans and Iain Rodger,
> *Anthroposophical Medicine*

> *Anthroposophy – from the Greek Anthropos (man) + sophia (wisdom) – is the name Steiner gave to his world-view."*
>
> Lois Cusick,
> *Waldorf Parenting Handbook*

Physical level (physical body)

Knowledge of the physical body comes from investigations in contemporary scientific medicine. Its therapeutic focus is surgery, intensive care, substitutive medication (replacement of missing substances through infusion or oral therapy), first aid, and the management of acute states.

Life functions level (etheric body)

This level is an understanding of the distinct qualities of life which cannot be analyzed in the same way as inert matter. These qualities alter the way physical substances work in the body and provide the link for all living entities to each other in the environment and the macrocosm. Life means the maintenance of complex interactions, functions, and rhythms which defy the tendency to death and decay of the physical body.

Soul level (astral body)

This level is the science of human consciousness and its laws as the basis of Thinking, Feeling, and Willing. The life of the soul is based on these activities, characterized by the polarities: conscious/unconscious, antipathy/sympathy, thinking/willing.

Spiritual level (the "I")

The "I" or ego is the power of integration and is linked to the forces working in every being and in the relationships between them. In ancient cultures spiritual therapies acted through incantations and ritual, when the "I" liberated itself from the body in ecstatic states or ritual sleep in temples. We should actively prepare to cross the threshold to the spiritual world consciously as a means of supporting our health.

"Cultural" childhood

"Natural childhood" is really "cultural childhood", for nothing in the human being can remain simply natural. We have to learn all the specifically human attributes, and this includes the preservation of health.

We are born without the three fundamental prerequisites of human behaviour: upright posture with the capacity to move freely, language, and thinking. These are not genetically inherited abilities. Quite the opposite. We acquire them throughout childhood in active and sometimes difficult learning processes. We inherit only the learning faculty – the possibility to learn these abilities – not the abilities themselves.

The imperfect human

Each human being is unique. We are all imperfect and we vary enormously in terms of our ability, behaviour, and learning ability. No person has ever been able to say of herself that she is perfect in the way that we can say this of an animal, say a pedigree dog. Who, after all, has ever been able to bring all possible human faculties to real perfection in the course of one lifetime? Even the most outstanding representatives of mankind, such as great poets and philosophers, admit most freely what is still lacking in their human development.

Thus it is a central part of being human that we will repeatedly experience ourselves as frail and imperfect: as "ill". In illness, we become a physical picture of what we still have to learn. In health, by contrast, we have an image of the perfection we will achieve in the far distant future. The healthy body is an image of the nature of human beings: upright, open, exercising free choice, with the heart in the middle and all forces working in the right place and at the

appropriate time, well ordered and controlled. Furthermore, as human beings we can have experiences through suffering and pain, provoking new questions and learning processes that transform us as individuals.

Ongoing development

Human beings show that the process of creation is not yet complete. Whereas many animals and plants have already been forced out of the human environment as a result of the ecological crisis and have sometimes been driven to extinction, we human beings are spreading all over the earth and demonstrating through our behaviour that we are still in a process of development. We even have to learn to preserve our environment on earth so that we can complete our development as individuals through learning.

QUESTIONS: CHOOSING PREVENTIVE MEASURES

When thinking about treating a particular child with preventive measures or a choice of therapy an anthroposophic paediatrician asks a number of questions:

● How can I strengthen the personality of the child through the measures I take?

● How do I support the child's own activity?

● What does the child need for her physical, psychological, and spiritual wellbeing?

● How do I help the child to use her body skilfully, to come to terms with it, and to learn to handle it?

● How do I activate the child's willingness to learn?

● How do I capture the child's attention and her interest?

▲ **Learning processes**
We are all born with the capability to learn, although the learning process may sometimes be difficult. This learning of skills continues throughout our lives and is part of our individual development.

"
Obviously, man is related to the animals, yet he is no naked ape. He belongs to a different species altogether, to the family of man. The human being, from the moment of fertilization onwards, has a different origin and different destiny from the animals…It is of the greatest significance."

Joan Salter,
The Incarnating Child

"
Man reveals his spiritual nature inasmuch as he is a thinking being: by thinking about his perceptions he acquires knowledge of his environment, and by reflecting about his actions he is empowered to introduce a reasonable coherence into his life."

Gilbert Childs,
Steiner Education in Theory and Practice

What does fever mean?

Feverish illnesses are a normal part of childhood and adolescence. Modern immunological research has reaffirmed the old folk wisdom that fever has meaning that contributes to healthy development. Today, we know the extent to which the physiological processes connected with fevers help activate the immune system and its development during childhood and adolescence. We human beings reach full immunity when we are able to deal with pathogens and harmful influences without developing illness.

Effects on the immune system

The immunological resistance of the child has further training with every fever that her body's own warmth regulation mechanisms successfully cope with. At the same time, fever stimulates and develops her immunological functions. Her immune system retains the ability to learn and adapt throughout her life and can even work as far as her genes, where it can induce new combinations and recombinations of genetic responses and reaction patterns.

This is borne out by the experience of many parents and doctors who have observed the strong degree to which the child can change, even to the extent of her outward appearance, through a pronounced illness such as measles, scarlet fever, or chicken pox. Afterwards, the child is as if reborn and may even describe herself in this way or say something along the lines of, "The world suddenly looks so fresh, everything looks so much more beautiful than before".

A practical approach to fever

Since a well-functioning immune system plays an important role in health, not least in dealing with non-feverish illnesses, a delicate approach in

> " Give me the power to produce a fever and I will cure any illness."
>
> Parmenides

> " Fever is half the striving of the organism against disease. It purifies the body like fire."
>
> Hippocrates

> " Fevers are a common condition of childhood, and so feared by some parents (and practitioners) that quite disproportionate measures are taken to avoid them. This fear is often misplaced. For many children (and adults) an occasional fever is beneficial, because it is a way of clearing any accumulated 'latent heat'."
>
> Julian Scott,
> Natural Medicine for Children

> " The warmth of the fever is analogous to the warmth that melts sealing wax and allows the impression of a signet ring to be stamped into it as a sign of the owner's identity."
>
> Dr Michael Evans and Iain Rodger,
> Anthroposophical Medicine

The positive aspects of fever

- The stimulation and training of the immunological resistance of the body

- The stimulation and training of thermo-regulation and, consequently, of the blood circulation in all the organs

- The combatting of bacteria and viruses. These are partly retarded in their growth, and partly (as a direct result of the fever reaction) damaged in their metabolism, and killed

the handling of fevers should be the focus of developmental paediatrics. A high temperature can occur very suddenly (particularly in infants and toddlers) or develop more slowly, when it is obvious the day before that the child is "incubating" something. We feel a kind of relief when the fever finally appears, because we can do something about it. Although temperatures of 41°C (106°F) are not unusual, we should be reassured that the child can cope with these high temperatures much better than we adults. The golden rule is: do not fight the temperature but treat the whole child. For if measures are introduced which lower the temperature, the body is deprived of the opportunity to cope with the illness, so increasing the dangers of complications.

Body response

A high temperature on its own does not pose a problem. We are, after all, only seeing the response of the body to one of a variety of possible disorders. Sometimes there is not even a pathogen – only a preceding agitation or excitement, or simply a case of "travel nerves". If a doctor immediately prescribes anti-fever drugs, they will directly affect the heat centre of the brain and so block the natural overall response, which the body was seeking to set in motion. Temperatures up to 39°C (102°F) do not provide sufficient grounds for action unless the child is prone to convulsions (see p. 275). There are several simple home care treatments we can learn to use in the event of the child developing a fever (see pp. 274–5). When the fever has subsided, however, it is good advice to see a doctor to determine the underlying illness, if any. Then we should not "rush" the child into getting better. She must have time to recover properly. Otherwise, she may suffer repeated bouts of the same illness, leading to a lowered resistance.

Fever treatment

Parents who are unsure of how to treat a high temperature should consult a doctor as a precaution to look for the underlying cause first and seek advice. But every parent or carer should learn in detail how to deal with a high temperature. These pages show what to do in the various stages of fever reaction.

▲ Sponging

Your child may feel sticky and uncomfortable. Sponge him gently with lukewarm water, especially face, hands, and feet.

STRATEGY: **HOW TO TREAT A RISING TEMPERATURE**

● When the temperature is rising (when arms and legs are still cold) wrap the child up warmly to help the body to reach the higher temperature it is seeking

● The child should drink as much as she wants. Hot drinks such as tea with honey and lemon can be very helpful

● Apply a cool wash cloth, possibly with a pleasantly scented essence, to her forehead (which feels hot, like the body) to provide the relief she now needs

● Once the fever has reached its climax, the body wants to give off the superfluous heat again. A very lively child may tend toward a more intense feverish reaction and may need fever-reducing measures in the form of compresses around the calves. This prevents the temperature rising further and usually reduces it slightly.

It is important, however, to check beforehand that the legs really are hot. Never apply a compress to cold legs as it would act as a cold stimulus and drive the temperature up further. Shivering fits, too, are an indication that the temperature is still rising, which means that measures to reduce it are also inappropriate

● First, protect the bed with a thick towel or plastic sheet. Dip two cotton towels into a bowl of water (between cold and room temperature) containing a little lemon juice

● Squeeze the towels well and wrap them around the child's calf, or the whole leg in the case of babies. Cover the towels with a piece of flannel or a woollen cloth, or a thick towel

● After 10 minutes the compress will have warmed up and needs to be replaced. Repeat this process three or four times, but remember to check each time that the legs still feel hot or thoroughly warm. Some 30 minutes after the final compress, take the child's temperature once more. If it has not yet fallen to the desired level, repeat the whole process, provided the legs are still warm

● A body wash, carried out bit by bit, may bring relief in acute fever situations and be pleasant for the child

● Afterwards, do not dress the child or cover her too warmly. Clothes and bed covers should be light and airy, but do not let the child become cold as this might produce a renewed rise in temperature

● If the child sweats a lot, change her clothes and sheets frequently. Air the bedroom regularly and keep the room temperature between 18°C (65°F) and 20°C (68°F) during the day, although it can be cooler at night

Convulsions

The concern that convulsions can be a harmful effect of a high temperature is unfounded. Large-scale studies have shown that the brain does not sustain damage from convulsions alone, but only through the underlying illness which accompanies the convulsion. While it is possible that a convulsive illness may manifest for the first time during a fever, it is never the result of the fever. However in cases where a convulsive illness is present, the child is more prone to convulsions when a fever occurs.

Children who have a tendency toward harmless fever convulsions are often particularly strong and healthy; when they suffer a real chill, their temperature rises too rapidly. Their convulsions do not recur during a feverish illness in which the temperature rise is more gradual. Of course, whenever a convulsion does occur, a thorough paediatric and neurological examination should follow. It is not a good idea to use chemical preventive medicines such as phenobarbitol since their side effects are completely out of proportion to their doubtful value.

Immunization

Global vaccination campaigns and the occasional complications of the illnesses of childhood have meant that they are no longer trivialized and seen as just "childhood illnesses", as they used to be. The classic examples – measles, scarlet fever, rubella, chicken pox, mumps, and whooping cough – vary a great deal in their appearance and seriousness, and are experienced by children with various degrees of intensity. If we examine more closely the way in which the body deals with these illnesses we can see that the same applies to them as to fevers: the child learns to take hold of herself in a new way, and re-works them. With the aid of the fever which accompanies most such illnesses there is thus a strong element of the body "reconstructing" itself. In the acute phase, the child will generally eat little and, at most, will drink something – so she will also lose some weight. Her body, which has been built up in her development so far, appears to be broken down again to a certain extent and then "reconstructed" during the illness and recovery.

Forces working together

There is also a more profound perspective. Consider what happens in conception, before the child matures fully in the womb so that she can be born. Many mothers and fathers know very well that the child which will be born into their family is already present in some way during the pregnancy. Often the child is the subject of dreams, or perceived in a flash, long before conception. A spiritual conception of the body seems to precede the physical conception and the start of the development of the embryo.

Rudolf Steiner's research confirms these pre-birth experiences. The human being, living in the four constituent elements of his being (the

CURES IN LATER LIFE
An increasing number of reports describe how chronic illnesses such as eczema, asthma, or multiple sclerosis, have been cured through a serious childhood illness suffered in later life. In 1991, *The Lancet* reported the cases of two adult sufferers of multiple sclerosis who contracted chicken pox. At the time of infection, both had entered the chronic progressive phase of their disease; one was wheelchair-bound, the other walked with two canes. Within six to eight weeks of infection, there was neurological improvement. A year later, both individuals were walking and taking part in all activities of daily living. One was able to jog. Six years and two years after infection, respectively, neither had had further relapse.

▲ Heredity
The embryo is the focus of a spiritual and physical union. The spiritual is the child's pre-birth self, the genetic and physical, her inheritance from her parents.

"I", soul organism, and etheric body are joined with the physical body on earth), gradually unites from conception with the developing embryonic life in the womb. Those specific forces and qualities inherited from the parents work together with those which belong to the child. Particularly in the first years, the individual forces of the child's being interact strongly with her inherited physical body.

This interaction expresses itself in the child's gradually developing immune system and in the childhood illnesses which sometimes provoke a violent fever. In the latter, the already-developed organ systems are baulked in their function and are then improved, transformed, and more adapted to the child's nature. Illnesses which affect the whole of the metabolism as deeply as the so-called childhood illnesses can provoke profound changes in the body (see box). The changes which take place during the illness are not restricted to those which can be externally measured and observed. The decisive factor lies in the careful handling of the fever reaction during the childhood illness (see pp. 274–5).

From a spiritual perspective, childhood illnesses are the means by which the individual adapts her inherited body to her own needs. As a result, her body can become an increasingly adapted and adequate instrument for the tasks which she has set herself on earth and which will unfold in the future. Obviously, immunization weakens or may even prevent this adaptation. The consequence is that the child no longer feels quite at home in her body and numerous colds or other illnesses may take the place of the childhood illnesses she has been unable to experience.

Parents who do not want their child to be vaccinated should inform themselves thoroughly about childhood illnesses and talk to a sympathetic doctor about their concerns.

Vaccination issues

Tempting as it may be to eradicate certain diseases through the strict vaccination of the whole population, experience shows that other diseases which were previously more rare take their place. In addition, there are some serious reservations about the effectiveness of vaccination strategies: measles is on the increase in the US (see right) and the number of adverse effects brought about by whooping cough and rubella vaccines has proliferated (see below right).

It is part of the nature of human beings that they seek – or are susceptible to – illnesses which they need to assist their development, either through overcoming or coming to terms with the disease. Anyone who takes seriously the supersensory nature of the human being may also trust that human beings bring their destiny with them. Serious complications in a childhood illness which produce permanent damage or even death are probably deeply founded in the destiny of the person concerned. Whether someone dies early or late is no chance event, but has meaning in the wider context of her overall development.

Science of the spirit

As parents and doctors we are called upon to do everything we can to help the child enter life healthily and to treat illnesses which occur as best we can. But we do not have the power to prolong life or to prevent serious blows of fate. Indeed, this is a recurring experience in intensive care units: no doctor can, in truth, **prolong** life. We can only offer survival opportunities in the form of infusions, medicines, and machines. If a human being really "wants" to die because her hour has come, there will be multiple organic failure and death will occur – even though none of the machines has been switched off.

MEASLES VACCINATION
Epidemiological evidence suggests that our vaccination strategy needs further critical questioning. Measles, for instance, has been on the increase again in the US during the early 1990s, despite a high level of vaccination. Predictably, the illness now mainly affects infants below vaccination age and young adults who were not vaccinated and are too old for vaccination now. In these groups, the complication rate is significantly higher than during childhood. The mortality rate of this epidemic was officially given as ten times higher than before the vaccination period. A good quarter of the deaths were among children below the age of one. Another quarter were among young adults between the ages of 19 and 33.

PERTUSSIS AND RUBELLA VACCINATION
In many US states rubella and whooping cough vaccinations are mandatory. Minor side effects are common and possible serious adverse effects are the subject of great controversy. In 1990, chronic arthritis was named as a possible adverse effect of the rubella vaccine. Possible adverse effects of whooping cough vaccine include anaphylaxis, erythema multiforme and other rashes; Guillain-Barre syndrome (polyneuropathy); protracted crying or screaming; and thrombocytopenia.

▲ A time for growth
Illness in childhood has an important role to play in building up the child's immune system for healthy adulthood. So we must "allow" the child to be ill and then give her enough time to convalesce thoroughly.

Our current mainstream medicine needs to be expanded through a science of the spirit. Anthroposophy, for example, illuminates the spiritual side of human existence in the form of reincarnation and destiny; illuminates it in the form of a science of spiritual existence as manifest in nature and in supersensory beings such as angels, archangels, or the majestic seraphim and cherubim. Religious traditions give an account of it, but they can only appeal to feeling and belief. Nevertheless, knowledge about this spiritual side of existence has to be acquired today if we want to do justice to human development and its associated conditions and necessities.

Studies show that the debate about the dangers and benefits of global vaccination strategies has not yet been concluded, although vaccination is currently promoted worldwide not only for medical but also for economic reasons. The key question today is: What can we give children to balance the vaccinations which have deprived the body of a developmental opportunity? What other possibilities are there to help the child imprint her personality on her body, to help turn her body into a suitable instrument? The answer is an education which promotes the soul and spiritual activities of the child in a specific way so that she learns to take hold of her body and which, from the soul aspect, helps her to penetrate it better and make it more individualized.

CHAPTER 19

Preventive medicine

Rudolf Steiner realized that the forces of growth and formative development in the embryo come from the etheric body at the life functions level (see p. 269). His findings can become the key to a new understanding of the link between education and medicine, between development of the soul and spirit and development of the physical body.

Merging forces

During childhood, these forces evolve into two parts, one continuing to fulfill its original function in the growth of the child, the other freeing itself from this development and becoming the spiritual force of thought. But because the human being still develops even when growth has reached completeness, the spiritual force is able to emerge later as the capacity for thought.

This discovery of the identity of the growing forces and the thinking activity has led to a new psychosomatic paradigm. For this link explains the findings of much recent immunological research: namely, that idealistic forms of thinking, a deeply religious life, or an open approach in thinking of the needs of the environment have a positive effect in stimulating the immune system.

The etheric body as bearer of the life and growth forces, and thus of the immunological reactions, is influenced by activity of not only the physical body but also of the soul and spirit. Inner warmth and light in the form of bright thoughts and true feelings have just as much of a healing effect as outer warmth and outer light have beneficial effects in climatotherapy. So it becomes clear why Steiner advised that the harmful effects of vaccination on the child could be balanced by an activating spiritual education.

Age-appropriate education

There are three fundamentally different educational stages (see also pp. 28–31). In the first seven to nine years, the development of the nervous system predominates. For healthy growth it requires an education encouraging physical movement and the development of a variety of skills. Major and minor motor activities, and good co-ordination of the senses with hands and feet are important. So there is nothing more harmful during this stage than to allow the child to sit motionless and passive in front of the television and accustom his eyes and ears to a wholly unnatural perceptual process (see also pp. 34, 53, 140–1, 223). Children who are protected from television and who are involved in meaningful creative and physical activities can practise to the full their sensory experiences, physical alertness, and skills in order to grow thoroughly accustomed to their body and its possibilities. They have a well co-ordinated nervous system and feel properly "at home" in themselves.

Would children not grow up just as physically healthy without such an educational approach? Outwardly they might; but in their soul and spirit they would be connected with their maturing body in a different way to the person whose soul and spiritual learning processes were linked to physical activities, each supporting the other.

A person educated in this way can handle his physical abilities in a much freer and more independent manner. He will not become either oppressed by his physical needs or dependent on them, and he will not be so easily bored. Education along these lines that encourages physical activity also offers the best method of preventing the many addictive illnesses prevalent today, which are often caused by boredom or the inability to deal with the Self actively.

> "It is of the greatest importance to know that man's ordinary forces of thought are refined formative and growth forces. Something spiritual reveals itself in the formation and growth of the human organism. The spiritual element then appears during the course of life as the spiritual force of thought."
>
> Rudolf Steiner and Ita Wegman,
> *Fundamentals of Therapy*

Our own temperaments

Dealing appropriately with the child's temperament is not only part of a healthy education (see also pp. 40–2). We adults must also be aware that we can affect his health through our own temperaments. If we often become angry and put him into a state of fear we upset his circulation, so that vaso-constriction occurs and the disposition to cold hands and feet develops. This leads to a tendency to metabolic disorders in later life.

If the sanguine temperament affects education in a one-sided manner there is far too little experience of the vigour that is needed to carry something through. This creates a lack of Will activity in later life. And if the child largely experiences melancholic adults, this will affect his rhythmic system. The alternation of joy and sadness cannot be practised and this sets the body on course to later diseases affecting cardiac rhythm and respiration. The effects of a phlegmatic temperament are easy to understand. The experience of someone taking an eternity to finish anything simply creates nervous tension in the observer.

Cultivation of rhythm

All organ functions of the human body possess their own rhythms. We are aware of the circadian, or daily, rhythms of most metabolic functions. But there are also weekly and monthly rhythms which we can recognize in the course of certain illnesses. The yearly rhythm is also important for the body. Just as embryonic and fetal development and the first trimester add up to one year, after which the physical body is no longer at such risk, so the yearly rhythm becomes evident as a rhythm which stabilizes the physical body. The experience of growing older also corresponds to the yearly rhythm, indicating the conclusion of a certain stage of development. The celebration of the child's birthday is therefore of great importance (see p. 244).

Caring for the biological clock

It is therefore decisive that our biological clock, this wonderful system of interweaving rhythms, is given the appropriate care at home and at school. Nothing is more beneficial for the child than properly regulated meal and bed times letting him feel safely embedded in the course of each day, knowing what comes next because his inner clock tells him. This also leads to the healthy interaction of the internal organs throughout later life. The daily greeting in the morning, the small goodnight ritual in the evening, linked with a verse or prayer, are invaluable even just from a rhythmical perspective, quite apart from the pleasant mood which is created and which is experienced with gratitude.

The weekly rhythm

The days of the week can be given their own emphasis. Certain things might occur only on Tuesdays, for instance, enabling the weekly rhythm to be imprinted more strongly on the child. Thus the inherent seven-day rhythm which is evident in the healing process of many infectious diseases (pneumonia, measles, typhoid) is supported in a positive way.

The monthly rhythm

Particularly important in school is the adherence to a monthly rhythm which has consequences for memory development. If, as happens in Waldorf schools for example, a certain subject is presented in a Main Lesson (see p. 320) over the course of four weeks, and with a new aspect added every day, while recalling and repeating what went before, this makes it easier for the child to absorb the whole thing. If later the child encounters particular aspects of the subject, it is easy for him to recall the whole context.

The yearly rhythm can be emphasized in the celebration of the festivals (see also pp. 254–5) and this can also support physical development. The constituent elements of the human being (see Chapter 18) possess an inner relationship to these rhythms. Daily rhythmical repetition directly strengthens the spirit (the "I") allowing us to be awake and alert, and is thus the vehicle of the human personality. Weekly repetition strengthens the soul as the vehicle for Thinking, Feeling, and Willing and our soul experiences as a whole, as well as for consciousness.

The four-week rhythm strengthens the life functions as the vehicle for the forces underlying growth and thinking, and thus also for memory and recall capacity. The yearly rhythm, in contrast, strengthens the physical body in its individual dynamic. The effort to cultivate these rhythms is an important contribution to the regulatory ability of the organism, and leads to a corresponding capacity to adapt to a wide variety of external circumstances.

Sleep

Enough sleep is one of the most important pre-requisites for health, both in childhood and in later life. There are individual variations in the amount of sleep needed, but we should not let the child decide when to go to bed. We should bring the day to a close together in a pleasant bedtime routine (see also p. 241).

It is important to reflect on the reality of the world the child enters during sleep. The process of going to sleep, with the slipping away of consciousness, occurs because the soul and the spirit disengage themselves from the nerve–sense system. The length of time we spend in the various stages of sleep, that is, in the spiritual spheres, varies. We run through the process several times during the night and it is supplemented by longer or shorter episodes of REM (rapid-eye-movement) sleep during which an increase in the regen-erative activity of the organism takes place. To help our child make the transition from the waking world to the sleeping world it is important that we pay attention to the spiritual side of sleep. Sleeping difficulties are widespread. It is one of the consequences of materialism that we fear the nocturnal world, because we open our-selves there to "assessment". A trusting surrender to this higher world is something which we have to learn anew. We should initiate this learning process for our child by radiating an atmosphere of trust and security. Sleep means surrender, being awake means individual activity.

"
From my head to my foot
I am the image of God.
From my heart to my hands
I feel the breath of God.
When I speak with my mouth
I will follow God's will.
When I see God
In Father and Mother,
In all dear people,
In animal and flower,
In tree and stone,
No fear shall I feel
But love will fill me
For everything around me."

Rudolf Steiner

◀ Rhythms and sleep
An experiment which monitored a baby's sleep rhythms for the first six months of his life (dark shading indicates sleep, and light wakefulness) revealed that after the first few chaotic weeks, a 25-hour rhythm emerged, changing to 24-hour, with most of the sleep at night.

How much sleep?
Babies and young children need adequate sleep if they are to have the strength to grow and develop.

	Night	**Day**
Newborn	20 hrs total	
1–2 yrs	12 hrs	1–2 hrs
2–6 yrs	11–12 hrs	Sleep not always necessary, but he should have a rest
6–9 yrs	10 hrs	Quiet times are necessary

Clothing

Children's clothes can be fun in colour and form, but they serve above all an important health-related function that is frequently forgotten. Small children and babies are very susceptible to changes in the environmental temperature and therefore need to be kept warm in cool weather and cool in warm weather. The right choice of clothes adjusts body temperature to the temperature of the environment. The smaller the child, the more important it is to use natural fibres such as wool, cotton, and silk, as only these can absorb moisture from sweat and thus prevent a feeling of coldness on the skin as a result of evaporation. This is important primarily because the body also has to learn to regulate its temperature as the child grows.

Thus, repeated cold stimuli on the skin as a result of sweat which has not been absorbed by synthetic fabrics can lead to a failure of the temperature regulating mechanism. The child's face and hands should come into contact with the ambient temperature and clothing should help the body preserve the optimum temperatures of the various organs to keep them healthy.

It is particularly important nowadays to cover the head, both in cool and warm weather. Not only does sunlight act more strongly as a result of the thinning of the ozone layer but also the development of the nervous system and the sensory organs can take place more harmoniously and undisturbed if the head is protected from the elements in this way. Elsewhere the body loses heat rapidly from the neck, the wrists, the backs of the knees, and the ankles.

CLOTHING CHECKLIST	Cool weather	Warm weather
Baby	• Wool hat (over the ears) • Wool vest/undershirt • All-in-one suit or wool tights/pantyhose and top • Wool jacket • Wool socks • Wool mittens • Wool shawl	• Cotton sunhat with brim (and sunscreen) • Cotton vest/undershirt • All-in-one suit or rompers • Cotton outdoor jacket • Cotton socks • Wool shawl
Toddler	• Wool hat • Wool vest/undershirt • Wool tights/pantyhose • Trousers/pants, shirt, sweater • Outdoor jacket with hood • Wool mittens	• Cotton sunhat with brim (and sunscreen) • Cotton vest/undershirt and underpants • Cotton shirt and sweater • Cotton trousers/pants or skirt • Outdoor jacket • Cotton socks
Child	• Wool hat and gloves • Wool or cotton vest/undershirt • Wool or cotton socks or tights/pantyhose • Trousers/pants or skirt, shirt, and sweater • Outdoor jacket or coat with hood	• Sunhat with brim (and sunscreen) • Cotton underpants • Wool/cotton shirt and sweater • Wool/cotton trousers/pants or skirt/dress • Outdoor jacket • Cotton socks

Food and diet

Foods are not only important for their fat, protein, carbohydrate and mineral content. Since the human etheric body is related to the whole of nature, it is affected differently by different types of food. As the body processes food, it has to overcome the residue of foreign life in the food and that is what actually strengthens the organism. The greater the care we take preparing food, the more the qualities associated with the etheric forces are preserved. Starch and protein from grain, for instance, contain different etheric forces than starch and protein from potatoes.

For the child to stay healthy he must be active. The highest level of self-activity is shown by the breastfeeding baby; even the drinking process itself is far more exhausting than if the baby simply sucks from a bottle. The lowest level of activity occurs if the milk is made from powder. This milk has been deprived of its etheric effectiveness to such an extent that it has become completely mineralized and it is too easy for the baby to digest the food.

QUESTIONS: FOOD

● Do you choose foods in season, as far as possible? These will strengthen the yearly rhythms of the physical body

● Does your food come from healthily grown plants and animals? Such foods contain greater vitality

● Do you combine a variety of foods so that any unbalanced nutrition is minimal and the child learns to digest everything?

● Do you accustom your child to regular mealtimes, with good intervals in between?

● Do you avoid allowing sweets and snacks between mealtimes as far as possible?

FOOD GROUPS	FOOD	NUTRIENT CONTENT
Protein (high)	Lamb, beef, chicken, pork, eggs, cheese, legumes, nuts	Protein, fat, iron, vits. A, D, B
Dairy products	Milk, yogurt, cheese	Protein, fat, calcium, vits. A, D, B2
Green/yellow vegetables	Cabbage, spinach, kale, sprouts, green beans, lettuce, squash, celery, courgettes (zucchini)	Calcium, chlorine, chromium, cobalt, copper, manganese, potassium, sodium
Citrus fruits	Tomatoes, oranges, melon	Vit. C
Other fruit and vegetables	Potatoes, corn, beets, carrots, cauliflower, apricots, pineapples	Carbohydrates, vits. A, B, C
Breads and cereals	Wholemeal bread, noodles, rice	Protein, carbohydrates, B vits., iron, calcium
Fats	Butter, margarine, vegetable oils	Vits. A, D

Treating the constitution

There are many different kinds of people in the world and just as many different kinds of children. As we watch our children grow up we may be aware that they have different constitutions which make them behave in characteristic ways. One child seems noisy much of the time, another is openly aggressive, while another seems cut off and dreamy. Are these differences part of character and personality and unalterable? Or can we do something to change the balance?

The restless child

We all know the lively, often small-headed, child, with his alert, restless eyes, who can hardly control his urge to move about. He may also have an unfortunate tendency to break things. It is a good idea to give a restless child regular, frequent, small meals of foods without artificial additives, but we should look into other measures as well. The restless child may not have enough opportunity to tire himself out constructively, through physical work and effort. Even a half-hour walk to school, or a game in the playground before school can give him the opportunity to sit quietly simply because he has used up some energy. It is also important to give him a good breakfast, otherwise he may be too hungry to concentrate.

Restlessness arises because the relationship between nerve and sense activity and metabolic activity is askew. An over-alert nervous system is often accompanied by a sluggish metabolic system with a lack of co-ordination between them. Some children also suffer alternating bouts of constipation and diarrhoea.

A warm compress (see left) applied to the stomach after a meal or before sleep stimulates the autonomic nervous system of the digestive organs and may help restlessness. In a compress, yarrow tea stimulates liver function, melissa tea stimulates blood flow through the whole of the intestinal area, caraway tea is used for wind, and essence of sorrel for general relaxation and the restoration of vitality.

STRATEGY: HOW TO APPLY A STOMACH COMPRESS

● Pour half a litre (1 pint) of boiling water over a handful of yarrow, cover, and stand for ten minutes. Meanwhile, fold a cloth to the correct size and place it on a larger cloth

● Strain the tea and pour it on to the compress. Squeeze out as much as possible

● Take the compress out of the larger cloth and place it hot on the stomach. Tie a cotton cloth around the body, plus a woollen cloth for the outer layer

● Place a hot water bottle on top and secure in place. Leave the compress in place for at least 30 minutes. If you leave it in place for longer, make sure that it does not get cold

The dreamy child

We may be familiar with a child who has dreamy eyes, and perhaps a large head, who gives the impression of not quite having arrived on earth yet. Often he is also a little awkward and clumsy and somehow "not quite there". It may be helpful to start the day with a cool rosemary wash of the face, body, and arms (see below). The stimulus provided by the water and the scent, combined with the parent's loving care, activates the functions of the nerve–sense system, which is too weak in relation to the metabolic system. The child will participate in school and in the home with greater alertness and security.

PROJECT: ROSEMARY BATH

● Add a few splashes of rosemary bath milk to lukewarm water. This has a stimulating scent and promotes blood flow

● Wash the child either while he is still sitting in bed or standing at the basin

● Continue this routine for at least a year to allow the process of constitutional change in the physical body to take place

The forgetful child

Care of the etheric organism is particularly appropriate in the forgetful child. This means imposing a regular rhythm on the day, particularly with regard to meal and sleep times. It is best not to use television, videos, computers, radios, and cassette players, since they only strengthen the child's forgetfulness and lack of concentration. This is because the child acquires the information passively and usually does not understand it because it is presented at a speed which has not been adapted for him. It is important to awaken strong feelings, particularly through artistic exercises; also through the telling of stories which are full of feeling and soul content and which can arouse the child's interest and sympathy. Everyone finds it easier to remember things which they can link with a personal interest or some inner experience. By contrast, anything assimilated only through the thinking rapidly disappears. So a powerful experience will enable the child to associate with the things he wants to remember.

STRATEGY: HELPING YOUR FORGETFUL CHILD

● Develop a definite routine: make sure the child eats and goes to sleep at the same times every day

● Limit his TV viewing as much as possible

● Let him experience strong feelings through painting, drawing, and other artistic activities, lively story-telling, and vivid, memorable activities

The fearful child

The most important thing is that parents should not become worried about the fearfulness of their child. The more we can organize the course of the day with the child in a calm and natural way, and the more regular the day's events are, so giving the child security, the faster his fearfulness will disappear. It is also important for the child to understand that the adult has learned to cope with fear, and continues to do so, and that one day he will be able to do the same (see also p. 97).

The angrily aggressive child

There is currently a great increase in violence and aggression in society. In the normal course of development the child learns to move, then to speak, and then finally to think intellectually. If the child remains at the stage of movement and does not learn to verbalize his wishes, aggression arises as a special form of speechlessness. Ensuring good progress in movement and speech is the most important preventive measure against aggressive behaviour. We adults know that as a rule it is only when words fail that people become speechless and throw something or hit out in anger. So the most important way to counter the increasing willingness to use violence is the cultivation of language. This is most effective if television is relegated to second place in the home and if there is greater emphasis on sympathetic and interesting conversations. But learning to think also requires conscious cultivation and support, for it is only when this inner aspect of life, one's own thinking, awakens that inner calmness and peace can follow.

STRATEGY: HELPING YOUR FEARFUL CHILD

● Try to keep your home calm and restful and establish a stable routine of daily activities. Even if you are not always a calm person, be aware that your fears can "rub off" on to your child. Rather than trying to conceal them, talk about them in a relaxed way

● Reassure your child with your loving care and presence

● Talk about your own childhood fears so that he can understand that you too were once a child with fears who overcame them successfully

"
When I was about five years old I was frightened of the rain. Every time it rained I thought it would flood. My father would take me out to watch the rainwater running into the drains in the street, to reassure me."

Catherine

STRATEGY: HELPING YOUR AGGRESSIVE CHILD

● Encourage your child to talk by engaging him in family conversations from an early age. Use mealtimes as a daily opportunity for family talk

● Don't be afraid of arguing heatedly, but try to draw out thoughtful, positive conclusions without upset

● Limit his TV viewing as much as possible

▲ The five constitutional types

The dreamy child is shown here in the centre. Around the outside, clockwise from top left, we have the fearful child, the restless child, the forgetful child, and the aggressive child.

PART 6

EDUCATION AND SCHOOLING

Professor Roland Meighan

*P*arents wanting an effective and morally healthy education for their children based on natural learning principles are in the same position as people wanting a more healthy vegetarian diet. The system may not always provide what we want and often has a vested interest in providing the opposite. So, like the vegetarian pioneers, parents wanting education of the kind outlined in this section will have to argue and organize to try to get it. This is why this section contains a lot of systematic argument rather than easy answers and ready-made solutions. It aims to brief parents well for the struggle to get natural learning available within a reconstructed education system and how to try to rescue bits from the wreck of the current system.

It also explains why home-based education features throughout, firstly because, like vegetarians, some families have decided they have no option but to do it themselves, and secondly, because their experience can teach us some valuable lessons about how to reform the system.

CHAPTER 20

Natural learning

The young child is a "natural" learner; she learns through imitation, by doing something after seeing or hearing it done by others. She busily gathers information and makes meaning out of the world. Her constant and universal learning activity, which is as natural as breathing, demonstrates that she is programmed to learn unless prevented from doing so.

A question of learning

By responding to a child's natural learning ability, and without any formal training, parents can help her master a number of complicated skills, such as walking, talking, writing, and reading. A child will walk or talk when she is ready (see p. 30), such skills do not have to be taught. The task of a parent is primarily to encourage and to support a child in her endeavours (see pp. 170–1).

Ideally, schools should pick up from where parents have brought their child in the early years. Many teachers of young children are able to accomplish this to a degree, but they are often hampered by a shortage of resources, and with classes of thirty or more are inevitably hardpressed to achieve anything like the personalized focus a parent can give. However, even in such large classes much can be achieved by a skilled teacher, and parents should continue to support their child's education by showing an interest in everything she is doing at school (see facing page). In addition, provide learning activities at home, for example invite your child to help you with chores such as washing up and gardening. Children love to "help" and these are opportunities for learning through imitation. Encourage your child to finish what she starts, and show sensitivity when she is concentrating on a task.

In general, all parents worry about whether their child is receiving the best education available; they want her potential to be fulfilled and look to schools to achieve this. A parent's worst nightmare is to watch a child lose curiosity, confidence, and enthusiasm for learning, but before blaming the school parents should look closely at their home life to see if any problems stem from there. Even if the problems do come from school, there is much a parent can do to help a child to cope (see above and p. 294).

Another common worry is that children may fail to acquire one of the key elements of learning at school – that of being personally responsible for managing their own activities. Without this, children become passively dependent on teachers as they grow older and pass through the educational system. Learning how to learn gives way to learning how to be taught.

Contribution of parents to natural learning

Managing her own learning is vital to a child's development. However, she needs the contribution of adults, particularly as "partners" in play experiences, and as encouraging supporters in the confidence-building process.

Parents as learning "coaches"

Educationalists see this "coaching" ability of parents as highly sophisticated and describe it as "dovetailing" into the child's behaviour. As a rule, parents do not implement a pre-determined plan of, say, language teaching; they do not sit their infants at desks to give lessons in language, because children learn language primarily through copying speech patterns (see pp. 30, 37, 72–3). Parents act as learning "coaches" by providing an example for their child to copy and by letting her learn for herself without constant interruption. The best early learning environment is one that a child can explore for herself.

Ideally, a parent should be nearby for the child to call upon for advice and assistance. Parents can foster and encourage a child's natural curiosity and innate desire to learn simply by showing an interest in whatever she shows them and talking about it with her. If supported and encouraged, a child will not only begin to make sense of her world but, through imitation, she will also acquire the attitudes and skills necessary for successful learning throughout life.

John Holt (see p. 293) warns us about the dangers of insensitive adult interference, which can hinder or halt a child's learning. Such interference can come from parents who are too eager to educate their child and give her a "head start", or it can come from an education system inappropriate to the needs of an individual child.

ESSENTIAL LEARNING REQUIREMENTS
What is the best way that a child can learn effectively? The answer differs from child to child according to variations in learning styles (see p. 298). However, some factors apply to all children. Three of these emerged in a study by H. G. McCurdy at the University of North Carolina:
- A high degree of individual attention given by parents and other adults, expressed in educational activities, accompanied by abundant affection
- Limited contact with other children, but plenty with supportive adults
- An environment rich in, and supportive of, imagination and fantasy

---

LEARNING DOS AND DON'TS

- Avoid criticizing or making negative comments about your child's ability. Labelling a child as "slow" can create a self-fulfilling prophecy of failure. Never adversely compare children

- Encourage persistence not mastery, and encourage your child to learn from her mistakes

- Never punish mistakes or threaten to withdraw love if your child fails to achieve goals

- Let your child set her own pace for learning and be available as a learning resource whenever you are asked

READING WITH YOUR CHILD

Reading is an essential ticket to learning, but learning to read is not a race. It doesn't matter when your child starts to read, as long as she comes to enjoy it. Your role is not to teach your child to read, but rather to help her learn to read.

● Build up a collection of interesting books at home and visit the public library. Select books with language that reflects everyday speech

● Read to your child while she looks at the pictures and text. In time, she will anticipate phrases and attempt reading by herself

● Let your child set the pace of reading and choose a time to read that suits her

● Let your child make mistakes without constantly interrupting and correcting her. Most children will go back and correct their own errors

● If your child asks for help, give her a clue rather than the actual word – children learn meanings from context. Adults skip words they are not familiar with and work out meaning from context; children do the same

PROFILE: JEAN PIAGET

Eminent Swiss psychologist, Jean Piaget (1896–1980) was one of the foremost researchers into the thought processes of children. He formulated a theory of developmental stages in children's thinking. He also stressed two fundamental ideas about learning. First, that children make meanings for themselves instead of merely receiving them passively from external sources; and second, that pupils acquire methods of learning and thinking rather than just absorbing set bodies of information which they can recall later. Piaget observed that children actively construct and arrange their knowledge as they develop their own personal interpretational scheme. He underlined the need to provide children with a wide range of first-hand experiences and to allow them time to think for themselves. If children readily accept everything they are told by adults, it prevents them from developing their own mental thought patterns.

"
When we speak of experience we must distinguish two different types, which will help us see that a child learns very little indeed when experiments are performed for him, and that he must do them himself rather than sit and watch them done..."

"
To me education is a leading out of what is already there in the pupil's soul. To Miss Mackay it is a putting in of something that is not there, and that is not what I call education, I call it intrusion."

Muriel Spark,
The Prime of Miss Jean Brodie

"
In the realm of education...this means that school children and students should be allowed a maximum of activity of their own, directed by means of materials which permit their activities to be cognitively useful."

Jean Piaget

Readiness for school

Most young children eagerly await the start of school. Their expectations have been fuelled by stories from family and friends of the pleasures in store. Most are happy at school and find it an interesting place to be. For others, disillusionment is swift and may be the result of a multiplicity of factors relating to the nature of the schooling, the inappropriate expectations of parents, or the "unreadiness" of the child. For some children going to school will be their first experience away from home and of being in a large group. Even for those with pre-school experience, the difference between a play-oriented nursery school and the organized teaching of a primary school classroom may come as a shock. The law tells us at what age children have to attend school, unless home-based education is chosen instead, but recognizing a child's readiness from observation of her behaviour and development (see facing page) is important.

▲ My new school
Before starting school, a child builds up her own picture of it, based on images in books and on television and adults' and siblings stories of their schooldays. This five year old drew herself and a friend in the classroom, but no teacher. There are pictures on the walls, and a fish tank on top of the cupboard, but no books.

Easing the transition to school

A child's curiosity and desire to have the school experience is vital, but this in itself is not sufficient to ensure a smooth transition into schooling. Most schools are conscious of the need to introduce children to some features of school before they start. Visits can be organized – teachers to homes, and parents and children to school – to meet the teachers and to explore the school. Some schools send personal letters to each child, and others invite them to join in an activity at the school, such as story time, either with or without a member of the family.

Parents are in a position positively to influence their child's response to schooling and it is important that their own negative feelings or memories of school, if any, are not transferred to her, consciously or subconsciously. The parents' interest, encouragement, and support of their child's experiences, and their willingness to get to know the teachers and participate in the life of the school, will enable them to share their child's educational experience more fully.

If things aren't going well...

Changes in a child's behaviour, for example, reduced enthusiasm and energy, increased irritability, loss of appetite, disturbed sleep, increased tearfulness, and suffering more minor illnesses than usual, may all be linked to problems at school. Most of these problems can be prevented by spending time preparing a child for school (see facing page), and most can be resolved through talking sensitively with the child.

PREPARING YOUR CHILD FOR SCHOOL

This is a question not of teaching your child to read or write, but ensuring that she starts school with confidence. A child's self-esteem and eagerness to learn could be undermined if she is not fully prepared for school life.

● Always talk positively about school, and never create anxiety by saying things such as, "Don't think you'll be allowed to do that at school"

● Support your child's growing independence by arranging visits to family or friends without you, and invite her friends home to play with her

● Ensure she can manage her own lavatory visits, can dress and undress herself, and do up her own shoes. To help her, buy easy-to-wear clothes and velcro-fastening shoes

● Spend time together doing things that are also done in school

● Ensure that your child knows something of what to expect, for example: the teacher, playtime and lunch-time procedures, and where the toilets are

STEINER'S THEORY ON READINESS

Steiner's insights show us that, during the first six years of life, the child is occupied with making her physical body her own. This process involves the employment of her "etheric body", which is responsible for growth, repair, and regeneration. By the age of six the reorganizing process is almost complete, evidenced by the shedding of the milk teeth. Some of the child's etheric forces now become available for the soul-spiritual functions, particularly the memory. Only then is the child mature enough for schooling that requires memory and intellect. Once the milk teeth have been shed, these powers can be called upon without detriment to the child's current or future wellbeing.

There is growing support for Steiner's views that children in many countries start school too early. The Gesell Institute of Human Development is campaigning to raise the age for starting school. It aims to introduce an extra "growth year" at nursery schools for children who need it.

"
I remember sitting on my chair in a very large room with big windows and wetting my pants. I was embarrassed and frightened until the teacher came and showed me a drawer full of clean, blue pants and reassured me – it didn't matter, it happened quite often, and the drawer of pants was there for us."

Linda, aged 32

"
I remember rows and rows of pegs, and being allocated one peg to hang my shoe bag from."

Rebecca, aged 22

ASSESSING YOUR CHILD'S READINESS FOR SCHOOL

It is not a child's age that indicates her readiness for school, but rather her developmental maturity. Use these questions to help assess your child's readiness:

● Is she happy to spend time with friends or family without you, and can she cope with meeting new people?

● Does she like playing with friends?

● Does she enjoy helping at home and does she finish what she starts?

● Is she interested in the idea of school? Does she want to read, write, paint, and draw?

● Does she enjoy listening to stories, and is she used to books at home?

● Does she know her surname, her home address, and telephone number?

● Can she hold a pencil?

● Can she visit the toilet unaccompanied and dress herself?

Individual differences in learning styles

We all have our own distinctive ways of learning. We probably developed them before school, at school, or even despite school; alternatively, we may simply have mixed together a number of different learning styles to suit our needs. Our motivation for learning and the effectiveness of our learning processes depends on how far the learning environment caters to our specific learning styles. This can have profound implications in schools, especially where the teacher–pupil ratio is high. For instance, if a teacher has thirty children in one class, and has forty-five minutes to carry out a standard lesson, it is unlikely that all the children will learn equally because the teacher will not be able to respond to their individual learning styles. Modern teaching methods try to overcome this by grouping children according to ability: the groups are small, the children work together in a co-operative way, and they can learn at their own pace.

We all may have wondered, at some time, how one child can be so different from another in the same family. Steiner recognized the differences between children and divided them into four groups according to their different temperaments (see pp. 40–3). The four temperaments: choleric, phlegmatic, sanguine, and melancholic, affect the way a child responds to a problem and may also affect the way she learns and how quickly she settles into school. Achievement in the classroom is not simply about intellectual ability, it is also about how a child feels. A child's self-image, her self-esteem, and how she responds to a challenge all influence her classroom success. The four temperaments have different learning requirements. A choleric, for example, abounds with energy and confidence

LEARNING STYLES
Researchers J. W. Keefe, R. Dunn, and S. A. Grigg have categorized a number of common learning styles. Use the list to assess the optimum learning conditions for your child.
- Deductive – she learns through reasoning from general principles to particular cases
- Inductive – she learns through reasoning from particular cases to form generalizations
- Visual – she learns through looking and seeing
- Auditory – she learns through hearing and listening
- Impulsive – she learns on the spur of the moment
- Reflective – she learns after a great deal of thought
- Dependent – she needs someone else to help learning
- Independent – she is able to learn without the help of others
- Noise levels – she needs a background hum, or peace and quiet
- Light conditions – she needs bright or low-intensity light
- Temperature conditions – she needs warmth or coolness
- Bodily positions – she learns best when sitting or lying
- Food intake – she learns best with a full stomach or empty stomach
- Bio-chronology – she learns best in the early morning (lark) or evening (owl)

UNDERSTANDING YOUR CHILD'S TEMPERAMENT

We are all, to a certain extent, victims of our own temperament (see pp. 40–3), and this is also true of children.

● Work with your child's temperament, and never against it. Do not try to introduce opposite qualities to those already present, or to attempt to modify behaviour to produce a "balanced" personality

● Seek ways to use the qualities of your child's temperament to advantageous effect. There is no point, for instance, in cajoling a melancholic child, who is in a blue mood, to cheer up

PROFILE: JEROME S. BRUNER

Professor of Psychology, Jerome S. Bruner, was born in New York in 1915. He maintains that learning is essentially of the same quality at the frontiers of knowledge as it is in the classroom. Children are researchers by nature and can, as research scientists do, make intelligent guesses and perform intellectual leaps from their intuitive understanding. Problem-solving through first-hand experience encourages this learning.

Bruner's idea of the spiral curriculum has provoked spirited debate. The basic ideas of any subject need to be developed in a person's consciousness. For example, a child's first encounters with money are about using coins to buy things, but spiralling round to this concept again and again produces a more sophisticated awareness of the complex "economics of money".

"
If a curriculum is to be effective in the classroom it must contain different ways of activating children…. A curriculum, in short, must contain many tracks leading to the same general goal."

J. S. Bruner,
Towards a Theory of Instruction

and soon becomes bored in a learning environment if not constantly stimulated by new experiences. A phlegmatic child, however, feels more comfortable with routine. She may be "slow-to-warm-up", and needs plenty of time to adjust to anything new, whether it is a toy, a place, or learning a new skill. These differences in optimum learning conditions need to be taken into account in school and at home to ensure that each child can achieve her full potential.

Steiner/Waldorf teacher training stresses that the key to good teaching is to "know thyself". Steiner teachers are encouraged to analyze their own temperaments and to use the insight gained to their advantage, instead of letting it use them.

"
The aim of education is the knowledge not of facts but of values."

William Ralph Inge,
in *Cambridge Essays on Education*

Absorbing culture

"Culture" means not only taste in music, theatre, or art, but the totality of shared and learned behaviour according to which the members of a society live. In fact, the culture of a society is the very thing that distinguishes it from every other society. All cultures break up into various sub-cultures, based on religion, gender, skin colour, social class, birth place, physical handicaps, and even left-handedness.

Children learn the culture around them in at least two ways. One is a conscious process that includes finding out, questioning, experiencing, and problem-solving. The second is a process more akin to absorption, in which learning – often attitudes or impressions – is more indirect, or even subconscious. Contrary to belief, children can, for example, absorb social and political knowledge. Children as young as four or five, when given a pile of pictures of people at work, will often arrange them in a way that reflects the pattern of their social class system. They cannot explain what social class is, but they have absorbed sufficient information in their everyday lives to grasp a basic pattern.

▼ **Actions speak louder than words**

The young child learns from what she experiences, absorbing and developing her attitudes by imitating the attitudes of those in her immediate environment. This poem is adapted from Children Learn What They Live *by D. L. Nolte.*

if If children live with fear they learn to be apprehensive...
If children live with pity they learn to feel sorry for themselves...
If children live with ridicule they learn to be shy...
If children live with jealousy they learn what envy is...
If children live with shame they learn to feel guilty...

alternatively,
if If children live with encouragement they learn to be confident...
If children live with tolerance they learn to be patient...
If children live with praise they learn to be appreciative...
If children live with acceptance they learn to love...
If children live with approval they learn to like themselves...
If children live with recognition they learn that it is good to have a goal...
If children live with sharing they learn about generosity...
If children live with honesty and fairness they learn what truth and justice are...
If children live with security they learn to have faith in themselves...
If children live with friendliness they learn that the world can be a nice place...
If you live with serenity your children will live with peace of mind...

if If children inherit a racist culture, they are likely to become racist...
If children are born into a class-ridden society, they tend to become classist...
If children experience a male chauvinist society, they often become sexist...
If they are encouraged to be competitive, they learn to become greedy for success, or selfish...
If they are required to spend 15,000 hours in the company of their peers,
    they may learn the tyranny of the peer group and become ageist in their outlook...
If they are compelled to learn religion, they may become dogmatists...

alternatively,
if If children live with tolerance, they may learn to resist racism...
If they experience fairness and justice, they may want a less class-ridden society...
If they encounter gender-equality, they may learn to get rid of their sexism...
If they experience co-operation, they can learn to share...
If their social life is broad, they may learn to resist the tyranny of the peer group...
If they are allowed to research alternative life-stances, they may become suspicious of dogmatism...

▶ Plan

In a Plan-Do-Review nursery or kindergarten, children as young as three have the freedom to plan activities with the support of an adult. Materials and equipment are arranged on low shelves that can be seen and reached by the children and they are encouraged to select what is most appropriate for their purposes. The early planning efforts usually involve the child talking with an adult about what she'd like to do, how to do it, and what materials to use.

◀ Do

The child carries out her plans for herself, and in her own time, asking for help and advice as she needs it. Working independently and following through her own plans help the child develop self-discipline to finish what she starts and encourages initiative and self-confidence.

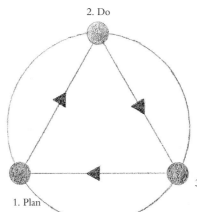

2. Do

1. Plan

3. Review

▲ Review

When children have completed their task, they are encouraged to reflect on their achievements. For very young children this may mean talking with an adult about what they have been doing. As they grow older and gain further experience they are encouraged to evaluate and justify their actions, not only to an adult but also to a small group of their peers who participate in the review process.

LONG-TERM BENEFITS OF HIGH/SCOPE

Research carried out in Ypsilanti, Michigan on a group of 27-year-olds who had experienced High/Scope, and a control group who had not, points to the long-term benefits of intensive, high-quality, preschool education.

● The High/Scope group developed a framework for success in adult life, and was able to interact more positively with people. The other group did not

● Female High/Scope group members were more likely to graduate

● Male High/Scope group members were more socially responsible in later life, and showed a reduction in criminal and anti-social behaviour

● "Graduates" of the scheme were less likely to have been to have needed help from the social services. Generally, they stayed in education longer and were in employment

---

Child-initiated learning: Plan-Do-Review

A new model of education called Plan-Do-Review, based on active, child-initiated learning and the idea that children learn most effectively when they are allowed to choose their activities within a structured environment, is the focus of much attention. The approach was developed and first used during the High/Scope Perry Preschool Project in Ypsilanti, Michigan. Children first decide and plan what they intend to do,

THE OUTCOMES OF ACTIVE, CHILD-INITIATED LEARNING
● A sense of personal control through opportunities to make decisions for themselves
● Active participation in first-hand experiences encourages problem-solving, reasoning, discovery, the acquisition of key concepts, and the development of a range of skills, including language skill
● Learning how to learn rather than learning how to be taught
● The development of traits important for lifelong learning – confidence, curiosity, initiative, independence, responsibility, and divergent thinking

▲ **Building plans**
Toby, aged four, draws a plan of a house, and with his mother decides what materials to use. He then starts building.

then carry out their plans, and finally reflect on what they did and what they have achieved. The Plan-Do-Review sequence provides a structure for each child's own self-initiated learning programme. Combining choice with routine in this way is particularly valuable for children with learning difficulties.

The long-term benefits of Plan-Do-Review, particularly to those from low socio-economic backgrounds, are significant (see facing page). The project presents a useful model that enables children to develop some autonomy in their learning. It requires a high adult–child ratio, involves parental participation, and may be modified to fit a range of settings and ages. The principles developed at Ypsilanti have been applied in schools in other countries, and they can also be applied to learning activities at home.

"

When children participate in an active learning curriculum, they develop self-control and self-discipline. This control is real power – not over other people or materials, but over themselves. Understanding what is happening in the surrounding environment, realizing that those around them are genuinely interested in what they say and do, and knowing that their work and effort have a chance of leading to success, gives a sense of control that promotes personal satisfaction and motivates children to be productive. While no single factor ensures success in life, the sense of personal control is certainly a major force."

L. J. Schweinhart and D. P. Weikart,
*A Summary of Significant Benefits:
The High/Scope Perry Pre-school
Study Through Age 27*

CHAPTER 21

Approaches to education

Current debates about choice in education tend to be stilted and to revolve around which authoritarian approach is best. But schools do not have to be slaves to authoritarianism; they can be run democratically, and learning itself can be a democratic process. Alternatively, there is the option of autonomous schooling and autonomous learning.

The three approaches

Genuinely child-centred education is largely confined to the first five years of childhood. It is practised when parents act as learning "coaches" (see p. 294) and also in many kindergartens, nurseries, and primary schools. In these instances, the autonomous approach and, at times, the democratic, are in operation, with the authoritarian used sparingly (see boxes, facing page).

In the book, *The School That I'd Like*, by Edward Blishen, teenage pupils report that they learn most effectively under a "nice strict" authoritarian regime rather than a "nasty strict" one. They go on to suggest that they would learn even more effectively still if they had some say in what went on in their school environment. They look back with longing to the schools they experienced as young children, where they learnt with enthusiasm and enjoyment.

The possibilities of democratic or autonomous learning are missing from the perceptions of children because they have no experience or awareness of them, and, in many cases, neither have their parents and teachers. We must look closely at the world of alternatives and begin to change the traditional educational culture, so that society is not doomed to repeat endlessly the same limited ideas of schooling and education.

"
We may get our way but we don't get their [the children's] learning. They may have to comply but they won't change. We have pushed out their goals and stolen their purposes. It is a pernicious form of theft which kills off the will to learn."

Charles Handy,
The Age of Unreason

"
All men who have turned out worth any-thing have had the chief hand in their own education."

Sir Walter Scott,
Letters of Sir Walter Scott, vol. 9

AUTHORITARIAN EDUCATION

In the various forms of authoritarian education, one person, or a small group of people, makes and implements the decisions about what to learn, when to learn, how to learn, how to assess learning, and the nature of the learning environment. These decisions are made in course-planning committees and accreditation boards, and often even before the learners have been recruited as individuals or have met as a group.

The authoritarian approach is teacher-centred. Knowledge is transmitted and pupils receive ready-made meanings. They engage in dependent study.

AUTONOMOUS EDUCATION

In autonomous education, the decisions about learning are made by the individual learners. They take responsibility for their own education, and manage their own learning programmes. They may seek advice from teachers, or look for ideas about what to learn and how to learn it by research and consultation. The autonomous approach is learner-managed learning. The teacher's task is to coach pupils so that they can teach themselves more effectively. Self-discipline, and learning the skills of how to learn and research for information are the essence of the autonomous approach. The aim is to develop personal confidence and competence.

DEMOCRATIC EDUCATION

The democratic approach is group-centred. It operates through power-sharing rather than authoritarian imposition. The learners as a group have the power to make some, most, or even all of the key decisions, since power is shared and not appropriated in advance by a minority of one or more. Pupils interpret knowledge and make their own meanings. Democratic education permits critical thought rather than belief. It promotes flexibility rather than rigidity, and admits variety rather than uniformity. Students engage in autonomous study. Ironically, many countries sustain the illusion that they are democratic, but democracy in educational practices is rare.

PROFILE: JOHN DEWEY

Philosopher John Dewey, born in the United States in 1859, saw both the autonomous and authoritarian approaches to curriculum selection as absurd. He felt that those who proposed leaving children to their own free fancies were as misguided as those who proposed that children should learn in an exclusively authoritarian environment. He thought schools should be a co-operative community with "a spirit of freedom and mutual respect", where discipline is not enforced, but evolves from the democratic participation of teachers and children. His emphasis was always on co-operative activity; learning to live and work together.

His Laboratory School, set up to test his theories, centred the curriculum around practical "occupations", such as cooking, and construction. Dewey wanted children to acquire the habit of active scientific inquiry and he felt that learning through experience was of lasting value.

The American public school system is today strongly based on the Dewey system, but is considered by many to have severe shortcomings. Educationalists are now looking to alternatives to improve the system.

"
If you simply indulge this impulse [to use pencil and paper] by letting the child go on indefinitely, there is no growth that is more than accidental. But let the child first express the impulse, and then through criticism, question, and suggestion bring him to consciousness of what he has done, and what he needs to do, and the result is quite different."

John Dewey

"
Education is what survives when what has been learned has been forgotten."

B. F. Skinner,
New Scientist, 21 May 1964

The combination of approaches

The autonomous, democratic, and authoritarian approaches to education can complement each other. Effective democratic learning can incorporate both the solo type of learner-managed learning and the collective form, in interaction with each other. The learning group can use the device of allocating tasks to individuals, and sometimes pairs and trios, which requires them to research and prepare material, activities, and sessions for themselves. The results of their solo or small-group activities can then be fed back into the main group programme.

In the past, the debate about education has often ended up with a case made out for one of the three approaches and rejection of the others. Enthusiasts for the authoritarian approach have usually scoffed at the other two. "Radical" or "alternative" sympathizers have often rejected the authoritarian approach. All three, however, have a part to play in the scheme of things. In the modern, complex world we need to be able to use each type of behaviour in turn, as appropriate, to cope with the different situations that we encounter.

RIGIDITY > > > > > > > > > > > > >< < < < < < < < < < < < **FLEXIBILITY**

Teachers are seen as:

Instructors	Facilitators	Consultants	Senior learners

Learners are seen as:

Raw material	Receptacles	Resistors	Clients	Partners	Autonomous	Democratic

Parents are seen as:

Spectators	Problems	Resources	Helpers	Partners	Educators

The Curriculum is:

Imposed/Competitive	Imposed/Confidence-building	Negotiated Democratic

The Aims are:

Obedience	Subject-learn	Skills-learn	Imagination	self-direct	Co-operate

The Organization for learning is by:

Classes	Individual work stations	Groups

The model of power in use is:

Authoritarian	Autonomous	Democratic

The Outcomes are:

Learning how to be taught	Learning how to learn	One-dimensional behaviour	Multi-dimensional behaviour	Received ideas	Imagination & creativity

▲ **Flexibility or rigidity?**
Is your school or education programme geared to produce rigid people or flexible people? If a school or an educational programme stays, for the most part, with the descriptions on the left-hand side, it is an authoritarian approach, which will tend to produce people with rigid mental sets and inflexible, one-dimensional behaviour patterns. The more a school or programme diversifies by venturing into the descriptions in the centre and right-hand side, the more flexible it becomes; it encourages a greater range of intellectual skills and also multi-dimensional behaviour.

"
Nothing in education is so astonishing as
the amount of ignorance it accumulates in
the form of inert facts."

Henry Brooks Adams,
The Education of Henry Adams

"
Students do not participate in choosing
the goals, the curriculum…. These things
are chosen for the students. This is in
striking contrast to all the teaching about
the virtues of democracy, the importance
of the 'free world', and the like. The
political practices of the school stand in
the most striking contrast to what is
taught. While being taught that freedom
and responsibility are the glorious features
of our democracy, students are experienc-
ing themselves as powerless, as having
little freedom, and as having almost no
opportunity to exercise choice or carry
responsibility."

Carl Rogers

"Mug-and-jug" teaching

The traditional instructor-teacher model is now widely regarded as ineffective. The teacher's task was seen as trying to get the mug to stay still while the jug poured in the selected facts. Rogers, Dewey, Russell, and others regarded this kind of teaching as futile. Its main effect was to give learners who could not respond to this treatment a lasting sense of failure.

In a world where knowledge is expanding and changing all the time, learning facts is of only limited value in the present, and often of even less value in the future. Learning how to learn, however, is always of value, and especially in the future. The task of the teacher is both delicate and demanding, and the good teachers teach us how to teach ourselves better. There is

A MODEST PLACE FOR THE AUTHORITARIAN APPROACH

According to English philosopher and social reformer Bertrand Russell (1072–1970), the general aim of education should be to enable children to learn to think; it is not simply to get them to mimic what their teachers think. This approach requires giving them access to the information and the mental habits necessary for forming independent judgements. Russell proposed that, although the ideal system of education is democratic, it is not instantly attainable due to the young child's lack of experience. The authoritarian approach, therefore, has a modest part to play.

> "
> *Authority in education is to some extent unavoidable, and those who educate have to find a way of exercising authority in accordance with the spirit of liberty. Where authority is unavoidable, what is needed is reverence…."*
>
> Bertrand Russell,
> *Principles of Social Reconstruction*

> "
> *In view of the fact that no authority can be wholly trusted, we must aim at having as little authority as possible, and to think out ways by which young people's natural desires and impulses can be utilised in education."*
>
> Bertrand Russell,
> *Sceptical Essays*

A DEMOCRATIC LEARNING CONTRACT

This group-learning contract could be adapted to suit any group of learners.

We, the learners, agree to:

● Accept group responsibility for our course, plan a programme of studies, implement it using teachers as resources, and review the outcome

● Take an active part in the learning of the group, and be constructively critical of our own and other people's ideas

● Keep a group log-book and other records, share the administrative duties, and review this contract periodically

little place in this kind of teaching for the perpetual authoritarian.

In fraught situations, however, people often revert to the authoritarian position. Obedience to a command is often paramount; while such phrases as "for your own good" and "because I say so" are neither democratic nor autonomous, all parents know that, sometimes, a child must comply with them. In many situations, the democratic saying "several heads are better than one" is likely to be true, and although power-sharing is time-consuming, it should lead to better, fairer, and mutually accepted decisions. Generally, families have moved away from the authoritarian model based on an autocratic male head, toward a more democratic and co-operative way of ordering their lives. Perhaps schools should follow suit.

STEINER'S EDUCATIONAL APPROACH

Steiner believed that educators should understand the need for developing pupils' faculties of Willing, Feeling, and Thinking. These requirements should be taken into account and reflected in the curriculum of every school. The age-groups to which these principles apply are, respectively, 0–7, 7–14, and 14–21. The corresponding educational strategies are: for the infant, imitation; for childhood, artistic creativity with emphasis on kind authority; and for adolescence, freedom and autonomy together with guidance and counselling.

Summerhill was founded in 1921 by A. S. Neill in Lyme Regis, UK, and moved to Leiston, Suffolk, in 1927. It is an international residential school for seventy-five children. The school is financed through fees and donations; it has no state funding.

The organization of the school is democratic: the pupils and staff meet weekly to make decisions about the day-to-day running of the school, and a Tribunal, run by volunteer children, deals with bad behaviour. The school tries to keep a balance of ages and sexes between five and eighteen: democracy works better when there is not a preponderance of one age or one sex.

Summerhill is both a "free" school and a libertarian school because of its stress on the freedom of the children to choose how they spend their time. Within its democratic framework the educational approach is autonomous: students decide what they learn and none of the lessons is compulsory.

▲ **Working together at Summerhill**
Education at Summerhill is about learning, not about being taught. The school is not just about academic achievement, it is about learning and getting on with people, and enjoying the learning experience.

"

I believe a free school is a place where, as long as children are not breaking the community's laws or hurting anyone else they are free to do as they please. The purpose of such schools is to turn out emotionally strong people who can go on to achieve whatever goal they set for themselves.... Part of the trouble is that people think freedom is easy. It is not. It is a complex thing needing understanding of the adult/child relationship in order to get it right. It also needs democratic structures that can help reduce the wear and tear on everyone concerned."

Albert Lamb,
a former pupil and teacher of
Summerhill

Breaking the mould

A few beacon schools are run on autonomous and democratic lines. For example, Sudbury Valley School in Massachusetts is run on purely democratic lines. In the UK, Summerhill operates on the principle that learners should be accorded some say, and some power in the nature of their education. The school is run and disciplined on democratic lines, and the autonomous approach is encouraged for learning, whereby the children are free to choose whether or not to go to lessons.

▲ **Playtime at Sudbury Valley**
Incidental learning that takes place out-
doors at Sudbury Valley is considered as
vital as that pursued indoors.

DEMOCRATIC LEARNING:
THE RESULTS
According to a research project
by Peter Gray and David
Chanoff at Sudbury Valley:
● Students had little difficulty in
being admitted to universities
● Students adjusted well to
other study programmes
● Students have been successful
in a wide range of careers
● Former students reported that
they appreciated being able to
develop their own interests
● Former students practised
democratic values in their lives
● Former students appreciated
the school's aim to encourage
personal responsibility, initiative,
and curiosity
● Students were able to
communicate well with people
regardless of status or age

PROFILE: SUDBURY VALLEY
SCHOOL, MASSACHUSETTS, USA

The school admits anyone who wants
to join between the ages of four and
nineteen. It is committed to a democratic approach in a setting where
children can feel comfortable and free
to pursue their own interests. It is
furnished more like a home than an
institution. The child's natural curiosity is the starting point for everything
that happens at Sudbury Valley.
There is no imposed timetable and
students initiate all their own activities. The staff, the buildings, and
equipment are there to answer their
needs. Age-mixing is the common
experience. There are no grades or
reports and the high-school diploma
is awarded solely on the basis of a
publicly defended thesis at a meeting
which is open to all members of the
school. The school is managed by a
weekly School Meeting where all
students and staff members have a
vote. A Judicial Committee deals
with problems of order.

The school gives one the realisation that
whatever you want you have to work for,
and my life since leaving SVS has been a
good example of that."

One respondent seemed to sum up the
benefits expressed by the whole group,
stating, 'I am attentive, communicate
well, look people in the eye, ask lots of
questions, work independently, and give
lots of effort to whatever I do.'"

Peter Gray and David Chanoff,
From an article following students from
Sudbury Valley School into their careers,
American Journal of Education

A map of education

Behaviour in the modern world is complex. Sometimes we need authoritarian types of responses and people who know when it makes sense to take orders or give them. At other times, we need the self-managing skills of autonomous behaviour and, at other times still, the co-operative skills of democratic behaviour. The world is multi-dimensional in its behaviour requirements and demands. An adequate education means helping people to grow to match it. Our present school system is, for the most part, uni-dimensional, it offers predominantly authoritarian experiences, especially as children grow older.

KEY
△ Autonomous approach
○ Democratic approach
□ Authoritarian approach

▶ **A map for guidance**
Most parents find that navigating their way through the educational maze, and choosing what is best for their child, is no easy task. The map lists the fundamental differences between the authoritarian, autonomous, and democratic approaches to education.

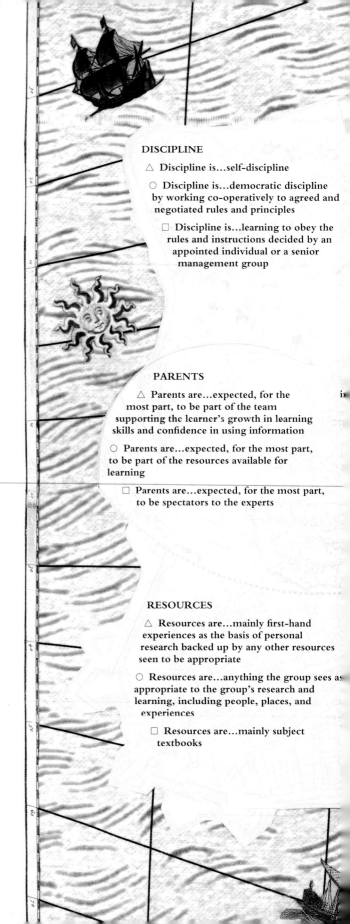

DISCIPLINE

△ Discipline is...self-discipline

○ Discipline is...democratic discipline by working co-operatively to agreed and negotiated rules and principles

□ Discipline is...learning to obey the rules and instructions decided by an appointed individual or a senior management group

PARENTS

△ Parents are...expected, for the most part, to be part of the team supporting the learner's growth in learning skills and confidence in using information

○ Parents are...expected, for the most part, to be part of the resources available for learning

□ Parents are...expected, for the most part, to be spectators to the experts

RESOURCES

△ Resources are...mainly first-hand experiences as the basis of personal research backed up by any other resources seen to be appropriate

○ Resources are...anything the group sees as appropriate to the group's research and learning, including people, places, and experiences

□ Resources are...mainly subject textbooks

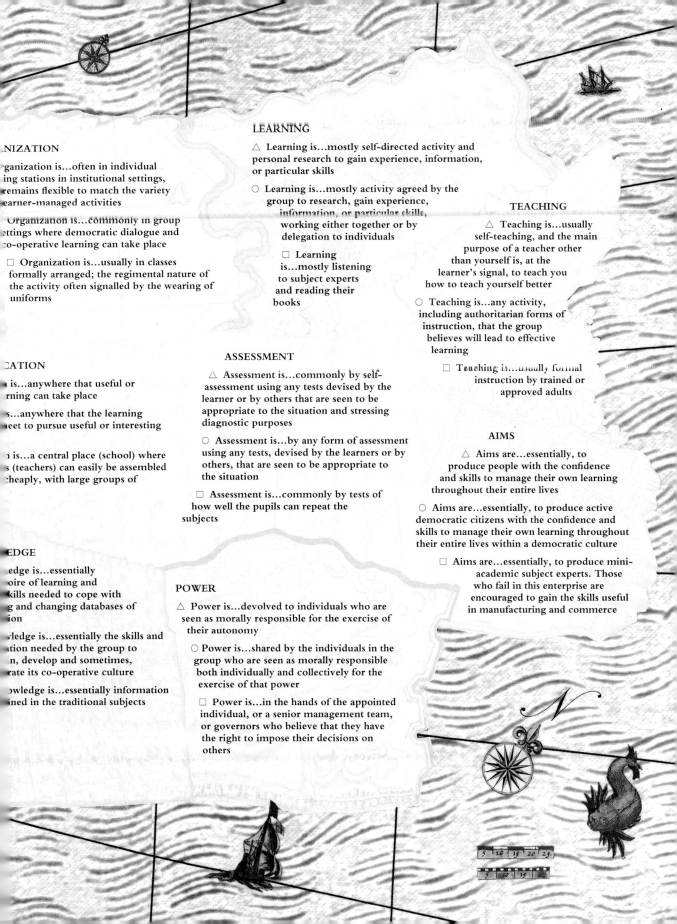

...NIZATION

...ganization is...often in individual
...ing stations in institutional settings,
...remains flexible to match the variety
...earner-managed activities

...Organization is...commonly in group
...ettings where democratic dialogue and
...co-operative learning can take place

☐ Organization is...usually in classes
formally arranged; the regimental nature of
the activity often signalled by the wearing of
uniforms

LEARNING

△ Learning is...mostly self-directed activity and
personal research to gain experience, information,
or particular skills

○ Learning is...mostly activity agreed by the
group to research, gain experience,
information, or particular skills,
working either together or by
delegation to individuals

☐ Learning
is...mostly listening
to subject experts
and reading their
books

TEACHING

△ Teaching is...usually
self-teaching, and the main
purpose of a teacher other
than yourself is, at the
learner's signal, to teach you
how to teach yourself better

○ Teaching is...any activity,
including authoritarian forms of
instruction, that the group
believes will lead to effective
learning

☐ Teaching is...usually formal
instruction by trained or
approved adults

...CATION

...a is...anywhere that useful or
...rning can take place

...s...anywhere that the learning
...eet to pursue useful or interesting

...n is...a central place (school) where
...s (teachers) can easily be assembled
...cheaply, with large groups of

ASSESSMENT

△ Assessment is...commonly by self-
assessment using any tests devised by the
learner or by others that are seen to be
appropriate to the situation and stressing
diagnostic purposes

○ Assessment is...by any form of assessment
using any tests, devised by the learners or by
others, that are seen to be appropriate to
the situation

☐ Assessment is...commonly by tests of
how well the pupils can repeat the
subjects

AIMS

△ Aims are...essentially, to
produce people with the confidence
and skills to manage their own learning
throughout their entire lives

○ Aims are...essentially, to produce active
democratic citizens with the confidence and
skills to manage their own learning throughout
their entire lives within a democratic culture

☐ Aims are...essentially, to produce mini-
academic subject experts. Those
who fail in this enterprise are
encouraged to gain the skills useful
in manufacturing and commerce

...EDGE

...edge is...essentially
...oire of learning and
...kills needed to cope with
...g and changing databases of
...ion

...ledge is...essentially the skills and
...tion needed by the group to
...n, develop and sometimes,
...rate its co-operative culture

...owledge is...essentially information
...ined in the traditional subjects

POWER

△ Power is...devolved to individuals who are
seen as morally responsible for the exercise of
their autonomy

○ Power is...shared by the individuals in the
group who are seen as morally responsible
both individually and collectively for the
exercise of that power

☐ Power is...in the hands of the appointed
individual, or a senior management team,
or governors who believe that they have
the right to impose their decisions on
others

CHAPTER 22

Choices in education

At several stages in their child's early years, parents are faced with serious decisions concerning her education. Many parents seek some form of early childhood service, either for child care or for the provision of pre-school educational experiences. All are faced with choices at primary and secondary level. This chapter explores the choices for pre-school care and alternative options to the traditional model of school.

Early childhood services

Many believe the family home is the natural place for young children, but this is not always possible or, indeed, desired by the parents. They may decide to find some form of pre-school care so that they can both work, or they may wish to extend their child's experience through pre-school education.

The nature and extent of the provision available varies from country to country. However, over-all, the range covers services that are primarily child care, where the security and wellbeing of the child is the first concern, and services that aim to provide appropriate educational experiences for the young child.

Child-minders and daycare homes

These primarily concentrate on child care. They are usually run by a mother with a young family of her own who offers child care for other children from a few months old to school age. Children often enjoy warm relationships (the carer is sometimes seen as a "second mother"), a wide variety of experiences, and stimulating interaction with their carer. Good carers are much sought after by working parents who wish for flexible care for their child, in a family setting.

Day nurseries and children's centres

These are staffed by professionals and provide daycare for babies and young children. Whilst the health and wellbeing of the children is of prime importance, the range of activities offered may promote language development and have other educational benefits. Day nurseries are run by individuals, local authorities, private companies, franchises, and voluntary organizations, and children may attend part-time or all day, so accommodating parents' work arrangements.

Playgroups and parent and toddler groups

These groups offer play experiences for pre-school children between the ages of two-and-a-half and five years. Playgroups are usually run by parent volunteers and some paid staff. Children attend one or more sessions a week, either with or without their parents. Many parents choose this option because of the opportunities it gives their child for social play and interaction with other children. Parents often enjoy the support they gain from meeting other parents.

Nursery schools and kindergartens

Highly qualified staff, a ratio of about one adult to thirteen children, the participation of parents, and the implementation of developmentally appropriate practice are the key factors in quality nursery education. Evidence suggests that nursery education gives children, particularly those from deprived backgrounds, a better chance of success in their school and adult lives (see also p. 302). In many European countries pre-school education is readily available and children do not start primary school until the age of six.

When investigating the nursery option, parents should ensure that enough time and opportunity is given to self-directed, creative, and imaginative play.

EARLY LEARNING: WHAT IT SHOULD BE

Research from many disciplines points clearly toward an education for the young child which in an ideal world is:

● Active: that gives plenty of hands-on involvement, rather than assuming passive receipt by the child

● Personally meaningful: that capitalizes clearly on what children are interested in

● Experimental: that plans for learning by doing, talking, experimenting

● Exploratory: that invites possibilities, delights in curiosity as a key motivator

● Developmentally appropriate: that is carefully suited to the age and stage of each child

● Pro-social: that provides for appropriate interaction and stresses co-operation rather than competition

● Creative: that encourages children to be inventive and imaginative

● Process-oriented: that recognizes the need to help children through complex processes in appropriate steps and stages

● Integrated: that is (as much as possible) holistic and not broken down into meaningless sub-skills

● Rigorous: that stresses child responsibility, initiative, and commitment; is conceptually developing and moving toward higher-order thought processes

Philip Gammage,
Early Childhood Education: Taking Stock

Two ideas are usually associated with German-born Froebel (1782): the Kindergarten and the value of play. He also established the first teacher-training college for women.

He believed education was concerned with three inter-related aspects of experience: activity, emotions, and intellect. Children learn by being active and this activity produces emotional as well as mental responses. To motivate a child, Froebel suggested starting not just with the child, but specifically with what a child can already do well.

Froebel believed that education starts with our relationship with the environment, Nature, and the people around us. He saw reflective imitation rather that thoughtless copying as the first step toward creativity.

While it is not possible to "teach" creativity, it is possible to arrange a situation that develops lateral thinking and fosters creativity. Play is important in developing such thinking, and according to Froebel, guided play is more important than unguided.

> *Play must...not be left to chance, for it is through play that the child learns and learns eagerly and with enjoyment."*

> *To awaken the pupil's urge for learning by concentration on what he can do well, is the highest and first goal of education of the people and especially the poor. This drive can easily be awakened in a free and tolerant situation, for every human being ultimately wants to be completely what his inclination and ability allows him to be."*

Friedrich Froebel

> *It is vital that the experiences provided for young children are in line with what we know about their development, about the intense critical periods within those sequences of development, and are in line with a view of the organism as active and exploring."*

Philip Gammage,
Early Childhood Education:
Taking Stock

Nursery education

There has never been agreement about what nursery education is and what it should aim to achieve. Not only is there confusion for the parents in choosing what might be most appropriate for their child's and their own needs, but there is also confusion among the policy makers, who all too often link nursery education with debates about whether mothers should work or not.

There is evidence from the High/Scope study (see pp. 302-3) to suggest that a good nursery education can have a positive effect on a child's later life, and it is certainly true that children from deprived homes will gain lasting benefit from the order and stimulation that a good nursery will provide. However, for the child from a secure, stable home, with a parent who provides and encourages creative and satisfying activities, the long-term effects of a nursery are less noticeable. What is clear, however, is that nursery provision should not be forced. Some children are simply not ready to be in a busy group environment or away from their parents.

PROFILE: MARIA MONTESSORI

Maria Montessori was born in Italy in 1870 where she became the first woman doctor. She worked with mentally and socially handicapped children. Her observations of young children led to the development of her methods, which are based on the idea that children learn from self-motivated activity within a highly structured environment. In her approach, prepared materials are organized in a planned sequence which enables children to work with a high level of independence. She believed that "play is child's work", and that young children travel through "critical" periods in their development when various concepts and skills are more easily acquired. But she only provided opportunities for exploratory play designed to promote the learning of specific skills and concepts, considering there to be no value in imaginative play. She rejected the value of fantasy since it did not present a true picture of reality. The rigid structures built in by Montessori did not allow for spontaneous, incidental learning, nor did they recognize the individuality of children.

Montessori's view of young children as intrinsically motivated, independent, active learners is acknowledged by many of those working with young children today.

According to the Montessori Society AMI, UK, "Montessori is an attitude: not simply a teaching system, not just a technique. One must have great love for and understanding of each individual child. Montessori is a spiritual attitude towards mankind and mankind begins with childhood".

▼ Caring and sharing

Caring for the creatures that share our planet is an accepted part of Montessori practice.

PROFILE: RUDOLF STEINER

Rudolf Steiner (1861–1925), outstanding philosopher, sociologist, educationalist, and "spiritual scientist", was the founder of Anthroposophy, "a path of knowledge which leads the spiritual in the human being to the spiritual in the universe". In the aftermath of World War I, he was invited to develop a form of education that would take into account the whole human being (body, mind, and spirit) and would lead to cultural renewal instead of to bigotry and destruction. Steiner opened his first school in 1919 for the children of the workers in the Waldorf Astoria cigarette factory in Stuttgart, Germany. The Waldorf Schools soon spread throughout Europe and worldwide.

Steiner gave many indications about the esoteric aspects of Christianity, but Steiner/Waldorf education is nonsectarian and for children from all religious backgrounds. In addition to creating new forms of education, Steiner's indications led to the establishment of anthroposophical medicine, bio-dynamic agriculture, and new artistic forms in painting, movement, and architecture.

" *So for the art of education it is a knowledge of the members of man's being and of their several development which is important. We must know on what part of the human being we have especially to work at a certain age, and how we can work upon it in the proper way.*"

Rudolf Steiner,
The Education of the Child

Steiner schools: techniques and methods

Steiner maintained that in teacher–pupil interaction "that which passes from soul to soul" is far more important than any kind of cold, intellectually conceived instruction – a mere passing on of information. All teaching method and strategy should be "warmed through" with feeling, with emphasis on maintaining the essentially human element present in all school "subjects". Steiner believed in "live" speech. During the early years, he felt, no book should come between teacher and class, since this practice breaks vital connections between them, rendering the creation of atmosphere almost impossible.

Steiner believed that it is not what is taught, but how it is taught, that is of paramount importance. The Steiner curriculum is not subject-based but child-based. Passing on information is less important than exercising the Soul-faculties of Thinking, Feeling, and Willing.

Each phase of a child's development should be reflected in the curriculum. For example, the fairy stories related in the first class gradually give

▲ Creative play in the sandbox
Digging and other outdoor activities encourage the development of a child's motor skills. A child's imagination can also run wild.

way to myth and legend, then to stories of the chroniclers, and on to the lives of historical characters, and finally to history proper.

Starting the day

In the nursery and lower school especially, the children are greeted individually by their class teachers. It is a good time for teachers to assess their pupils' physical and emotional state. The day begins with the recital in chorus of the morning verse, the class and teacher standing in a circle with all hands joined. The words call attention to our inner and outer worlds in a mood of gratitude for our blessings. If it is a child's birthday, this is celebrated by singing the well-known birthday song, and, perhaps, with flowers, cards, a home-baked cake, or a candle lit in honour of the occasion.

The emphasis throughout the day, for both children and teachers, is on fostering social values, courtesy, and consideration for others, and being truly happy and productive in their work.

FEATURES OF A STEINER KINDERGARTEN

- Designed for children aged three to six
- The nursery mimics the home environment
- The nursery is designed on a small physical scale to match the scale of a young child
- The walls are painted pinky yellow or light orange. There are no artificial colours
- Walls are decorated with children's paintings and drawings
- There is an outside play area with a sandbox or climbing apparatus to develop motor skills
- The toys are made of natural materials such as wood and bees' wax. They are very simple, to encourage imaginative play
- Nursery rhymes and fairy tales are important
- A daily, weekly, and seasonal rhythm is followed
- There is a daily mix of play and rest, creativity and receptivity, free play and listening. Early morning is set aside for the special activity
- A weekly timetable assigns a theme to particular days of the week. For example, there is a fairy-tale day, a eurythmy day, and a music day
- The seasons and festivals and children's birthdays are celebrated. There is a seasonal tableau in the classroom
- Class teachers are aware of each child's temperament
- Class teachers get to know the family background and circumstances of their pupils through regular parent/teacher meetings

"

I used to think of Waldorf education as the most undamaging system, and then the more I looked into it, I found that it was the most beneficial system we've got.... If there is any one thing that the Waldorf system does, it nurtures, protects and develops beautifully the intelligence of the true child."

Joseph Chilton Pearce,
author of *Magical Child* and
Crack in the Cosmic Egg

▼ Able fingers, able mind
Steiner schools encourage children to become skilled in crafts. Steiner believed that finger dexterity at a young age helps prepare the brain to cope with dexterity of thought. Initially, children learn to crochet, knit, and garden, and progress on to more intricate crafts.

A day in a Steiner elementary school

Ideally, all "brain-work" is done during the mornings, with less intellectual activities occupying the afternoons. The Main Lesson takes up most of the morning. A theme, chosen by the class teacher, is developed during the Main Lesson over several consecutive weeks. This practice is more effective than that of a more traditional, fragmented school timetable, since it facilitates in-depth treatment of the selected topic. The Main Lesson subject, particularly in the lower school, is treated in a creative way, which involves drawing, painting, modelling, singing, acting out stories, or a school trip.

Steiner/Waldorf teachers prepare their material to the point of complete mastery; this serves to enhance their authority. If textbooks are continually being consulted, the unconscious feeling arises in the children that if the teachers have not taken the trouble to learn their subject, why should the pupils bother?

The importance of eurythmy, art, and craft
Steiner referred to eurythmy (see also p. 165) as "soul gymnastics", and the importance he attached to it may be judged from the fact that it was the only compulsory subject in the first Steiner/Waldorf School. Activities such as art, craft, and playing a musical instrument encourage self-expression and are ways of getting children to "think with their fingers". They are all activities that involve the limbs and, therefore, the Will and since all require practice, they are also good training for the Feelings. Through being creative, children exercise their imagination which leads to a mobility of Thinking, as well as a greater capacity for coping with the joys and woes of adult life.

▲ **Celebrating at the Sheiling Community, Ringwood, England**

The Camphill Movement, which caters for children and adults with special needs, has shown that, given help and support, mentally disabled and handicapped people can enjoy fuller lives and brighter futures.

Writing and reading

First, the children form the letter shapes with their bodies, or they walk the path of enlarged letter-forms on the floor, or "draw" them in the air (see also p. 176). The shapes of the consonants are incorporated into blackboard illustrations of stories, before being "abstracted". The vowels are taught by associating their sounds with the expression of feelings, for example, Ah! Oh! Ooh! Ugh! Children start by printing words that they already know, perhaps from a rhyme that is already familiar. Writing, by occupying the hands as well as the eyes, engages the Will, whereas reading is a relatively passive activity.

PROFILE: CAMPHILL SCHOOLS

In 1940 an Austrian doctor, Dr Karl Konig, founded The Camphill Rudolf Steiner Schools to provide curative education for children with special needs. In 1955 he supported the start of a village community for handicapped adults at Botton, on the North York Moors, England.

Children with mental and physical difficulties have a life to fulfill, in spite of their afflictions, and it is the special task of the curative teacher to help them to fulfill it. Camphill schools do this by celebrating the uniqueness of each child. They practise a multi-disciplinary approach to curative education, combining the work of doctors, nurses, teachers, therapists, musicians, artists, and craftspeople. The fundamental principle behind all activities at Camphill schools is communication and working together. Positive, direct, and lively contact between staff and children leads to a full and vibrant life for both parties.

"

By accepting at last that we as a family had special needs, we began to function in a more positive way. We managed, after much searching to find more appropriate schooling for Marcella (at a Camphill school), although this involved the sacrifice of letting her go away to boarding school. But even this had other benefits: when Marcella came home during the holidays, we had lots of energy for her; and we had more time for our own needs and those of the rest of the family when she was away. The holidays became a lot of fun, rather than a time to be dreaded."

Elaine, Marcella's mother

Education Now is a UK-based publishing co-operative that reports on
initiatives in education occurring
worldwide. It opposes the traditional
educational approaches that promote
uniformity, dependency, and, for
many, a lasting sense of failure.
Education Now believes that people
learn best when they are self-motivated, take responsibility for their
own learning, and when teachers and
learners trust and listen to each other.
Education should be seen as a life-
long process.

According to its Statement of
Purpose, April 1993, Education
Now's vision of education includes:

● A focus on the uniqueness of individuals, of their learning experiences,
and of their varied learning styles

● Support of education in human-
scale settings (home-based, small and
mini-schools, schools-within-schools,
flexi-schools, and flexi-colleges)

● Recognition that learners have the
ability to make both rational and
intuitive choices about their own
education

● Advocacy of co-operative and
democratic organization of places of
learning

● Belief in the need to share national
resources so that everyone has a real
choice in education

● Acceptance of Einstein's proposal
that imagination is more important
than knowledge in our changing
world

● Adoption of the Universal
Declaration of Human Rights and
the European Convention for the
Protection of Human Rights and
Fundamental Freedoms

Alternative education

Many people feel that the word "education" has
come to mean "what teachers do with children
in school" and little else. A more positive
response to the educational predicament worldwide involves developing personal autonomy
along with responsible democracy. The education system needs to be re-thought to produce
more flexible, inquiring, tolerant, and confident
citizens. We need to get away from imposed systems that produce rigid, dependent people, and
use more flexible, choice-based approaches.

People can discuss alternatives to existing
forms of education through such groups as
Education Now, Education Otherwise, and
Human Scale Education in the UK, and
National Coalition of Alternative Community
Schools (NCACS) in the USA. These groups
have international links and aim to stimulate and
inform educational debate.

In the 1990s, the ideas of these groups are
moving from the radical margins toward centre
stage. For example, large corporations in the US,
such as Nabisco and Citibank, have started to
support alternative approaches with grants.

Nabisco's chairman, Louis Gerstner, says that
their scheme is designed to enable those "entre-
preneurs and risk-takers in education to break up
the institutional gridlock that has stifled innova-
tion and creativity". Known as Next Century
Schools, the scheme has been given a generous
grant to "find bold ideas and see if they work".

Citibank has given their first grant to the
Coalition of Essential Schools, a group of 500
schools, whose aim is to pursue a flexible curriculum related to pupils' abilities and interests.
The object is to train teachers to be "coaches",
and for pupils to be active participants in deciding what and how they learn.

TEN PRINCIPLES OF NATURAL LEARNING

These principles are a celebration of natural learning. Use them as a basis to think about and amplify your own ideas and assumptions about schooling and education.

- Schooling and education are not the same thing

- Education is an octopus and not a snake – education is a complex problem and not a simple problem at all, however inconvenient this may be

- Uniform approaches to all are intellectual death to some

- Deep learning is needed more than shallow learning

- An information-rich society allows a variety of learning locations

- Rigid systems produce rigid people and flexible systems produce flexible people

- With information doubling in quantity about every ten years we need a different kind of learning

- Effective teaching requires much more than being an instructor

- What we want to see is the learner in pursuit of knowledge and not knowledge in pursuit of the learner

- Open learning resource centres need to replace traditional schools

PROFILE: NCACS

Shifts toward alternative education are also taking place in the USA. Many of the ideas form the agenda of the National Coalition of Alternative Community Schools (NCACS), a non-profit-making coalition of schools, groups, families, and individuals. It brings members together and gives them strength, encouragement, new ideas, experiences, and a sense of community in their common endeavours. It is dedicated to providing confident, imaginative, independent thinkers, and a globally oriented education, which will not only cope successfully with the society in which we live, but will also enable change for the better.

BASIC OBJECTIVES

- To support an educational process that is alternative in intention, working to empower people actively and collectively to direct their lives

- To support an educational process that is alternative in form, requiring the active control of education by the students, parents, teachers, and community members who are most directly affected

- To support an educational process that is alternative in content, developing tools and skills to work for social justice

Human scale education

The scale of an educational setting ranges from a single family operating home-based education, through the small school operating as an extended family, to the large institution operating with hundreds of families. The scale of the educational environment itself does not automatically tell us the pattern of education adopted. A family can operate a very rigid form of authoritarian education, and a large institution can implement the democratic/autonomous techniques involved in mini-schooling or in the schools-within-schools approach developed in the USA.

In the UK, the educational charity Human Scale Education (HSE) exists to encourage human scale values in education in all schools and educational settings, however large or small. The charity believes that the child should be at the centre of the educational process not the curriculum, the school, or the requirements of the economy. Since each child is an individual with different needs this calls for a wide variety of schools, and a diversity of learning experiences and opportunities. The common requirement in any learning environment is that the child is treated with respect, and as an individual, and is encouraged to develop meaningful relationships with adults. These aims can be best achieved when the children are in small groups.

Small is beautiful

Most parents, whatever style of education they favour for their child, would choose a small, intimate school with small classes in preference to a large and probably more impersonal one. So too would most pupils and most teachers. Human Scale Education supports small schools in both urban and rural settings and actively encourages the setting up of new ones.

> HUMAN SCALE
> EDUCATION SUPPORTS:
> ● Small schools, mini-schooling and schools within schools, and flexi-schooling
> ● Creation of schools with a family, rather than a "factory", feel
> ● Encouragement of teachers to act as both friends and mentors
> ● Tailoring of the curriculum to each individual child
> ● Involving parents as partners in the process of education

---

Mini-schools

HSE also believes that inside all the large schools are numbers of small, personal, family-style schools waiting to be liberated. The idea behind mini-schooling is to reorganize a large school into a cluster of small learning communities, or a federation of mini-schools. Each mini-school has its own small team of teachers, a defined student population of about 100 pupils, some autonomy over the use of time, some resources of its own, and a base in the school. From time to time, the pupils of a mini-school will visit other parts of the campus to use special facilities, such as the gymnasium. A mini-school teacher may also sometimes visit other groups as a specialist teacher. There is continuity in mini-schools

▲ **A small school in operation**
*The children and teachers of Dame
Catherine's School, Ticknall, England.*

because teachers and pupils stay together, and are therefore able to build good relationships with each other, based on mutual respect, caring, and trust. The aim is to create a sense of community and a sense of belonging.

Schools within schools

This type of mini-schooling deliberately sets up mini-schools that have different educational approaches under one roof. Thus, one may be authoritarian, another autonomous, and another democratic: together they provide choice of approach. Parents, pupils, and teachers can choose the approach most suited to their needs and can change it as desired. In fact, it is a proto-type of flexi-schooling (see p. 332) in action.

(see p. 332)

PROFILE: DAME CATHERINE'S SCHOOL, TICKNALL, ENGLAND

Dame Catherine Harpur established a trust to provide a small school in Ticknall for local children in 1744. Later, it was taken over by the Local Education Authority, who closed it in 1987, because it was seen as too small. The parents immediately re-opened it as a non-fee-paying parent–teacher co-operative venture for five-to-sixteen year olds. It now has about fifty children on roll.

The school's educational approach, developed by the parents and teachers, puts the emphasis on small groups and a curriculum that is adapted to suit individual needs. In a weekly tutorial, each child's assignments are agreed with the teacher. The children keep a log-book of work completed. The aim, which is fundamental to natural learning, is to enable children to learn how to learn. Autonomous learning is supported and coached by sensitive adults. At the weekly school meeting, children can express their views about the school.

The philosophy is based on the development of the whole person – body, mind, and spirit – in a family-like atmosphere, with teachers as both friends and mentors, and parents as active partners in their child's education. Close parental involvement in teaching, as well as in organization and fund raising is encouraged. Parents take the children swimming, to the library, and help in the classroom. They clean, repair, and maintain the school building and run the Catherine Wheel gift shop to help raise funds.

Home versus school

In 1926, Bertrand Russell wrote, "There must be in the world many parents who...have young children whom they are anxious to educate as well as possible, but reluctant to expose them to the evils of most educational institutions". Even though schools have changed considerably since Russell's day, many parents and teachers are unimpressed with the outdated model of compulsory and regimented schooling being offered.

Survival and a vision

Replacing regimented schooling with a more healthy variety based on natural learning may prove to be a long process. There are a few institutions that can be held up as beacons of healthy schooling, but many parents with high hopes for their children's education may have to compromise or find other alternatives. Until we achieve a more intelligent schooling system a dual policy is essential – parents and teachers need both a sense of survival and a vision. They need an awareness of the reality, and constructive ways of coping with and limiting the damage, but also a dream toward which to work.

Most people believe that schooling is compulsory and are quite taken aback to learn otherwise. In the UK the law is clear: education is compulsory, but schooling is not. Parents have primary responsibility for their children's education, and although most delegate this to schools they need not do so. In the UK, the USA, and many other countries, more and more parents are choosing to educate their children at home. In the USA over a million families are now "home-schoolers". In the UK between 5000 and 10,000 families are operating home-based education, with similar numbers in New Zealand, Canada, and Australia.

The motives for home-based education

Families educating the home-based way display considerable diversity in motive, methods, and aims. According to research initiated at the University of Birmingham in the UK, the main motivation for parents educating at home in 1977 was desperation. Since then, however, there has been a change in motivation and many parents plan from the outset to educate their children at home. For others, the feeling that school can have a negative moral effect on their child's behaviour is a major motivating force. Other parents are distressed to find that their children are the victims of playground bullying. Home-based education is sometimes chosen for children who demand a more academic form of education than that available in schools. In other cases, it is chosen for children who have been unhappy or unsuccessful in a traditional school.

The principles of home-based education

Families use the home as a springboard into a range of community-based activities and investigations. They do not merely copy the "day prison" model operated by many schools. A society rich in sources of information and with access to a variety of media does not need learning to take place in a single location. Diversity is the key: home, work places, museums, libraries, and schools. Learning activities out and about in the community give children more social contacts with people of all ages, and more varied encounters, which improve their social skills, and reduce peer dependency. Home-based education respects the principles of natural learning (see p. 323). It encourages autonomous, self-directed learning and the development of self-sufficiency skills. Home-based education can be implemented at any time during a child's pre-school, primary, or secondary years.

Education for the 21st century is not a list; it's not a set of guidelines; it's not a curriculum. It's a way of thinking. In the years that lie ahead, beware the rule-bound; they live by lists and would have others live by them. Beware the categorisers, who divide children and curricula and loyalties into neat little domains over which they can rule in myopic comfort; there are no divisions in education worth taking seriously.... We need instead to construct for ourselves (and for the children in our charge) patterns with which to make sense of the world. We must sell understanding, not information. We must be wise, not just smart."

Robert Cole,
A Wish for My Child

School is the Army for kids. Adults make them go there, and when they go there, adults tell them what to do, bribe and threaten them into doing it, and punish them when they don't."

John Holt,
Alternatives in Education

Why not make schools into places where children would be allowed, encouraged, and when they asked, helped to explore and make sense of the world around them in ways that interested them?"

John Holt,
Teach Your Own

PROFILE: PAUL GOODMAN

The writing of New York born Paul Goodman (1911–1972) was at first ignored, then ridiculed, and finally acclaimed as visionary. His book *Growing Up Absurd* became a best-seller and *Compulsory Miseducation* set in motion a fierce debate about the effects of schooling.

In Goodman's view, the philosophical aim of education is to get children to be "society makers" who belong to one humanity. He proposed that the more schooling we impose, the less education we get. He thought schooling was a mass superstition, because it was believed that education could only be achieved in school-type institutions. He observed that subjecting young people to institutionalized learning tended to stunt their natural intellectual development and turned out regimented, competitive citizens. Goodman encouraged the natural learning patterns of the family and the community as experienced in a child's early years, and promoted the type of learning relationships fostered in master–apprentice traditions.

He saw school as artificial, whereas education was a natural experience. He set up Schools Without Walls and the New York Street School.

Education is a natural community function and occurs inevitably..."

It is in the schools and from the mass media, rather than at home or from their friends, that the mass of our citizens in all classes learn that life is inevitably graded; that it is best to toe the mark and shut up; that there is no place for spontaneity, open sexuality, free spirit."

Paul Goodman

Home-based education

A book entitled *Anything School Can Do You Can Do Better*, by Maria Mullarney, sounded like an unlikely claim to make before the evidence became available (see box), but it is now considered to be, more or less, accurate.

Many have reservations about home-based education, for example the lack of social life and social interaction for children, but research suggests that home-schoolers are ahead of their schooled peers in terms of social maturity.

Other criticisms about home schooling focus on the difficulty of organizing games or science experiments, and the lack of materials. However, with over one million families involved in home-based education in the USA, the provision of materials is a growing phenomenon. A publishing house is devoted to home schoolers, a research centre produces the journal *Home School Researcher*, and a number of companies have developed materials specifically for this market.

Undervalued parents

Schools often take the attitude that if home-based education is to be tolerable, families should learn from the "professionals". However, evidence demonstrates that schools often have more to learn from the flexibility of practice of many families, than vice versa. Generally, parents are undervalued as educators in schools. Parents are often seen as useful fundraisers or valuable teaching helpers, but teachers do not always see how they can amplify and extend the work of the parents with their child.

In most home-schooling families, one parent at least is a qualified teacher. However, of greater importance than a teaching qualification is that the family has energy and imagination to make home-based education work.

THE EVIDENCE FOR HOME SCHOOLING
Educationalist Larry Shyers has been studying the effects of home schooling in the USA. His research shows that compared to their schooled counterparts home-schooled children:
● Are more socially mature
● Have a far wider range of social skills
● Have fewer behavioural problems
A study by Thomas Smedley supports Shyers's findings and suggests possible reasons for this greater social maturity:
● The classroom is mostly one-way communication, involving few meaningful interchanges. In home-based education the opposite is the case
● Schools are products of the factory age with uniform products running on the conveyor belt toward the standardized diploma. Home-based education works toward more personalized educational outcomes
● An unnatural aspect of school is age segregation. Learning to get along with peers alone does not prepare students for the varied interactions of life. Home-based education avoids this, since people of various ages are encountered in a way that more accurately mirrors the variety of society
● The emphasis of home-based education is on self-discipline and self-directed learning. This creates confident young people who adapt well to new situations and people

"My schooling not only failed to teach me what it professed to be teaching, but prevented me from being educated to an extent which infuriates me when I think of all I might have learned at home by myself."

George Bernard Shaw,
in *The Freethinker's Guide to the Educational Universe*

"Home schoolers as a rule have no quarrel with teachers.... My feeling is that most teachers are dedicated, caring people with a very difficult job to do.... Our reservation is about the system of schooling."

David Smith,
Parent-generated Home Study in Canada

"The important issues in regard to home schooling are not the numbers, the statistics, the grades, the finances, the qualifications. The important issues are character, morals, motivation, self reliance, self esteem, service, and wisdom."

David Smith,
Parent-generated Home Study in Canada

"No one should undertake to home-school without coming to terms with this fundamental truth: it is the fabric of your own life you are deciding about, not just your child's education."

David Guterson,
Harpers Magazine, November 1990

PROFILE: EDUCATION OTHERWISE

This UK-based membership organization was established in 1977 and since then has been gradually growing in size and influence. It provides support and information for families whose children are being educated outside school, and for those who wish to uphold the freedom of families to take full responsibility for the education of their children.

The principal aims of EO are to:

● Encourage learning outside the school system

● Reaffirm that parents have the primary responsibility for their children's education and that they have a right to exercise this responsibility by educating them out of school

● Establish the primary right of children to have full consideration given to their wishes and feelings about their education

"Home schooling reminds us that learning is a much more fluid process than we might have realized.... We learn from the living model of life as it happens."

Pederson and O'Mara,
Home School Researcher, vol 8 no 4

"I was very pleased with our year... I felt listened to, much more than in any other school I have been associated with, and feel that input from the participants is important to the continued success of the program."

Kathy Litman, commenting on the
Santa Rosa Independent Study Programme

Flexi-time

A newcomer in the educational field is already mounting a potential challenge to full-time, home-based education. Some families are pioneering a more flexible form of education – flexi-time, which is a programme that is partly school-based and partly home-based. Other forms of more flexible schooling, which use learning resource centres, have come to be described as "flexi-schools" (see p. 332).

For some parents, and their children, the best learning arrangement uses a flexi-time scheme, with the child spending part of the time at home, and part of the time at a more traditionally run school. Some flexi-time arrangements are relatively easy to achieve, especially when large blocks of time are spent either at school or at home. For example, the primary years may be devoted to home-based education and the secondary years given over to school, or vice versa. Some children alternate between home and school on a yearly or semester basis.

The most difficult type of flexi-time to arrange is a flexible weekly timetable. This is commonplace in nursery schools and also in higher education, but most schools refuse to allow flexi-time. Gradually, however, there are more cases of successful negotiations for flexi-time being reported in the UK. In the United States, Independent Study Programmes (ISPs) provide this kind of weekly based flexi-time and are becoming increasingly popular (see box). Some local authorities, both in the UK and US, organize this way for children with special needs, using the Portage Scheme (see facing page).

A few families have one child in school and another out, with options to change in either direction as experience and the needs of each child develop, and events unfold.

INDEPENDENT STUDY PROGRAMMES (ISPS)
Each ISP varies because it is the result of a negotiation between a specially trained member of staff from the school and a family. The programme that emerges states how much time will be spent learning in school and how much learning at home and elsewhere. It is an agreement about what learning is to be attempted in each setting, and how it is to be monitored. The responsibilities of all parties (students, family, and school), are written into a contract, which is reviewed periodically.

"
"Much of our expenditure on teachers and plant is wasted by attempting to teach people what they do not want to learn in a situation that they would rather not be involved in."

Colin Ward,
New Humanist, September 1977

"
...the best learning happens in real life with real problems and real people and not in classrooms with know-all teachers."

Charles Handy,
The Age of Reason

"
Education is not the filling of a pail, but the lighting of a fire."

W. B. Yeats,
in *The Freethinker's Guide to the Educational Universe*

Flexi-time and the law

The position in law in the UK is that there are two absolute rights in education: either to educate at home, or to use a school. Flexi-time is a relative right. A school or Local Education Authority may agree to flexi-time, but if permission is refused, no reason has to be given. Each arrangement has to be negotiated afresh, and so parents may have to explain patiently that it is permissible, plenty of people have done it, and that it does work very well if the will and the vision are there.

PROFILE: THE PORTAGE HOME VISITING SCHEME

In both the USA and UK a flexi-time approach is used for special education. It is known as the Portage Scheme, after the small town in Wisconsin, USA, where it was initially set up. This scheme was designed to bring educational and developmental aids to pre-school children with mild and moderate learning difficulties. The principle aim of the scheme is to enable parents to teach their children in their own homes. Home teachers visit once a week, identify, and agree with the parents which new skills their child should learn next. After a demonstration by the teacher, and a trial run by the parent, the agreement is written down on an activity chart to allow monitoring of progress.

The evaluation reports of the project show that the scheme helps parents systematically to teach their handicapped children and record their progress. The model recognizes and validates the view that children learn very effectively when parents are closely involved in the teaching. Portage parents often "graduate" and become visiting home teachers themselves once their own children have gone to school.

Flexi-schooling

Flexi-schooling is when a school has become more flexible in one dimension or in more of its activities so that negotiation of a programme that takes into account the wishes and needs of the family and child can take place. Flexi-schools are being renamed "learning resource centres" to avoid confusion with the traditional image of school. They are places of freedom to learn. They are places where children are allowed, encouraged, and when they ask for it, helped to make sense of the world around them in ways that interest them.

Flexi-schools are there for everyone to use. They are used by families who school their children at home to augment their programmes of study, and by students of any age who come to the centre for particular classes. Workshops and special activities such as music and drama are arranged on request. Facilities are available for group meetings, large and small, and for all kinds of activities for people of all ages.

Flexi-schooling is a complicated idea and it sounds rather demanding to implement, so why is it worth trying? We are living in a changing world. Its technologies and its cultures continue to develop and become more complicated. Knowledge continues to grow and existing knowledge is shown to be partial and sometimes in error. Rigid people cannot cope with the reviewing, revising, and re-learning that is necessary to be effective in the modern world. "Flexible" people have a better chance of coping, as do those who know how to find out for themselves, and can manage their own learning. Flexi-schooling allows diversity and encourages the idea that a variety of educational ideas and experiences have a legitimate part to play in one person's educational programme.

> "
> *The schools we need today must be institutions which abandon any and all attempts to limit the free pursuit of knowledge that every child, and every adult, engages in naturally, without any outside goading."*
>
> Daniel Greenberg,
> *A Voice for Children, Winter 1992*

> "
> *No teacher ever said: 'Don't value uncertainty and tentativeness, don't question questions, above all don't think!' The message is communicated quietly, insidiously, relentlessly and efficiently through the structure of the classroom: through the role of the teacher, the role of the student, the rules of their verbal game, the rights that are assigned, the arrangements made for communication, the 'doings' that are praised or censured. In other words, the medium is the message."*
>
> N. Postman and C. Weingartner,
> *Teaching as a Subversive Activity*

▲ **Uppattinas Resource Center**
The center is run on the principle that learning and education take place everywhere: Uppattinas is a place for personal growth, learning, and sharing.

A worthwhile world

Adults perhaps need to exercise a little humility about their achievements and their efforts in the world so far. Paul Goodman says: "...there is no right education except growing up into a worthwhile world. Our excessive concern with the 'problems of education' at present simply means that the grown-ups do not have such a worthwhile world."

If we do not have a worthwhile world yet, nor worthwhile schools, we will have to build them both. Schools need to become communities engaged in the task of improving themselves, their members, and their worlds.

PROFILE: **UPPATTINAS EDUCATIONAL RESOURCE CENTER, PHILADELPHIA, USA**

The re-creation of the Uppattinas school came after a long and painful struggle when members faced up to the fact that there just weren't enough students who could pay sufficient fees, or families who could work hard enough to make up the shortfall in finances to run it as a "school". But, it was possible to sustain the buildings and preserve the integrity of the commitment to open education through establishing it as a Learning Resource Centre. The centre director, Sandy Hurst, explained that it could be "a place to which people came who truly wanted to learn and to share what they had learned".

Everyone is welcome and the facility is open to community members as and when they need it. Programmes are limited only by the interests and needs of those involved. Workshops have been organized, ranging from music improvisation to American Indian survival skills, projects on environmental concerns and classes spanning literature to first aid.

The Uppattinas center is:
A "doing" centre for all ages
A repository for tools for doing things
A repository for records of things done
A place for sharing
A source of helpers
A centre for people from all cultures
A source for participant-controlled learning
A centre for all who believe in life-long learning

Matching your child to a school

Finding a path through the labyrinth of a national education system and choosing a school for your child can be a daunting, often intimidating, task for any parent. At first, there seem to be so many choices: home-based education or flexi-schooling; large schools or small; authoritarian, democratic, or autonomous education; day or boarding school; state or private school; single-sex or mixed. Choice in education involves educational approach, finances, ethics, and scale, but then we realize that some hard facts of life – national regulations, personal expense, examinations, geographical location – narrow those choices down dramatically. The school should be the choice of the family, the parents in consultation with the child. Subsequent family reviews of the wisdom of the choice should take place, and agreement reached if it needs to be changed

School represents a new stage in a child's life, but it should also be a continuation and gradual transformation of pre-school life. If parents have made this rich, healthy, and without stress they will also want these qualities at school.

The quality of the relationships within the school, the nature of its organization, and the experiences it offers will influence a child's ability to adjust to school life. Children are very sensitive to the pervading "atmosphere" of a school. To feel secure and happy they need smiling faces, kindness, and sympathetic support. The school should allow for the development of independence and responsibility. The provision of experiences that excite curiosity, and encourage investigation and talk, enables children to gain enjoyment and satisfaction from their activities. School brochures explain aspects of school life to parents, but they are no substitute for visiting the school and getting a feel of it in person.

WHAT IS YOUR CHILD LIKE?
Use the following questions to think about your child's character and what she needs in a learning environment. Is she:

Quiet or lively?
Thoughtful or selfish?
Passive or bossy?
Industrious or lazy?
A leader or a follower?
Able to work on her own
or only under supervision?
Able to work as part of a group?
Vocal, or never voices her opinion?
Compliant or headstrong?
Able to concentrate well or easily distracted?
Able to work in noise or needs silence?
Easily bored or perseveres until
a task is finished?
Accustomed to finding things easy or does she struggle to accomplish things?
Articulate, and was she an early or late talker?
Musical, artistic, or sporty?
Active or lethargic?
Adept at number work?
Adept at letter work?
Able to draw well or does she find it
difficult?
Enthusiastic about making things?
Healthy or unhealthy?
A self-starter or does she need
encouragement?

THE SCHOOL ENVIRONMENT

Is there order or chaos?
Is it friendly or austere?
Is it noisy or quiet?
Is it clean and tidy, or in need of redecoration?
Is the playground asphalt or grass?
Is there an ecology corner?

THE STAFF

Do you like the principal's attitude toward parents?
Are the teachers well presented or untidy?
Are they experienced but jaded, or inexperienced but enthusiastic?
What is the staff turnover?
Are there temporary teachers?
What is the female to male teacher ratio?
What is the staff to pupil ratio?
Are there any teaching assistants?

ORGANIZATION

How is the school funded?
Is there a uniform?
Is it single-sex or mixed?
Are the classes large or small?
Are there parallel classes?
Is there streaming?
How many children are there with special needs?
How are very "bright" children handled?
Do boys and girls play together?
Is there fighting in the playground?
What is the racial balance?
Is bullying or racism addressed or ignored?
What types of punishment are used?
Is there any truancy or expulsion?
What opportunities do parents have to contact teachers?
Is parental involvement in the classroom encouraged?
Is there an active parent-teacher association (PTA)?
Is there contact with the local community?
Do the pupils receive regular health checks?

THE CURRICULUM

Does the school operate the National Curriculum or equivalent?
What is the attitude toward testing, sports, and religion?
What reading and mathematics schemes are used?
Are there drama/art/music/crafts/computer facilities?
Is homework expected?
Are there outings and field trips?
Is there preparation for, and links with, secondary schools?
Is flexi-time a possibility?

◀ **How to choose a school?**
Use the list (left) to help you think about and assess the possible options open to you when choosing a school for your child. Trust your gut reactions: does the school strike you as a stimulating place and inspire you with confidence? Is it solid, reliable, and secure? Remember that you are choosing a school for your child, not for yourself. Can you visualize your child there?

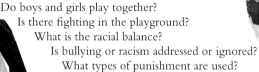

Resources

SELF HELP, PARENTING

Adoptive Families of America
3333 Hwy 100
North Minneapolis MN 55422

Center for Parent Education
55 Chapel St
Newton MA 02160

Compleat Mother
Box 209
Minot ND 58702
(journal)

Depression After Delivery
PO Box 1282
Morrisville PA 19067

The Doula
PO Box 71
Santa Cruz CA 95063
(journal)

Full-Time Dads
PO Box 577
Cumberland ME 04021
(journal)

Informed Birth & Parenting
PO Box 3675
Ann Arbor MI 48106

Joyful Child Journal
PO Box 5506
Scottsdale AZ 85261

La Leche League International
9616 Minneapolis Ave
Franklin Park IL 60131

Mothering
PO Box 1690
Santa Fe NM 87504
(quarterly magazine and Mothering Friends Network)

Mothers of Preschoolers International
4175 Harlan St #105
Wheat Ridge CO 80033
(MOPS Christian support groups)

Mothers' Resource Guide
PO Box 38
South Milwaukee WI 53172

Mothers' Underground
3047 N Lincoln Ave
Suite 360
Chicago IL 60657
(journal)

National Association for Family Day Care
725 Fifteenth St
NW Suite 505
Washington DC 20005

National Association of Mothers' Centers
336 Fulton Ave
Hempstead NY 11550

National MOMS Club
814 Moffatt Circle
Simi Valley CA 93065
(115 chapters for at-home mothers)

National Organization of Mothers of Twins Clubs
PO Box 23188
Albuquerque NM 87192

The Nurturing Parent
PO Box 6191
Bismarck ND 58506
(newsletter)

Parents Anonymous
6733 S Sepulveda Blvd #270
Los Angeles CA 90045
Tel: 1-800-421-0353

Parents without Partners
8807 Colesville Rd
Silver Spring MD 20910

Positive Pregnancy and Parenting Fitness
51 Saltrock Rd
Baltic CT 06330

Postpartum Support International
927 N Kellogg Ave
Santa Barbara CA 93111

Priority Parenting
PO Box 1793
Warsaw IN 46581
(newsletter)

Services for the Nurturing of Children
1100 Irvine Blvd
Suite 173
Tustin CA 92680

Single Mothers by Choice
PO Box 1642
Gracie Square Station
New York NY 10028

Stepfamily Association of America Inc
602 E Joppa Rd
Baltimore MD 21204

Twins Magazine
PO Box 12045
Overland Park KS 66282

CRAFT SUPPLIERS

Bartlettyarns
PO Box 36
Harmony ME 04942

Chaselle Inc
9645 Gerwig Lane
Columbia MD
(arts and crafts)

A Child's Dream
PO Box 2203
Shingle Springs CA 95682

Earth Guild
37 Haywood St
Asheville NC 28801
(natural dyes, spinning, and weaving)

Handworks
Route 1
Box 138
Afton VA 22920
(kits for children)

Hearth Song
PO Box B
Sebastopol CA 95473
(beeswax for modelling and crayons, watercolors)

Mountain Sunrise
279 Swanzey Lake Rd
Winchester NH 03470
(plant-dyed fleece, felt, yarn)

Sureway Trading Enterprises
826 Pine Ave
Suites 5 & 6
Niagara Falls NY 14301
(silk)

Triform Fiber Arts Workshop
RD4 Box 151
Hudson NY 12534
(wool products)

Weir Dolls
2909 Parkridge Drive
Ann Arbor MI 48103

West End Woolen Mill
R D 2 Ephrata PA 17522

Wilde and Wooly
3705 Main St
Philadelphia PA 19127

TOYS, GAMES AND PLAY

Animal Town Game Company
PO Box 485
Healdsburg CA 95448

Back to Basics Toys
2707 Pittman Dr,
Silver Spring MD 10910

A Child's Dream
PO Box 2203
Single Springs CA 95682

Community Playthings
Route 213
Ritton NY 124/1

Hearth Song
PO Box B
Sebastopol CA 95473

Heartwood Arts Educational Toys
2768 Route 208
Walden NY 12586

Marvelous Toy Works
RR1
Box 124A
Stillwater PA 17878

Meadow View Imports
PO Box 407
Wyoming RI 02898

North Star Toys
617 North Star Route
Questa NM 87556

Nova
817 Chestnut Ridge Rd
Chestnut Ridge
NY 10977

Pagoda People
PO Box 2055
Boulder CO 80306

Pecos Pine
242 E Main Street
Suite 8
Ashland OR 97520

Vidar Goods
PO Box 808
College Park MD 20740

Weir Dolls
2909 Parkridge Drive
Ann Arbor MI 48103

MUSICAL INSTRUMENTS

Choroi Karen Klaveness
4600 Minnesota Ave
Fair Oaks CA 95628

Harps of Lorien
HC81 Box 610
Questa NM 87556

Hearth Song
PO Box B
Sebastopol CA 95473

Song of the Sea
47 West Street
Bar Harbor ME 04609

NATURAL FIBER CLOTHING

After the Stork
3002 Monte Vista NE
Albuquerque NM 87106

Cotton Dreams
2962 NW 60th Street
Ft Lauderdale FL 33309

Footnotes
65 Bow St
Portsmouth NH 03801

Garnet Hill
Franconia NH 05380

Hanna Anderson
1010 NW Flanders
Portland OR 97209

Kottage Kids
Red Meadow Lane
Polebridge MT 59928

Motherwear, Inc PO Box 114
Northampton MA 01061

Nature's Little Shoes
254 9th St NE
Washington DC 20002

Royal Silk
PO Box 5051
Clifton NJ 07015

Trade Wind
PO Box 380
Summertown TN 38483

Vermont Country Store
PO Box 3000
Manchester Center VT 05255

Winter Silks
PO Box 130
Middleton WI 53562

NON-DISPOSABLE DIAPERS

Baby Bunz & Co
PO Box 1717
Sebastopol CA 95473

Babyworks
11725 NW West Road
#2 Portland OR 97229

Bio Bottoms
PO Box 1060
Bodega Ave
Petaluma CA 94953

Eco-Baby
4145 Clares St
Suite F
Capitola CA 95003

Mainely Baby Bottoms
PO Box 1068
Brunswick ME 04011

The Natural Baby Company
816 Sylvia St 800B
Trenton NJ 08628

Simple Alternatives
817 S 1st St
Cottage Grove
OR 97424

BABY CARRIERS

Baby Wrap Products Inc
PO Box 100584
Denver CO 80250

California Diversified Manufacturing
PO Box 635
San Clemente CA 92674

Co-op America Order Service
126 Intervale Road
Burlington VT 05401

Parenting Concepts
PO Box 1437
Lake Arrowhead CA 92352

Rebozo Way
6063 Ethel Ave
Van Nuys CA 91401

ECOLOGICAL HOUSEHOLD PRODUCTS

ECO Design Co
1365 Rufina Circle
Santa Fe NM 87501

Seventh Generation
Colchester VT 05446

HEALTH

American Holistic Medical Association and
American Holistic Nurses' Association
4101 Lake Boone Trail
Suite 201
Raleigh NC 27607

Anthroposophical Nurses Association of
America
215 E Main St
Elkton MD 21921

Anthroposophical Therapy and Hygiene
Association (ANTHA)
241 Hungry Hollow Road
Chestnut Ridge NY 10977

Association for Pre- and Perinatal
Psychology and Health
1600 Prince St #500
Alexandira VA 22314

The Bradley Method
PO Box 5224
Sherman Oaks CA 91413

Cascade Health Care Products
141 Commercial St
NE Salem OR 97301

Doulas of North America (DONA)
1100 23rd Avenue
East Seattle WA 98112

Global Maternal Child Health Association
PO Box 366
West Linn OR 97068

Herbs for Kids
2050 Fairway Dr
Suite 106
Bozeman MT 59715

Homeopathic Educational Services
2124A Kittredge
Berkeley CA 94704

Homeopathy Overnight Inc
4111 Simon Rd
Youngstown OH 44512
(1-800-ARNICA 30)

Immunization Resource Guide,
Patter Publications
PO Box 204
Burlington IA 52601

Informed Homebirth
PO Box 3675
Ann Arbor MI 48106

International Cesarean Awareness Network
(ICAN)
PO Box 152
Syracuse NY 13210

International Childbirth Education
Association
(ICEA)
PO Box 20048
Minneapolis MN 55420

International Lactation Consultants
Association
201 Brown Ave
Evanston IL 60202

Midwives Alliance of North America
(MANA)
PO Box 175
Newton KS 67114

Mothering
PO Box 1690,
Santa Fe NM 87504
(publishes Vaccinations. The Rest of the
Story)

National Association of Childbirth Assistants
205 Copco Lane
San Jose CA 95123

National Center for Homeopathy
801 N Fairfax St
Suite 306
Alexandria VA 22314

National Organization of Circumcision
Information Resource Centers
(NOCIRC)
PO Box 2512
San Anselmo CA 94979

National Vaccine Information
Center/Dissatisfied Parents Together
(NVIC/DPT)
512 W. Maple Ave
Suite 206
Vienna VA 22180

Natural Elements
PO Box 3299
Santa Cruz CA 95063

New Atlantean Press
PO Box 9638,
Santa Fe, NM 87505
(publishes books on vaccination)

Physician's Association for Anthroposophical
Medicine
(PAAM)
PO Box 66609
Portland OR 97290

Weleda Inc
PO Box 249
Congers NY 10920

EDUCATION

Alliance for Parental Involvement in
Education
(AllPIE)
PO Box 59
East Chatham NY 12060

Brook Farm Books
PO Box 246
Bridgewater ME 04735
(The Home School Source Book)

Child and Man
Barbara Richardson
529 W Grant Place
Chicago IL 60614
(British Waldorf journal)

Childhood
RR1 Box 2675
Westford VT 05494
(Waldorf-based journal)

Clonlara Home Based Education Program
1289 Jewett
Ann Arbor MI 48103

Global Alliance for Transforming Education
4202 Ashwoody Trail
Atlanta GA 30319

Growing without Schooling
2269 Massachusetts Ave
Cambridge MA 02140

Home Education Press
PO Box 1083
Monasket WA 98855

Home Study International
PO Box 4437
Silver Spring MD 20914
(Christian-based curriculum)

Homeschool Associates
116 Third Ave
Auburn ME 04210

The Homeschool Gazette
Route 3
Box 500
Leighton AL 35646

Homeschooling Today
PO Box 956
Lutz Fl 33549
(journal; Christian oriented)

Human Scale Education Movement
96 Carlingcott
Bath BA2 8AW
United Kingdom
("small is beautiful" approach to schooling via
smallschooling, minischooling, and flexischooling)

Institute for Democracy in Education
Ohio University
313 McCracken Hall
Athens OH 45701

Mothering
PO Box 1690
Santa Fe, NM 87504
(publishes Schooling at Home)

National Coalition of Alternative
Community Schools
PO Box 15036
Santa Fe NM 87506
(includes home-schooling)

National Homeschool Association
PO Box 157290
Cincinnati OH 45215

Oak Meadow School
PO Drawer Q
Blacksburg VA 24060
(elementary school curriculum with Waldorf influence and home teacher training)

Parents as Teachers
9374 Olive Blvd
St Louis MO 63132

The Sycamore Tree
2179 Meyer Place
Costa Mesa CA 92627
(homeschool curriculum, catalog)

Renewal, A Journal for Waldorf Education
AWSNA
3911 Bannister Rd
Fair Oaks CA 95628

Rethinking Schools
1001 East Keefe Ave
Milwaukee WI 53212
(magazine)

Waldorf Kindergarten Newsletter
1359 Alderton Lane
Silver Spring MD 20906

Teacher Education Courses for
Waldorf/Steiner Schools
Antioch
New England

Waldorf Teacher Training
Roxbury St
Keene NH 03431

Chicago Extension Program of the Waldorf
Institute
1651 W Diversey
Chicago IL 60614

Rudolf Steiner Centre
9100 Bathurst
Toronto
Ontario
Canada L3T 3N3

Rudolf Steiner College
9200 Fair Oaks Blvd
Fair Oaks CA 95628

Rudolf Steiner Institute
PO Box 0990
Planetarium Sta
New York NY 10024
(summer courses in Maine)

Waldorf Institute of Southern California
17100 Superior St
Northridge CA 91325

Waldorf Institute of Sunbridge College
260 Hungry Hollow Rd
Chestnut Ridge NY 10977

Waldorf Teacher Development Association
8211 Hendrie
Hungtington Woods MI 48070

SCHOOLS

Albany Free School
8 Elm Street
Albany NY 12202

Association of Waldorf Schools of North
America (AWSNA)
3911 Bannister Rd
Fair Oaks CA 95628

City as School
16b Clarkson Street
New York NY 10014

Summerhill School
Leiston
Suffolk
United Kingdom
(free school founded by A S Neill)

Waldorf Kindergarten Association of North
America
1359 Alderton Lane Ave
Silver Spring MD 20906

SPECIAL NEEDS

Association for a Healing Education
Box 300A
Glenmoore PA 19343
(Steiner oriented)

Association for Children and Adults with
Learning Disabilities
4256 Library Rd
Pittsburgh PA 15234

Association of Birth Defect Children
5400 Diplomatic Circle
Suite 270
Orlando FL 32810

Attention-Deficit Disorder Association
4300 West Park Blvd
Plano TX 75093

Federation for Children with Special Needs
95 Berkeley St
Suite 104
Boston MA 02116

International Camphill Seminar in Curative
Education,
Camphill Special School
RD 1 Box 240
Glenmoore PA 19343
(Steiner oriented)

MUMS
(Mothers United for Moral Support)
150 Custer Court
Green Bay WI 54301

PUBLISHERS AND MAIL-ORDER BOOK SERVICES

Anthroposophic Press
RR4 Box 94A1
Hudson NY 12534

Bear & Co Publishing
PO Box 2860
Santa Fe NM 87504

Birth and Life Books
141 Commercial St
NE Salem OR 97301

Cascade Health Care Products
141 Commercial St
NE Salem OR 97301

Celestial Arts
PO Box 7327
Berkeley CA 94707

Chinaberry: Books and Other Treasures for
the Entire Family
2780 Via Orange Way
Suite B
Spring Valley CA 91978

The Crossing Press
PO Box 1048
Freedom CA 95019

Home Education Press
PO Box 1083
Tonasket WA 98855

Informed Birth & Parenting Books
PO Box 3675
Ann Arbor MI 48106

Lura Media
PO Box 261668
San Diego CA 92196

Mercury Press
241 Hungry Hollow Rd
Chestnut Ridge NY 10977

Mother and Home Books
Westerdale Rd
RR1 Box 122
Woodstock VT 05091

Natural Resources
4081 24th St
San Francisco CA 94114

Optimal Family Health Catalog
PO Box 398
Monroe UT 84758

Rudolf Steiner College/
St George Publications
9200 Fair Oaks Blvd
Fair Oaks CA 95628

Rudolf Steiner School Press
15 East 79th St
New York NY 10021

Sudbury Valley Press
2 Winch St
Framingham MA 01701

Further Reading

CHILD DEVELOPMENT

Aeppli, W, *The Care and Development of the Human Senses*, Steiner Schools Fellowship, 1993

Baldwin, R, *You Are Your Child's First Teacher*, Celestial Arts, Berkeley, California, 1989

— *Special Delivery*, Celestial Arts, Berkeley, California, 1986

Baldwin, R and Palmarini, T, *Pregnant Feelings*, Celestial Arts, Berkeley, California, 1986

de Beauvoir, S, *The Second Sex*, Everyman, 1993

Beck, J, *How to Raise a Brighter Child* (out of print)

Berrien Berends, P, *Whole Child/Whole Parent*, Harper & Row, 1983

Bettelheim, B, *The Uses of Enchantment*, Knopf, New York, 1976

Brazelton, T Berry, *Infants and Mothers: Differences in Development*, Dell, New York, 1986

— *Touchpoints*, Viking, 1992

Britz-Crecelius, H, *Children at Play – Preparation for Life*, Floris Books, Edinburgh, 1986

Childs, G, *Steiner Education in Theory and Practice*, Floris Books, 1991

Chilton Pearce, J, *The Magical Child*, E P Dutton, New York, 1977

— *Crack in the Cosmic Egg* (out of print)

— *Evolution's End*, Harper Collins, 1993

Cusick, L, *Waldorf Parenting Handbook*, Rudolf Steiner College/St George Publications, 1984

Erikson, E, *Life Crises in the Child* (out of print)

Elkind, D, *The Hurried Child*, Addison Wesley, 1989

— *Miseducation: Preschoolers at Risk*, Alfred A. Knopf, 1984

Fraiberg, S, *The Magic Years, Understanding the Problems of Early Childhood*, Methuen, 1968

Fromm, E, *The Art of Loving*, George Allen and Unwin, 1985

— *Voyage Through Childhood Into The Adult World: A Description of Child Development*, Pergamon Press, London, 1969

Gesell, A, *The First Five Years of Life*, Methuen, London, 1954

Gesell, A, et al, *Infant and Child*, Hamish Hamilton (out of print)

Glas, N, *Conception, Birth and Early Childhood*, Anthroposophic Press, New York, 1973

Glöckler, M, & Goebel, W, *A Guide to Child Health*, Floris Books, Edinburgh, 1990

Haller, I, *How Children Play*, Floris Books, Edinburgh, 1991

Hostler, P, *The Child's World*, Penguin, 1959

Kazantzakis, N, *Report to Greco*, Faber, 1973

Knight, M et al, *Teaching Children to Love Themselves*, Spectrum, 1982

Konig, K, *The First Three Years of the Child*, Anthroposophic Press, New York, 1969

Leach, P, *Baby and Child*, Penguin, 1988

Leboyer, F, *Birth Without Violence*, Collins, 1983

Liedloff, J, *The Continuum Concept*, Penguin, 1986

Lievegoed, B, *Phases of Childhood*, Floris Books, Edinburgh, 1987

— *Phases, Crisis and Development in the Individual*, Rudolf Steiner Press, 1979

zur Linden, W, *A Child is Born: Pregnancy, Birth and Early Childhood*, Rudolf Steiner Press, 1973

Maslow, A, *Toward a Psychology of Being*, Van Nostrand, 1969

Miller, A, *The Drama of Being a Child*, Virago, 1987

Miedzian, M, *Boys will be boys: breaking the link between masculinity and violence*, Virago, 1993

Moore, R S and D N, *Better Late Than Early*, Reader's Digest (out of print)

Nilsson, L, *A Child is Born*, Faber, 1977

Piaget, J, *The Moral Judgment of the Child* (out of print)

Roazen, P, *Freud and his Followers*, Da Capo, 1992

Rogers, C, *On Becoming a Person*, Houghton Mifflin, 1961

— *Personal Power*, Constable, 1978

— *Freedom to Learn for the 80s*, Charles E. Merrill, 1983

Sacks, O, *The Man Who Mistook His Wife For A Hat*, Duckworth, 1985

Salter, J, *The Incarnating Child*, Hawthorn Press, Stroud, 1987

Scott Peck, J, *The Road Less Travelled*, Arrow, 1983

Steiner, R, *The Four Temperaments*, Anthroposophic Press, 1976

— *Education of the Child in the Light of Anthroposophy*, Rudolf Steiner Press, 1985

Stern, D, *Diary of a Baby*, Fontana, 1991

— *The First Relationship: Infant and Mother*, Open Books, 1989

Strauss, M, *Understanding Children's Drawings*, Rudolf Steiner Press, 1979

Vygotsky, Lev, *Thought and Language*, MIT Press, 1986

Winnicott, D W, *The Child, the Family and the Outside World*, Penguin, 1991

SPIRITUALITY

Carson, A (ed), *Spiritual Parenting in the New Age*, The Crossing Press, California, 1989

Gibran, K, *The Prophet*, Heinemann, 1993

Harwood, A C, *The Way of a Child*, Rudolf Steiner Press, 1974

Jones, M (ed), *Prayers and Graces*, Floris Books, Edinburgh, 1987

Silverstein, S, *Child Spirit*, Bear & Co, New Mexico, 1991

Steiner, R, *Prayers for Mothers and Children*, Rudolf Steiner Press, London 1983

— *The Spiritual Ground of Education*, Anthroposophical Publishing Co, London, 1960

— *Verses and Meditations*, Rudolf Steiner Press, London, 1985

SELF-HELP

Baldwin, R and Palmarini, T, *Pregnant Feelings*, Celestial Arts, Berkeley, California, 1986

Berrien Berends, P, *Whole Child/Whole Parent*, Harper & Row, 1983

Bettelheim, B, *A Good Enough Parent*, Pan, 1987

Coplen, D, *Parenting*, Floris Books, Edinburgh, 1982

Crowe, B, *Your Child and You*, Unwin, 1986

Faber, A and Mazlish, E, *How to Talk so Kids Will Listen*, Avon, New York, 1980

— *Siblings Without Rivalry*, Avon, New York, 1987

— *Liberated Parents, Liberated Children*, Avon, New York, 1990

Fromm, E, *The Art of Loving*, Allen & Unwin, 1985

Jackson, D, *Three in a Bed*, Bloomsbury, 1990

Jolly, H, *The Book of Child Care*, Allen & Unwin, 1985

Leach, P, *The Parents' A to Z*, Penguin, 1988

Skynner, R and Cleese, J, *Families and How to Survive Them*, Methuen, 1983

Sokolov, I and Hutton, D, *The Parents' Book*, Thorsons, 1988

Spock, Dr B, *Baby and Child Care*, Dutton, New York, 1985

Steiner, R, *The Four Temperaments*, Anthroposophic Press, New York, 1987

Thevenin, T, *The Family Bed: an Age Old Concept in Child Rearing*, Avery Publishing, New York, 1985

Walker, P and F, *Natural Parenting*, Bloomsbury, 1987, and Interlink, New York, 1988

Wipfler, P, Series of booklets from Parents Leadership Institute:

Listening to Children
Playlistening
Reaching for your Angry Child
Healing Childrens' Fears
Crying, Tantrums and Indignation
Listening: a Tool for Powerful Parenting, 1989
Special Time: Listening to Children, 1990
Leading a Parent Resource Group, 1990
Listening Partnerships for Parents, 1991
available from Parents' Leadership Institute, PO Box 50492, Palo Alto, California 94303, USA

Series from The Rosendale Press, London 1992 and 1993, written by workers at the Tavistock Clinic:

Understanding Your Baby, Lisa Miller
Understanding Your 1 Year Old, Deborah Steiner
Understanding Your 2 Year Old, Susan Reid
Understanding Your 3 Year Old, Judith Trowell
Understanding Your 4 Year Old, Lisa Miller
Understanding Your 5 Year Old, Lesley Holditch
Understanding Your 6 Year Old, Deborah Steiner
Understanding Your 7 Year Old, Elsie Osborne

FESTIVALS

Barz, B, *Festivals with Children*, Floris Books, Edinburgh, 1987

Carey, D and Large, J, *Festivals, Family and Food*, Hawthorn Press, Stroud, 1982

Fitzjohn, S et al, *Festivals Together*, Hawthorn Press, Stroud, 1993

Green, M, *A Calendar of Festivals*, Element, Dorset and Massachusetts, 1991

van Leeuwen, M and Moeskops, J, *The Nature Corner: Celebrating the Year's Cycle with a Seasonal Tableau*, Floris Books, Edinburgh, 1990

Lenz, F, *Celebrating the Festivals with Children*, Anthroposophic Press, New York, 1986

Seasonal Project Series (Spring, Summer, Autumn, Winter, Christmas, Easter), Wayland, Hove, 1989

Starting Points Series (Spring, Summer, Autumn, Winter), Franklin Watts, London and New York, 1989

Steiner, R, *The Festivals and their Meaning*, Rudolf Steiner Press, London, 1981

NATURE

Cornell, J B, *Sharing Nature with Children*, Exley Publications, UK, 1990 and Ananda Publications, California, 1979

Johnson, C M, *Discovering Nature with Young People*, Greenwood Press, London, 1988 and Connecticut, 1987

Kraul, W, *Earth, Water, Fire and Air*, Floris Books, 1990

van Leeuwen, M and Moeskops, J, *The Nature Corner: Celebrating the year's cycle with a seasonal tableau*, Floris Books, Edinburgh, 1989

Litvinoff, M, *Earthscan Action Handbook*, Earthscan, London, 1990

Masheder, M, *Windows to Nature*, World Wide Fund for Nature, 1990

— *Let's Enjoy Nature*, Merlin Press, London, 1994

Petrash, C, *Earthwise*, Floris Books, Edinburgh, 1993, or *Earthways*, Gryphon House, USA, 1993

CRAFTS

Bridgewater, A and G, *Easy to Make Decorative Kites*, Dover Publications Inc, New York, 1985

Brown, R, *Things to Make from Autumn Seeds and Leaves*, Jade Publishers, Haslemere, UK, 1989

Burns, E, *Hanky Panky*, 7351 Mesa Dr, Aptos, California 95003, 1980

Cooper, S et al, *The Children's Year*, Hawthorn Press, Stroud, 1986

Craft Supplies Directory, M R S Projects (LMI), Projects House, 36 Radnor Ave, Welling, Kent, DA16 2BX

Gardner, H, *Artful Scribbles: The Significance of Children's Drawings*, Jill Norman, London, 1980 and Basic Books, New York, 1982

Kellogg, R, *Children's Drawing, Children's Minds*, Avon, New York, 1979

Make and Play Series, Kingfisher Books, London, 1990

More Children's Art and Crafts, The Australian Women's Weekly Home Library, Australian Consolidated Press, Sydney, Australia and Australian Consolidated Press (UK) Ltd (0604) 760456

Petrash C, *Earthwise*, Floris Books, Edinburgh, 1993, or *Earthways*, Gryphon House, USA, 1993

Reinckens, S, *Making Dolls*, Floris Books, Edinburgh, 1989

van Steenderen, L, *Making Dolls and Dolls' Clothes*, Exley Publications, Watford, 1988

Strauss, M, *Understanding Children's Drawings*, Rudolf Steiner Press, 1979

STORY TELLING

Gersie, A, *Storytelling in Times of Change*, Green Print, 1991

Gersie, A and King, N, *Storymaking in Education and Therapy*, Jessica Kingsley Publishers, London, 1990

Steiner, R, *The Interpretation of Fairy Tales*, Anthroposophic Press, New York, 1943

ANTHOLOGIES

Asbjornsen and Moe, *Norwegian Folk Tales*, Grondhal Dreyer Forlag, Norway, 1992

Barratt, S and Hodge, S, *Tinderbox, 66 songs for children*, A & C Black, 1982

Grimm, J, *The Complete Grimm's Fairy Tales*, Routledge, London, 1975

Jacobs, J, *English Fairy Tales*, David Campbell Publishers Ltd, 1993

McCaughrean, G, *The Orchard Book of Greek Myths*, Orchard Books, London, 1992

Ransome, A, *Old Peter's Russian Tales*, Cape, 1984

Sherlock, *West Indian Folk Tales*, Oxford University Press, 1966

The Golden Goose and other Grimms Fairy Tales, Floris Books, Edinburgh, 1992

Zahlingen, B, *Plays for Puppets and Marionettes*, Acorn Hill Children's Center, 9500 Brunett Ave, Silver Spring, MD 20901, USA

NURSERY RHYMES

Beck, I and Williams, S, *Round and Round the Garden; Oranges and Lemons; Pudding and Pie; Ride a Cock Horse*, Oxford University Press, 1992

Cope, W, *Twiddling Your Thumbs*, Hand Rhymes, Faber & Faber, 1988

Michael Foreman's Mother Goose, Walker Books, London, 1991

Scott, A, *The Laughing Baby: remembering nursery rhymes and reasons*, Bergen and Garvey, 1987

PLAY AND TOYS

Bettelheim, B, *The Uses of Enchantment*, Knopf, 1976 and Penguin, 1991

Bond, T, *Games for Social and Life Skills*, Stanley Thornes, 1990

Bonel, P, *Playing for Real*, National Children's Play and Recreation Unit, 1993

Brandes, D, *Gamester's Handbook Two*, Stanley Thornes, 1990

Brandes, D and Phillips, H, *Gamester's Handbook*, Stanley Thornes, 1990

Britton, L, *Montessori Play and Learn*, Vermilion, London, 1992

Britz-Crecelius, H, *Children at Play*, Floris Books, Edinburgh, 1972

Bruce, T, *Time to Play in Early Childhood Education*, Hodder & Stoughton, 1991

Crowe, B, *Play is a Feeling*, Unwin, 1986

Deacove, J, *Sports Manual of Non competitive Games*, Family Pastimes, 1982

Haller, I, *How Children Play*, Floris Books, Edinburgh, 1987

Jackson, L, *Childsplay*, Thorsons, 1993

Judson, S, *A Manual on Non-violence and Children*, New Society Publishers, 1983

Kreidler, W, *Creative Conflict Resolution*, Scott Foreman, 1984

Masheder, M, *Let's Play Together*, Green Print, London, 1989

— *Let's Co-operate*, Peace Education Project, London, 1991

McToots, *Kids' Book of Games*, Beaver Books, 1982

Michaelis, B and D, *Learning through Non-competetive Activities and Play*, Learning Handbooks, 1977

Millar, S, *The Psychology of Play* (out of print)

Newson J and E, *Toys and Playthings*, Penguin, 1979

Opie, I and P, *The Singing Game*, Oxford University Press, 1988

— *Children's Games in Street and Playground*, Oxford University Press, 1969

Orlick, T, *The Co-operative Sports and Games Book*, Writers and Readers, 1979

— *The Second Co-operative Sports and Games Book*, Pantheon Books, 1982

Parachute Games, Peace Education Project, 6 Endsleigh St, London WC1H 0DX, 1994

Parker, J and Olsen, S, *Parachute Games*, Peace Education PEP Talk, No 17, 1988

Piaget, J, Play, *Dreams and Inititation in Childhood*, Norton, New York, 1962

Schneider, T, *Everyone's a Winner*, Little Brown & Co, 1976

Sobell, J, *Everybody Wins*, Walker & Co, 1984

Sternlicht, M and Hurwitz, A, *Games Children Play*, Reinhold, 1980

Storms, G, *Handbook of Music Games*, Hutchinson, 1979

Winnicott, D, *Playing and Reality*, Pelican, 1974

TELEVISION, COMPUTERS

Bonel, P, *Playing for Real*, National Children's Play and Recreation Unit, 1993

Large, M, *Who's Bringing Them Up?* Hawthorn Press, Stroud, 1990

Postman, N, *Amusing Ourselves to Death*, Viking, New York, 1985

Provenzo, E F, *Video Kids: Making Sense of Nintendo*, Harvard University Press, 1991

Setzer, V, *Computers in Education*, Floris Books, Edinburgh, 1989

Winn, M, *The Plug-in Drug*, Bantam Books, New York, 1977

EURYTHMY

Dubach, A, *Principles of Eurythmy*, Rudolf Steiner Press, Bristol (out of print)

Spock, M, *Eurythmy*, Anthroposophic Press, New York, 1980

Steiner, R, *Eurythmy as Visible Speech*, Rudolf Steiner Press, Bristol, 1984

— *An Introduction to Eurythmy*, Anthroposophic Press, New York (out of print)

— *Curative Eurythmy*, Rudolf Steiner Press, London, 1983

HEALTH AND HEALING

Atkins, E, "Fever, Its History, Cause and Function", *The Yale Journal of Biology and Medicine*, **55** (1982)

van Bentheim, T, et al, *Caring for the Sick at Home,* Floris Books, Edinburgh, 1987

Bott, V, *Anthroposophical Medicine,* Rudolf Steiner Press, 1978

— *Anthroposophical Guide to Family Medicine* (out of print)

Evans, M and Rodger, I, *Anthroposophical Medicine,* Thorsons, 1992

Glöckler, M and Goebel, W, *A Guide to Child Health,* Floris Books, Edinburgh, 1990

Should I Have My Child Vaccinated? Anthroposophical Medicine Association in the UK, Rudolf Steiner House, 35 Park Road, London, NW1 6XT

Hauschka, M, *Fundamentals of Artistic Therapy,* Rudolf Steiner Press, London, 1985

Howson, C, et al, *Report of the Committee to Review Adverse Effects of Pertussis and Rubella Vaccines,* Nat Acad Publishers, 1991

Husemann, F and Wolff, O (ed), *The Anthroposophical Approach to Medicine* (3 Vols), Anthroposophic Press, New York, 1989

Leroi, R, *Illness and Healing,* Temple Lodge Press, London, 1988

Leviton, R, *Anthroposophic Medicine Today,* Anthroposophic Press, New York, 1988

Levy, J, *Exercises for our Baby,* (trans E Gleasure), Collins, 1978

Lievegoed, B, *Phases of Childhood,* Floris Books, Edinburgh, 1987

Mees, L F S, *Blessed by Illness,* Anthroposophic Press, New York, 1983

Mendelsohn, R, *How to Raise a Healthy Child...In Spite of Your Doctor,* Ballantine, New York, 1984

Moskowitz, R, *The Case Against Immunisation,* National Center for Homeopathy, 1500 Massachusetts Avenue NW, Washington DC, 20005, USA

Homeopathic Medicines for Pregnancy and Childbirth, North Atlantic Books, Berkeley, California, 1992

Scott, J, *Natural Medicine for Children,* Unwin Hyman, 1990 and Avon, New York, 1990

Stanway, Dr A, *The Natural Family Doctor,* Select Books, 1993 and Simon & Schuster, 1987

Steiner, R, *Health and Illness,* Vols 1 and 2, Anthroposophic Press, New York, 1981

Steiner, R and Wegman, I, *Fundamentals of Therapy,* Rudolf Steiner Press, London, 1983

Twentyman, R, *The Science and Art of Healing,* Floris Books, Edinburgh, 1992

Walker, P, *The Book of Baby Massage,* Bloomsbury, 1988 and Simon & Schuster, 1988

Weihs, T, *Children in Need of Special Care,* Souvenir Press, London, 1977

Wolfram, E, *Paracelsus* (out of print)

Wootan, G and Verney, S, *Take Charge of Your Child's Health,* Crown, New York, 1992

NUTRITION

Hauschka, R, *Nutrition,* Rudolf Steiner Press, Bristol, 1983

Kitzinger, S, *Breastfeeding Your Baby,* Dorling Kindersley, London and Knopf, New York, 1989

— *The Experience of Breastfeeding,* Penguin, 1987

La Leche League, *The Womanly Art of Breastfeeding,* La Leche League International, Illinois and London, 1981

zur Linden, W, *When a Child is Born,* Rudolf Steiner Press, 1980

Pryor, K, *Nursing Your Baby,* Harper and Row, New York, 1973

Schmidt, G, *The Dynamics of Nutrition,* (trans G F Karnow) Biodynamic Literature, Wyoming, 1980

Stanway, Drs P and A, *Breast is Best,* Pan, 1993

Steiner, R, *Nutrition and Health,* Rudolf Steiner Press, 1987

EDUCATION

Ashton-Warner, S, *Teacher,* Simon & Schuster, 1963

Ball, C and M, *Education for a Change,* Penguin, 1973

Barbiana, School of, *Letter to a Teacher,* Penguin, 1970

Blishen, E (ed), *The School That I'd Like,* Penguin, 1969

Britton, J, *Education Towards Freedom,* Pelican Books, 1972

Bruner, J, *Towards a Theory of Instruction,* Norton, 1966

— *On Knowing. Essays for the left hand,* Harvard University Press, 1964

— *Under Five in Britain,* Blackwell, 1983

Buckman, P (ed), *Education Without Schools,* Souvenir Press, London, 1973

Cole, R, *A Wish for my Child* (out of print)

Carlgren, F, *Education Towards Freedom,* Lanthorn Press, East Grinstead, 1972

Chanan, G and Gilchrist, L, *What School is For,* Methuen, 1974

Croall, J, *Neill of Summerhill: The Permanent Rebel,* Routledge, 1983

Curle, A, *Education for Liberation,* Routledge, 1979

Dewey, J, *Art as Experience,* Capricorn Books, New York, 1958

— *The Child and the Curriculum,* University of Chicago Press, 1963

— *Democracy and Education,* Macmillan, New York, 1916

— *Experience and Education,* Collier, New York, 1963

Dewey, J and E, *Schools of Tomorrow,* Dutton, New York, 1962

Donaldson, M, *Children's Minds,* Croom Helm, 1978 and Fontana, 1978

Education Rights Handbook, The Children's Legal Centre Ltd, 20 Compton Terrace, London N1 2UN, 1987

Elkind, D, *The Hurried Child,* Knopf, New York, 1984

— *Miseducation: Preschoolers at Risk,* Knopf, New York, 1987

van der Eyken, W and Turner, B, *Adventures in Education,* Penguin, 1969

Ferrer, F, *The Origins and Ideals of the Modern School,* Watts, 1913

Freire, P, *Pedagogy of the Oppressed,* Penguin, 1972

Gammage, P, *Early Childhood Education:Taking Stock,* Education Now, Derbyshire, 1993

Gatto, J T, *Dumbing Us Down: The Hidden Curriculum of Compulsory Schooling,* New Society Publishers, Philadelphia, 1993

Goodman, P, *Compulsory Miseducation,* Penguin, London, 1971

— *Growing Up Absurd,* Gollancz, 1961

Handy, C, *The Age of Unreason,* Arrow Books, London, 1991

Harber, C, et al (eds) *Alternative Educational Futures,* Holt, Rinehart and Winston, 1984

Harber, C and Meighan, R, *The Democratic School,* Education Now, Derbyshire , 1989

Holt, J, *How Children Learn,* Penguin, 1970

— *How Children Fail,* Penguin, London, 1971

— *Instead of Education,* Penguin, London, 1976

— *Learning all the Time,* Lighthouse Books, 1989

— *Teach Your Own,* Lighthouse Books, 1982

— *Never Too Late,* Education Now, Derbyshire, 1992

Inge, W R, *Cambridge Essays on Education* (out of print)

Lister, I, (ed) *Deschooling,* Cambridge University Press, 1974

Meighan, R, *Flexischooling,* Education Now Books, Derbyshire, 1988

Meighan, R, et al, *Theory and Practice of Regressive Education,* Educational Heretics Press, Nottingham, 1993

Meighan, R and Toogood, P, *Anatomy of Choice in Education,* Education Now, Ticknall, Derbyshire, 1992

Miller, A, *For Your Own Good,* Virago, London, 1987

Montessori, M, *The Absorbent Mind,* Dell, New York, 1969

Moore, R and D, *School Can Wait* (out of print)

Mullarney, M, *Anything School Can Do, You Can Do Better* (out of print)

Neill, A S, *That Dreadful School,* Herbert Jenkins, 1937

— *Summerhill,* Penguin, 1968

Peachey, J Lorne, *How to Teach Peace to Children,* Herald Press, 1981

Postman, N and Weingartner, C, *Teaching as a Subversive Activity,* Penguin, 1971

Prutzman, P, et al, *The Friendly Classroom for a Small Planet,* Avery Publishing Group, 1978

Randle, D, *Teaching Green,* Merlin Press, London, 1989

Rogers, C, *Freedom to Learn for the 80's,* Charles E Merrill, 1983

Russell, B, *Education and the Social Order,* Allen & Unwin, 1968

— *On Education,* Allen & Unwin, 1926

— *Principles of Social Reconstruction,* Allen & Unwin, 1980

— *Sceptical Essays,* Routledge, 1991

Russell, D, *The Tamarisk Tree 2: My School and the Years of War,* Virago, 1980

Schweinhart, L J and Weikart, D P, *A Summary of Significant Benefits: The High/Scope Perry Pre-school Study Through Age 27*

Scott, Sir W, *Letters of Sir Walter Scott, vol 9* (out of print)

Shaw, G B, *The Freethinker's Guide to the Educational Universe* (out of print)

Shute, C, *Compulsory Schooling Disease,* Educational Heretics Press, Nottingham, 1993

Smith, D, *Parent-generated Home Study in Canada* (out of print)

Spark, M, *The Prime of Miss Jean Brodie,* Penguin, 1969

Wright, N, *Assessing Radical Education,* Open University Press, 1989

STEINER EDUCATION

Aeppli, W, *Rudolf Steiner Education and the Developing Child,* Anthroposophic Press, New York, 1986

Childs, G, *Steiner Education in Theory and Practice,* Floris Books, Edinburgh, 1991

Edmunds, L F, *Rudolf Steiner Education – the Waldorf Impulse,* Rudolf Steiner Press, Bristol, 1962

Grunelius, E, *Early Childhood Education and the Waldorf School Plan,* Waldorf School Monographs, Spring Valley, New York, 1984

Harwood, A C, T*he Recovery of Man in Childhood, A Study in the Educational Work of Rudolf Steiner,* Hodder & Stoughton, London, 1958

— *The Way of a Child,* Rudolf Steiner Press, Bristol, 1974

Lissau, R, *Rudolf Steiner, An introduction,* Hawthorn Press, Stroud, 1987

Spock, M, *Teaching as a Lively Art,* Anthroposophic Press, New York, 1979

Steiner, R, *Practical Course for Teachers,* Rudolf Steiner Press, Bristol, 1937

— *The Roots of Education,* Rudolf Steiner Press, Bristol, 1968

— *Practical Advice for Teachers,* Rudolf Steiner Press, Bristol, 1970

— *Human Values in Education,* Rudolf Steiner Press, Bristol, 1971

— *Education of the Child in Light of Anthroposophy,* Rudolf Steiner Press, Bristol, 1975

— *The Renewal of Education,* Steiner Schools Fellowship Publications, Sussex, 1981

— *An Introduction to Waldorf Education,* Anthroposophic Press, New York, 1985

— *Education as a Social Problem,* Anthroposophic Press, New York, 1984

SPECIAL NEEDS

Clarke, P et al, *To a Different Drumbeat: a practical guide to parenting children with special needs,* Hawthorn Press, Stroud, 1989

Konig, K, *In Need of Special Understanding,* Camphill Press, Botton, 1987

Pietzner, C, *Questions of Destiny: Mental Retardation and Curative Education,* Anthroposophic Press, New York, 1988

Pietzner, Cornelius (ed), *A Candle on the Hill: Images of Camphill Life,* Floris Books, Edinburgh, 1990

Steiner, R, *The Exceptional Child: A Way of Life for Mentally Handicapped Children,* Rudolf Steiner Press, London, 1970

Weihs, A, et al, *Camphill Villages,* Camphill Press, Botton, 1989

Weihs, T, *Children in Need of Special Care,* Souvenir, London, 1977

Index

Acknowledgements

AUTHORS' ACKNOWLEDGEMENTS

John B. Thomson

I would like to acknowledge all I have learned from my own children and the children and colleagues at Elmfield Steiner School, over a period of 25 years. I am also grateful for the furtherance of my education by the students in the Foundation and Teacher Training programmes at Emerson College. I am especially grateful to my wife, Marie-Claire, for her patient support.

Tim Kahn

I have gained my understanding of human behaviour through my involvement in two self-help organizations, Re-evaluation Counselling and Parent Network. The many years of support that I gave to and received from others helped me gain the insight to write my section. Margaret Gault and Nechamah Inbar-Bonanos are the two people who repeatedly helped me find my direction and made invaluable suggestions on reading my manuscript. Lia (my wife) and Sarah and Ben (my two children) supported me with great understanding during my months of writing.

Lynne Oldfield

I wish to acknowledge the constant inspiration of the works of Rudolf Steiner: the encouragement of Erika Grantham, the UK representative to the International Waldorf Kindergarten Association and Gabriel Kennish; the support of David, Rachel, Sophia and my mother Olive Wyatt, without whom none of this would have been possible.

Roland Meighan

I was most fortunate in being able to draw on the considerable experience and expertise of Janet Meighan in the field of early childhood education in the writing of the Education and Schooling section.

PUBLISHER'S ACKNOWLEDGMENTS

Gaia Books would like to thank Rahima Baldwin (consultant to Informed Homebirth/Informed Birth and Parenting, and to the Garden of Life Birth Centre in Ann Arbor, Michigan, USA) for commenting on the text; Dr Jenny Josephson for acting as consultant on Health and Healing; Dr Michael Evans and Christian von Arnim for translating Health and Healing from the German; Dr Gilbert Childs for writing additional text on Steiner education for Education and Schooling; Jane Lord from Strid Cottage and Barden Old School Montessori Centre, Bolton Abbey, Skipton, UK, for her contribution to Education and Schooling; Helena Petre for research; Mary Warren for the index; Jenny Banfield, Mike Bingle, Suzy Boston, and Lyn Hemming for editorial and production work; Fiona Carnie of Human Scale Development, Dr Grahame Curtis-Jenkins; Professor Margaret Donaldson; Poppy Green; Greenprint for permission to reproduce games from *Let's Play Together* by Mildred Masheder; Colin Hodgetts from The Small School, Hartland, Devon, UK; Alan Jones from Caldo Gap Press; Bryan Masters; Diana Miles from the Holistic Education Network; Mothering Magazine (USA); Mel Parr; Jane Read from the Family Childhood Collection at the Froebel Institute; everyone at *Resurgence*; Ivan Sokolov; Tamar Swade; Professor Kathy Sylva; Professor Colwyn Trevarthen; Graeme Whiting; Kathryn Willder.

Gaia Books would also like to thank the following for being models, drawing illustrations, and providing equipment for photographic shoots: Catherine Asdrubal, Cathy, Michelle, and Phil Atkinson, Mary Barton, Sam and Beth Cotterrell, Fiona and Lucy Bennet, Max Bickford, Zoë Billingham, Ashlyn Bird, Ken Brown, Tom Burns, Gemma Butler, James, Jessica, Michelle, and Rachel Chinn, Kayleigh and Luke Collins, Lawrence Cripps, Mary and Steven Curtis, Sophie Foxen, Tilly Geoghan, Joanna, Jack, and Hal Godfrey Wood, Robin Goodwin, Francesca, James, and Robert Gregory, Nicola Grove, the Guenot family, Christine and Tobias Haseler, Leah Haslam, Natasha Hall, George, James, Stephanie, and Susan Hemming, Doris Horn, Jessie Hoskin, Julien Hunt, Samuel Jeffery, Sarah, Felix, Miles, and Dorcas Kiernan, Georgia Lafferty, Laurent and Martine Lecourt, Max Lines, Hannah Lippman, Danny McKenzie and family, James Mahdiyone and Colette Wilson, Lizzie Mason, Isabelle, Rebecca and Neil McDougal, Godfrey, Okailey, Okaikoi, and Jennie Mensah, Marcus Moore and Hannah Eadie, Harry and Rhys Morgan, Miles Mylius, Alexandra Mylius Pate, Daniel and Tristan Pate, Mary Oliver, Anna, Lucy, Richard, and Simon Pearce, Alice, Celia, Harry, and William Phipps, Luke Porter, Anna Pouncey, Gabriel Raeburn, Lesley Raignault, Jasmine Shaw, Emma Skelton, Vita Taylor, Eleanor, Naomi, and Steve Teague, John, Peter, and Rachel Varah, Noah Wace, Emily, Crispin, and Stephanie Walker, Angie, Daniel, Kevin, and Milly Webb, Leon Wilson, the children of Muswell Hill Quaker Meeting for lending the Earthquakers game; pupils and staff at Hotwells Primary School, Bristol; Stroud Valley Infant School, Stroud; St Werbergh's Park Nursery School, Bristol, including Louis Morgan; The Lindens Waldorf Family Centre, Stroud, including Alexander, Amos, Bronwyn, Cherry, Francis, Pablo, Raphael, Rebecca, and Topaz, Cory Fairhurst for his assistance at photographic shoots.

PHOTGRAPHIC CREDITS

All photographs by Steve Teague except: p. 25 Magnum, Costa Manos; pp. 59, 82 Format, Maggie Murray; pp. 77, 266, 270–1 Gaia Books, Fausto Dorelli; p. 111 Format, Joanne O'Brien; pp. 246 and 260 Magnum, Paul Fusco; p. 261 Magnum, Eli Reed; p. 265 Magnum, Ian Berry; p. 293 Holt Associates, Cambridge, Massachusetts, USA; p. 295 Jean Piaget Archives, University of Geneva, Switzerland; p. 299 Professor Jerome Bruner, New York, USA; p. 306 Terry E Smith, *Washington Post* and *Resurgence* No 154, Sept/Nov 1992, p. 9; p. 308 Maria Kilcoyne, Constable Publishers, Constable and Co Ltd, London, UK; p. 310 Summerhill School, Suffolk, UK; p. 311 Daniel Greenberg, Sudbury Valley School, Massachusetts, USA; pp. 314, 317 Jane Lord, Strid Cottage and Barden Old School Montessori Centre, Bolton Abbey, Skipton, UK; p. 316 Early Childhood Collection, Froebel Institute College, London, UK p. 317 (top) Maria Montessori Training Organisation, AMI, London, UK; p. 318 Rudolf Steiner Bookshop © Philophisch Anthroposophischer; pp. 319, 320 Maxima Skelton; p. 321 Paul Penrose, Penrose, Dorset, UK; p. 325 Dame Catherine's School, Ticknall, UK; p. 327 Peter Moore and Colin Ward; p. 333 Uppatinas School, Glenmore, Pennnsylvania, US.

ILLUSTRATIONS

Danny McKenzie pp. 28, 32, 33, 41–3, 65, 69, 72, 85, 101, 115, 117, 122–3; **Giovanna Pierce** pp. 12, 22–3, 35, 40, 50–1, 52, 64, 67, 74, 80, 81, 90–1, 92, 93, 99, 100, 103, 106–7, 109, 113, 139, 162–3, 180, 196–7, 232, 242–3, 248–9, 250–1, 277, 280, 289; **Ann Savage** pp. 45, 46–7, 89, 219, 220, 237, 238, 240, 253, 256–7, 260–1, 264–5, 302; **Nancy Tolford** pp. 18–19, 38–9, 56–7, 73, 88, 224–5, 233, 234–5, 290–1, 304, 312–13; **Joe Robinson** pp. 66, 131, 143, 146–7, 150, 154, 158, 164–5, 167, 168–9, 176, 181, 184–5, 188–9, 197, 198–9, 210, 212, 217, 268, 279, 274, 283, 286–7.